Careers in Building Construction

Careers in Building Construction

Editor
Michael Shally-Jensen, Ph.D.

SALEM PRESS
A Division of EBSCO Information Services, Inc.
Ipswich, Massachusetts

GREY HOUSE PUBLISHING

Publisher's Cataloging-In-Publication Data
(Prepared by The Donohue Group, Inc.)

Careers in building construction / editor, Michael Shally-Jensen, PhD. --
  First edition.

    pages : illustrations ; cm. -- (Careers in--)

  Includes bibliographical references and index.
  ISBN: 978-1-61925-862-4 (hardcover)

  1. Building--Vocational guidance--United States. 2. Construction industry--Vocational
guidance--United States. I. Shally-Jensen, Michael, editor. II. Series: Careers in--

TH159 .C375 2015
690.023

First Printing

PRINTED IN THE UNITED STATES OF AMERICA

CONTENTS

PUBLISHER'S NOTE

Careers in Building Construction contains twenty-six alphabetically arranged chapters describing specific fields of interest in this industry. Merging scholarship with occupational development, this single comprehensive guidebook provides building construction students with the necessary insight into potential careers, and provides instruction on what job seekers can expect in terms of training, advancement, earnings, job prospects, working conditions, relevant associations, and more. *Careers in Building Construction* is specifically designed for a high school and undergraduate audience and is edited to align with secondary or high school curriculum standards.

Scope of Coverage

Understanding the wide net of jobs in building construction is important for anyone preparing for a career within it. *Careers in Building Construction* comprises twenty-six lengthy chapters on a broad range of occupations including traditional and long-established jobs such as Architect, and Construction Manager, as well as in-demand jobs: Solar Energy Installer, Surveyor, and Civil Engineer. This excellent reference also presents possible career paths and occupations within high-growth and emerging fields in this industry.

Careers in Building Construction is enhanced with numerous charts and tables, including projections from the US Bureau of Labor Statistics, and median annual salaries or wages for those occupations profiled. Each chapter also notes those skills that can be applied across broad occupation categories. Interesting enhancements, like **Fun Facts**, **Famous Firsts**, and dozens of photos, add depth to the discussion. A highlight of each chapter is **Conversation With** – a two-page interview with a professional working in a related job. The respondents share their personal career paths, detail potential for career advancement, offer advice for students, and include a "try this" for those interested in embarking on a career in their profession.

Essay Length and Format

Each chapter ranges in length from 3,500 to 4,500 words and begins with a Snapshot of the occupation that includes career clusters, interests, earnings and employment outlook. This is followed by these major categories:

- **Overview** includes detailed discussions on: Sphere of Work; Work Environment; Occupation Interest; A Day in the Life. Also included here is a Profile that outlines working conditions, educational needs, and physical abilities. You will also find the occupation's Holland Interest Score, which matches up character and personality traits with specific jobs.

- **Occupational Specialties** lists specific jobs that are related in some way, like Landscape Drafter, Urban and Regional Planner, and Architectural Drafter. Duties and Responsibilities are also included.

- **Work Environment** details the physical, human, and technological environment of the occupation profiled.

- **Education, Training, and Advancement** outlines how to prepare for this field while in high school, and what college courses to take, including licenses and certifications needed. A section is devoted to the Adult Job Seeker, and there is a list of skills and abilities needed to succeed in the job profiled.

- **Earnings and Advancements** offers specific salary ranges, and includes a chart of metropolitan areas that have the highest concentration of the profession.

- **Employment and Outlook** discusses employment trends, and projects growth to 2020. This section also lists related occupations.

- **Selected Schools** list those prominent learning institutions that offer specific courses in the profiles occupations.

- **More Information** includes associations that the reader can contact for more information.

Special Features

Several features continue to distinguish this reference series from other career-oriented reference works. The back matter includes:
- Appendix A: Guide to Holland Code. This discusses John Holland's theory that people and work environments can be classified into six different groups: Realistic; Investigative; Artistic; Social; Enterprising; and Conventional. See if the job you want is right for you!
- Appendix B: General Bibliography. This is a collection of suggested readings, organized into major categories.
- Subject Index: Includes people, concepts, technologies, terms, principles, and all specific occupations discussed in the occupational profile chapters.

Acknowledgments

Special mention is made of editor Michael Shally-Jensen, who played a principal role in shaping this work with current, comprehensive, and valuable material. Thanks are due to Allison Blake, who took the lead in developing "Conversations With," with help from Vanessa Parks, and to the professionals who communicated their work experience through interview questionnaires. Their frank and honest responses provide immeasurable value to *Careers in Building Construction*. The contributions of all are gratefully acknowledged.

EDITOR'S INTRODUCTION

Industry Overview

The construction industry continues to grow. One area, in particular, that has shown growth is "green" construction, or the erecting of buildings using materials and processes that are environmentally friendly and energy efficient. Buildings constructed today are very different from those built 100 years ago. As interest in protecting the environment grows, green, or sustainable, buildings have become more common. Creating these buildings requires skilled workers, including architects, construction managers, carpenters, plumbers, heating and cooling technicians, steel workers, and many others.

Studies have shown that green building construction in the United States rose from being a $3-billion industry in 2005 to an approximately $50-billion industry in 2010. Moreover, calculations show the size of the same industry today (2015) to be between $120 billion and $145 billion. And these figures are for the *nonresidential* sector alone. The construction of large projects, such as hospitals, office complexes, and government buildings—increasingly built to green standards—has advanced the construction industry in general, and green construction in particular. Similar growth applies to the housing industry, where more and more homeowners are demanding green construction.

As the size of the industry continues to grow, so too will its workforce. According to a McGraw-Hill Construction study, green construction supported more than 660,000 US workers in 2011, representing about 35 percent of all construction jobs. In light of ongoing industry growth, the expectation is that today's percentage of green jobs stands at around 50 percent, or more—and these estimates do not include employment for suppliers of green building materials and products, an industry that should also experience increased growth as demand for their goods rises. Although green building techniques are used in both residential and industrial construction, commercial construction remains the largest player in the industry's growth.

Occupations

No states mandate or license workers to work on green buildings exclusively. But many organizations, both national and local, offer training for construction trades with a focus on green construction. Workers seeking to enter the construction industry, or those who are already proficient in their trade but looking to add green skills, should check with the National Center for Construction Education and Research (NCCER) or visit a local employment, trade, or union center for training opportunities.

Design Occupations. The workers who design buildings must be open to new ideas and technologies and seek to be innovative yet practical. Designers of green buildings work together to make their projects as environmentally friendly as possible. These workers are required to be knowledgeable about both standard construction techniques, such as the number of load-bearing columns needed to support a structure, as well as new ones, such as maximizing water conservation and indoor air quality. To make buildings that appeal to both their owners and the public, designers have to achieve a balance between the qualities of visual appeal and sustainability. Let us look at a few of these so-called design occupations.

Architects design buildings and other structures. They are responsible for the overall look of buildings, but an architect's work goes beyond appearance. Buildings must also be functional, safe, and economical, and must suit the needs of the people who use them. Architects use computer-aided design and drafting (CADD) software and other technologies to design and manage projects. They often work closely with engineers, interior designers, landscape architects, and other professionals. Architects spend a great deal of their time coordinating information from, and the work of, others engaged in the same project.

Civil engineers design and supervise the construction of roads, buildings, airports, tunnels, dams, bridges, and water supply and sewage systems. Their work requires them to consider many factors, from the construction costs and expected lifetime of a project to government regulations and environmental hazards. The major specialties of civil engineering are structural, water resources, construction, transportation, and geotechnical engineering.

Landscape architects plan the location of roads and walkways and the arrangement of flowers, shrubs, and trees. They analyze the natural elements of a site, such as the climate, soil, drainage, vegetation, and slope of the land. Landscape architects also assess existing buildings, roads, walkways, and utilities to determine what improvements are necessary. At all stages, they evaluate the project's impact on the local ecosystem.

Building Construction Occupations. Constructing a building is a complicated task. Workers who are new to the job will have to perform many different chores, and even experienced workers working in a new area, such as green construction, might have to develop new skills. Also, when constructing green buildings, workers might find themselves using unusual design schematics or materials that are different from what they are used to. Working together, however, the job gets done in the end. Here are some examples of these occupations.

Construction managers plan, direct, coordinate, and budget a wide variety of construction projects. They may supervise an entire project or just one part of a large project. As coordinators of all building and construction processes, construction managers select, hire, and oversee specialty trade contractors, such as carpenters, plumbers, and electricians. They supervise the construction process from beginning to end and make sure it is completed on time and within budget. They often meet with owners, engineers, architects, and others working on the project.

Construction laborers perform a wide range of tasks on construction sites. They use a variety of equipment, including pavement breakers, jackhammers, and small mechanical hoists. For some jobs, construction laborers use computers and other high-tech input devices to control robotic pipe cutters and cleaners. They often assist workers in the specialty trades, including carpenters, plasterers, and masons.

Construction equipment operators use bulldozers and other heavy machinery to move construction materials, earth, and other heavy objects at construction sites. They use machines to clear and grade land prior to construction. Construction equipment operators also dig trenches to lay sewer and other utilities, and they hoist heavy construction materials.

Specialty Trade Occupations. Along with designers and construction crews, skilled trades workers are needed to complete the erection of a building. These workers use their unique sets of skills to perform their specific tasks. Their duties vary with their specialty and the project.

Carpenters construct, install, and repair structures made from lumber, or standard lengths of cut and planed wood. Those who erect the basic frame of a wooden structure are sometimes called framers. In accordance with the building plans and drawings, carpenters measure, mark, cut, and join together boards, planks, and other wood materials. They use hand and power tools, such as chisels, planes, saws, drills, sanders, and nail guns to complete their work, always checking for accuracy as they go.

Electricians do both installation and maintenance work on the power and lighting systems of buildings. When working in construction, electricians check their construction drawings to determine where to place equipment, such as circuits and outlets. After finding the proper locations, they install and connect wires to circuit breakers, transformers, outlets, or other components and systems. When installing wiring, electricians use both hand tools—such as screwdrivers and wire strippers— and power tools—such as drills and saws. Electricians also are responsible for testing the new components.

Heating & Cooling Technicians install, maintain, and repair heating, ventilation, and air-conditioning (HVAC) systems. HVAC systems vary among buildings, but all are composed of many mechanical, electrical, and electronic components, such as motors, fans, and pumps. Following construction drawings, technicians install heating and air-conditioning systems by putting in fuel and water supply lines, air ducts and vents, pumps, and other components. They may connect electrical wiring to controls and check the unit to confirm that it works properly.

Plumbers install piping, valves, gauges, fixtures, drains and other plumbing hardware in new buildings. To conserve resources, plumbers lay out their materials and fit the piping into the building's structure. They measure and mark areas in which pipes will be installed and connected, while checking for obstructions, such as electrical wiring. Plumbers must be knowledgeable of building codes and different system options.

Brickmasons and stonemasons use brick, natural stone, concrete blocks, mortar, and other materials to build structures such as fireplaces, chimneys, walls, and walkways. They may work on small projects such as stone paths, or on large office buildings. Masons cut the necessary stones or bricks, lay out the planned designs, prepare the site for construction, and assemble a structure that is visually appealing and meets the needs of the client. They may also perform repairs or reconstruction on preexisting brickwork.

Conclusion

If the growth of the construction industry continues, as it is expected to do, more buildings will be erected and more workers will be needed to erect them. Moreover, more and more of these buildings will be built to green standards. Construction is able to provide jobs to people with a broad range of education and experience levels. Many of the occupations in building design, such as architects and civil engineers, do require a bachelor's degree or postgraduate training, whereas many of the construction and trade occupations can be learned through on-the-job training or an apprenticeship. New opportunities will continue to arise in construction generally and in green construction in particular. The better skilled one is at plying one's trade, the better will be the range of opportunities in the future.

—Michael Shally-Jensen, Ph.D.

Sources

Green Outlook 2011: Green Trends Driving Growth. New York, McGraw-Hill Construction, 2010. Available at
http://construction.com/market_research/.
Greenbuild: Growing Green Building Market. New York: McGraw-Hill Construction, 2011. Available at
http://www.usgbc.org/articles/greenbuild-growing-green-building-market-supports-661000-green-jobs-us%E2%80%94-third-design-and-co
Liming, Drew. *Careers in Green Construction*. Washington, DC: Bureau of Labor Statistics, 2012. Available at
http://www.bls.gov/green/construction/
National Center for Construction Education and Research. www.nccer.org/

Architect

Snapshot

Career Cluster: Building & Construction, Architecture & Construction

Interests: Design, drawing, drafting, computer technology, communicating with people

Earnings (Yearly Average): $74,520

Employment & Outlook: Faster Than Average Growth Expected

OVERVIEW

Sphere of Work

Architects design and sometimes oversee the construction of a wide array of buildings and other structures. They plan homes, offices, government buildings, schools and educational complexes, and other

buildings and complexes according to safety, function, and budget specifications, as well as the needs of the client. Once an architect creates the blueprints for the project, he or she may coordinate with construction crews during all stages of the project to ensure that it is built to plan and stays within budget. About one-fifth of licensed architects are self-employed, a higher than average percentage compared to other careers,

while the remaining 80 percent work for larger firms, construction companies, and government agencies.

Work Environment

Architects spend most of their work days in an office setting, where they meet with clients, draft blueprints and reports, and coordinate with contractors, engineers, and other architects. They may frequently visit work sites to review the progress of a particular project, monitor the types of materials used, and meet with contractors and workers. Building sites can present physical risks, such as exposed wiring and exposure to dust and debris. Architects may work long hours at the office, drafting blueprints and drawing models.

Profile

Working Conditions: Work Indoors
Physical Strength: Light Work
Education Needs: Bachelor's Degree, Master's Degree
Licensure/Certification: Required
Opportunities For Experience: Apprenticeship, Military Service, Part-Time Work
Holland Interest Score*: AIR

* See Appendix A

Occupation Interest

Architects must be comfortable taking a leadership role in construction, renovation, or preservation projects. They take the general ideas and needs of a client and use both creativity and spatial design expertise to transform those ideas into a reality that construction contractors can execute. People who seek to become architects should be attracted to careers that combine both engineering knowledge and imagination.

Historically, architects drew blueprints by hand. However, today they use innovative computer technologies, such as 2-D and 3-D drafting, modeling, and design tools and software, almost exclusively to design and draw blueprints. The profession attracts individuals able to work independently as well as collaborate with others.

A Day in the Life—Duties and Responsibilities

Prior to the project's initiation, an architect meets with clients to establish the budget, project objectives, and client requirements. Using this information, the architect begins pre-design activities, such as conducting environmental impact assessment studies and feasibility reports, preparing cost analysis and land-use studies, establishing design requirements and constraints and, where necessary, helping in the selection of construction sites. Once pre-design is complete, the architect works with his or her staff to prepare blueprint drawings and generate ideas to present to the client. It is not unusual for several plans to be presented before the architect and client agree on a final version, so architects should be prepared to design and execute multiple drafts of a plan for any project.

When the client approves of the architect's proposals, the architect begins the construction phase of the project. He or she develops final construction plans, which include structural systems and other design components such as electricity, plumbing, heating, ventilation, and air conditioning, ventilation (HVAC), and landscaping. The architect may also be responsible for choosing building materials and awarding construction bids on behalf of the client. Once the crews have been organized and building begins, the architect may coordinate consistently with these groups at the construction site to ensure that the project is proceeding according to schedule, budget, and design specifications. He or she may also spend time with local government officials to ensure the project complies with building and fire codes, zoning laws, and other ordinances. Finally, the architect may make changes to the plan (and, if so, coordinates with the construction contractors regarding these changes) as asked by the client.

Duties and Responsibilities

- Referring to building codes and zoning laws
- Working with drafters to prepare drawings for the client
- Developing detailed drawings and models
- Presenting designs to the client for approval
- Translating the design into construction documents
- Selecting a builder or contractor
- Supervising the construction of the building

OCCUPATION SPECIALTIES

Marine Architects

Marine Architects design and oversee the construction and repair of marine craft and floating structures, such as ships, barges, submarines, torpedoes and buoys.

Landscape Architects

Landscape Architects plan and design the development of land areas for projects, such as recreational facilities, airports, highways, hospitals, schools and sites that are planned for residential, commercial and industrial development.

School-Plant Consultants

School-Plant Consultants formulate and enforce the standards for the construction of public school facilities. They develop legislation relative to school building sites and school design and construction.

Architectural Drafters

Architectural Drafters prepare detailed drawings of architectural designs and plans for buildings, according to the specifications, sketches and rough drafts that are provided by architects.

Landscape Drafters

Landscape Drafters prepare detailed scale drawings and tracings from rough sketches or other data provided by a landscape architect.

Sustainable/Clean Energy/Green Building Architects

Sustainable/Clean Energy/Green Building Architects design buildings that use clean energy technologies to meet new environmental standards.

WORK ENVIRONMENT

Physical Environment

Architects spend most of their time in an office environment, whether as part of an architectural firm, a home office, or the headquarters of a developer or construction company. A significant amount of time may be spent at building sites, supervising the construction process and discussing the project with contractors. Some architects also spend time at local town and city halls and offices, securing permits and filing compliance reports with government officials.

Relevant Skills and Abilities

Communication Skills
- Speaking effectively
- Writing concisely

Interpersonal/Social Skills
- Being able to work independently

Organization & Management Skills
- Coordinating tasks
- Managing people/groups
- Paying attention to and handling details
- Performing duties which change frequently

Research & Planning Skills
- Creating ideas
- Using logical reasoning

Technical Skills
- Performing scientific, mathematical and technical work

Human Environment

Architects work with a wide range of clients, which includes homeowners, but more often developers and building owners. They may work on a daily basis with construction workers, general contractors, and other professionals (such as plumbers, electricians, and interior designers). Some architects work closely with public officials, including fire marshals, health and building inspectors, and environmental officials, ensuring compliance with local and state laws, regulations, and ordinances.

Technological Environment

Architects predominantly work with computer modeling tools and software to create blueprints and construction plans. They must be familiar with computer-aided design and drafting (CADD) and building information modeling (BIM) technologies as well as other 2-D and 3-D systems. They must also understand the construction tools and materials necessary for the project, as well as have an understanding of building methods. A thorough comprehension of how to execute environmental impact statements related to any project is increasingly a necessity.

EDUCATION, TRAINING, AND ADVANCEMENT

High School/Secondary

High school students interested in becoming architects should take courses that will help develop their spatial design capabilities. These classes include geometry, algebra, physics, industrial arts, drafting, and computer science. It is also useful for students to study history to gain a better understanding of period architecture and art. Because communication with clients and contractors is a critical aspect of the architectural design and building processes, students are encouraged to take courses that build verbal and communication skills.

Suggested High School Subjects
- Algebra
- Applied Math
- Applied Physics
- Arts
- Blueprint Reading
- College Preparatory
- Computer Science
- Drafting
- English
- Geometry
- Graphic Communications
- History
- Industrial Arts
- Mathematics
- Mechanical Drawing
- Physics
- Trigonometry

Famous First

The first woman to receive a patent for her architectural design was Harriet Morrison Irwin. She designed a two-story hexagonal house in 1869 and it was characterized by a central hallway which connected all the rooms. The house design was not only accepted, but built on West Fifth Street in Charlotte, North Carolina. Harriet Morrison Irwin was also the sister-in-law of General Stonewall Jackson.

College/Postsecondary

Most states require that architects have a professional-caliber degree in architecture in order to receive their licenses. These degrees are considered to include the five-year Bachelor of Architecture degree and the two-year Master of Architecture degree. Advanced degrees increase the individual's competitiveness as a candidate for employment and can help them specialize in certain fields of architecture. Some schools offer graduate-level degrees in "green" or environmentally sustainable architectural design.

Related College Majors

- Architectural Drafting
- Architectural Environmental Design
- Architecture
- Drafting, General
- Engineering, General
- Landscape Architecture
- Naval Architecture & Marine Engineering

Adult Job Seekers

Architects who complete their degree training must then complete internships working under the direction of an established architect. These internships can lead to full-time employment. Experienced architects may apply directly for open positions. All architects are advised to join a professional trade association or organization, such as the American Institute of Architects (AIA).

Professional Certification and Licensure

Architects are required to become licensed in order to practice architecture. This license is gained by obtaining a professional degree, completing an internship, and passing the Architect Registration Examination (adopted by all states and administered by the National Council of Architectural Registration Boards, or NCARB).

Additional Requirements

 Architects are expected to have strong computer skills, both for office management and writing proposals and for 2-D and 3-D CADD and BIM usage. Additionally, architects should have exceptional communication skills, visual design acuity, creativity, and spatial intelligence (necessary in engineering and drafting).

Fun Fact

The world's most complex architecture is a 9-foot tall, 2,000 pound series of columns made from cardboard created by Swiss architect and programmer Michael Hansmeyer.

Source: http://www.fastcodesign.com/1663306/the-worlds-most-complex-architecture-cardboard-columns-with-16-million-facet

EARNINGS AND ADVANCEMENT

Salaries vary according to the type of firm and its geographic location. Architects with well-established private practices generally earn more than salaried employees in architectural firms. Architects starting their own practices may go through a period when their expense is greater than their income.

Median annual earnings of architects were $74,520 in 2014. The lowest ten percent earned less than $44,940, and the highest ten percent earned more than $121,910.

Architects may receive paid vacations, holidays, and sick days; life and health insurance; and retirement benefits. These are usually paid by the employer.

Metropolitan Areas with the Highest Employment Level in this Occupation

Metropolitan area	Employment	Employment per thousand jobs	Hourly mean wage
New York-White Plains-Wayne, NY-NJ	9,650	1.79	$40.72
Chicago-Joliet-Naperville, IL	3,630	0.97	$37.06
Washington-Arlington-Alexandria, DC-VA-MD-WV	3,500	1.47	$41.90
Los Angeles-Long Beach-Glendale, CA	3,280	0.81	$42.69
Boston-Cambridge-Quincy, MA	3,000	1.67	$42.74
Dallas-Plano-Irving, TX	2,520	1.13	$38.87
Houston-Sugar Land-Baytown, TX	2,470	0.87	$40.96
Seattle-Bellevue-Everett, WA	2,280	1.53	$36.54
Denver-Aurora-Broomfield, CO	1,910	1.44	$36.37
Philadelphia, PA	1,780	0.96	$38.75

Source: Bureau of Labor Statistics

EMPLOYMENT AND OUTLOOK

There were approximately 107,500 architects employed nationally in 2012. One in five architects was self-employed. Employment is expected to grow faster than the average for all occupations through the year 2022, which means employment is projected to increase 15 percent to 20 percent. Employment is affected by the level of activity in the construction industry and the cyclical changes in the economy. Competition will continue to be keen for jobs in the most prestigious firms, which offer good potential for career advancement. Prospective architects who gain experience in an architectural firm while they are still in school will have a distinct advantage in obtaining an intern-architect position after college graduation. The demand will be higher for architects who are skilled in "green" or sustainable design, which puts an emphasis on the use of environmentally friendly practices and materials.

Employment Trend, Projected 2012–22

Architects, except landscape and naval: 17%

Architects, surveyors, and cartographers: 15%

Total, all occupations: 11%

Note: "All Occupations" includes all occupations in the U.S. Economy. Source: U.S. Bureau of Labor Statistics, Employment Projections Program

Related Occupations
- Civil Engineer
- Construction Manager
- Drafter
- Landscape Architect
- Marine Engineer & Naval Architect
- Mechanical Engineer
- Surveyor & Cartographer
- Urban & Regional Planner

Related Military Occupations
- Marine Engineer

Conversation With . . .
JORDAN ZIMMERMANN

Associate
Arrowstreet, Boston, Massachusetts
Architect, 7½ years

1. What was your individual career path in terms of education/training, entry-level job, or other significant opportunity?

I grew up around my dad's design/build landscape architecture firm in Memphis. I didn't gravitate towards the plant science aspect of his work, but I shared the same talent and interest in design of the built environment. Interior design and architecture were the natural alternative avenues for me. I received a Bachelor of Science in interior design from Murray State University in Kentucky. One of my professors, Mr. Michael Jordan, was an architect who gave us an assignment to design an airport. This was a pivotal project for me, as I realized I loved designing both the exterior and interior of buildings—and developed the opinion that neither can be designed in a vacuum. After graduation, I worked for an architecture firm in Memphis before attending Washington University in St. Louis for a master's degree in architecture. There, I studied design not only in the Midwest, but also spent a full semester in Helsinki, Finland, and another in Seoul, South Korea. My now-husband brought me to Boston, where I have found a meaningful and growing career in architecture.

2. What are the most important skills and/or qualities for someone in your profession?

Architecture requires a natural eye for design and interest in science, art, and history. More important, it requires the ability to work collaboratively with clients who don't always understand design. Every day is a new challenge. Years ago, I thought everyone was silly, telling me not to pursue architecture unless I wanted to work excessive overtime for a small salary. However, they were mostly right. If you're truly passionate about it, though, you'll pursue it anyway–like I did.

3. What do you wish you had known going into this profession?

I believe I was prepared for working as an architect. Graduate school was the toughest part. I wish I had known that working smarter and with very clear intentions, instead of working longer hours, would have gotten me further in school. I had amazing professors at Washington University, but I spent too much time guessing what everyone else wanted me to do instead of focusing on my own interest in projects. In the real world, you are challenged with so many practical constraints. I always wish I could go back to some of those school projects now and not worry about the constraints.

4. Are there many job opportunities in your profession? In what specific areas?

You can use your architecture license to design any building type you can imagine. Many architects become experts in specific areas, such as health care or student life buildings. Others are more generalists. Some architects are best in design roles, creating concepts and programming for buildings. Others function in a technical role—they figure out the details such as how to keep water out of the building. Integration of sustainable design is a growing area in the industry. Boston and other coastal cities are facing the reality of rising sea levels and vulnerability to flooding. Architects play a role in the future of coastal development. There are a lot of opportunities and challenges in this area.

5. How do you see your profession changing in the next five years? What role will technology play in those changes, and what skills will be required?

3D modeling has changed the industry significantly in the past ten years. We are now able to 3D print practically anything, from scaled study models to full-size building elements. This has changed the design process and has advanced full-scale building techniques.

6. What do you enjoy most about your job? What do you enjoy least about your job?

You cannot possibly master every building type in one career. My colleagues with thirty years of experience still have opportunities to learn. It's exciting and exhausting at the same time. What I enjoy least is the inconsistency of work load. Both the industry and individual firms are either overwhelmingly busy or depressingly slow. It's the nature of project-based work that's dependent on the market.

7. Can you suggest a valuable "try this" for students considering a career in your profession?

In order to understand architecture, you need to understand the history of it. Books like *Ten Books on Architecture, Devil in the White City*, and *The Eyes of the Skin* are good recommendations. It's important to read about the past but also be aware of current design progress and leaders around world. *ArchDaily, Dezeen* and other publications are easily accessible online. More specifically, Harvard University has a career discovery summer program that gives students a taste of design studio without a long-term commitment. Other schools may offer something similar.

SELECTED SCHOOLS

Many colleges and universities offer programs related to the study of architecture; a number of them also have schools or programs specifically devoted to this field. Some of the more prominent undergraduate programs in architecture are listed below.

Cal Poly, San Luis Obispo
San Luis Obispo, CA 93407
Phone: 805.756.2311
www.calpoly.edu

Cornell University
Ithaca, NY 14850
Phone: 607.254.4636
www.cornell.edu

Pratt Institute
200 Willoughby Avenue
Brooklyn, NY 11205
Phone: 718.636.3600
www.pratt.edu

Rhode Island School of Design
2 College Street
Providence, RI 02903
Phone: 401.454.6100
www.risd.edu

Rice University
6100 Main Street
Houston, TX 77005
Phone: 713.348.0000
www.rice.edu

Southern California Institute of Architecture
960 E. 3rd Street
Los Angeles, CA 90013
Phone: 213.613.2200
www.sciarc.edu

Syracuse University
900 South Crouse Avenue
Syracuse, NY 13244
Phone: 315.443.1870
www.syr.edu

University of Texas, Austin
Austin, Texas 78712
Phone: 512.471.3434
www.utexas.edu

University of Southern California
Los Angeles, CA 90089
Phone: 213.740.1111
www.usc.edu

Virginia Tech
Blacksburg, VA 24061
Phone: 540.231.6000
www.vt.edu

MORE INFORMATION

American Institute of Architects
1735 New York Avenue, NW
Washington, DC 20006-5292
800.242.3837
www.aia.org

Association of Collegiate Schools of Architecture
1735 New York Avenue, NW
Washington, DC 20006
202.785.2324
www.acsa-arch.org

Association of Licensed Architects
22159 North Pepper Road, Suite 2N
Barrington, IL 60010
847.382.0630
www.alatoday.org

National Architectural Accrediting Board, Inc.
1735 New York Avenue NW
Washington, DC 20006
202.783.2007
www.naab.org

National Council of Architectural Registration Boards
1801 K Street NW, Suite 700K
Washington, DC 20006
202.783.6500
www.ncarb.org

Society of American Registered Architects
14 E. 38th Street
New York, NY 10016
888.385.7272
www.sara-national.org

Michael Auerbach/Editor

Brickmason/ Stonemason

Snapshot

Career Cluster(s): Building & Construction, Architecture & Construction
Interests: Construction, architecture, design, working with your hands
Earnings (Yearly Average): $47,650
Employment & Outlook: Much Faster Than Average Growth Expected

OVERVIEW

Sphere of Work

Brickmasons and stonemasons use brick, natural stone, concrete blocks, mortar, and other materials to build structures such as fireplaces, chimneys, walls, and walkways. They may work on small projects such as stone paths, or on large office buildings. Masons cut the necessary stones or bricks, lay out the planned designs, prepare the site for construction, and assemble a structure that is visually appealing and meets the needs of the client. They may also perform repairs or reconstruction on preexisting brickwork.

Work Environment

Stonemasons and brickmasons typically work at project sites with strict safety protocols, including mandatory hard hats and equipment checks. They spend the majority of their day outdoors in all types of weather conditions. The work of stonemasons and brickmasons is physically demanding, requiring them to be on their feet for extended periods of time and lift heavy materials such as brick and stone. There is also a danger of physical injury due to this heavy lifting, cuts from sharp tools and stone fragments, and falls from scaffolding. Stonemasons typically work a forty-hour week, although those hours may vary based on the type of job performed, the weather, and other factors.

Profile

Working Conditions: Work both Indoors and Outdoors
Physical Strength: Medium Work
Education Needs: On-The-Job Training, High School Diploma with Technical Education, Apprenticeship
Licensure/Certification: Usually Not Required
Opportunities For Experience: Apprenticeship, Part-Time Work
Holland Interest Score*: ERS, REI, RES, RIE, RSE

* See Appendix A

Occupation Interest

Brickmasons and stonemasons should be detail oriented, have a strong sense of spatial awareness, and enjoy working with their hands. Jobs for both stonemasons and brickmasons are plentiful, with demand for these craftsmen expected to increase over the next few years at a rate higher than that of other professions. A large number of masons are self-employed or own their own businesses, which means that they set their own schedules, and should therefore be highly organized and motivated.

A Day in the Life—Duties and Responsibilities

Brickmasons and stonemasons consult with clients and general contractors to understand customers' aesthetic preferences and structural needs. These consultations include reviewing project blueprints and drawings and taking into account the client's budget for stonework. Based on this information, masons determine the type of equipment that will be needed and order the stones and other materials.

When the initial consultation is complete, brickmasons and stonemasons prepare the project site, a process which varies depending on the type of work being done. For example, a brickmason must decide whether to use poles or corner leads (complex pyramids of bricks) to mark the corners of the structure. Brickmasons and stonemasons also cut and prepare the bricks or stones that will be used, polishing or shaping them as necessary. Once the site is ready, they lay the foundation for the project with a binding material such as mortar, which is generally a combination of sand, water, and cement. The masons then stack or arrange the bricks or stones in place, using mortar to hold them together, until the project is complete. Upon completion, masons cut away excess mortar and clean up the structure for final presentation to the customer.

Duties and Responsibilities

- **Measuring distances**
- **Determining the alignment of brick or stones**
- **Cutting bricks and chopping stones to size**
- **Spreading mortar to serve as a base and binder**
- **Tapping bricks to align, level and place them in mortar**
- **Finishing mortar joints between bricks or stones**

OCCUPATION SPECIALTIES

Firebrick and Refractory Tile Bricklayers

Firebrick and Refractory Tile Bricklayers build, rebuild, reline or patch steam boilers, furnaces, cupolas or ovens using fire resistant (refractory) brick or tile and mortar.

Sewer Bricklayers

Sewer Bricklayers lay brick, concrete blocks or shaped tile to construct sewers and manholes.

Brick Chimney Builders

Brick Chimney Builders lay brick or tile to construct or repair industrial smokestacks or chimneys.

Marble Setters

Marble Setters cut and set marble slabs in walls or floors of buildings and repair or polish previously set slabs.

WORK ENVIRONMENT

Physical Environment

Brickmasons and stonemasons work primarily on project sites, most of which are located outdoors. They must lift heavy objects, use a variety of sharp tools, and be on their feet or knees in all types of weather during the course of their work.

Relevant Skills and Abilities

Organization & Management Skills
- Coordinating tasks
- Following instructions
- Managing people/groups
- Paying attention to and handling details

Technical Skills
- Working with machines, tools or other objects

Unclassified Skills
- Performing work that produces tangible results

Human Environment

In addition to their clients, brickmasons and stonemasons regularly interact with architects, construction personnel, interior designers, apprentices, construction supply company representatives, and other masons.

Technological Environment

Brickmasons and stonemasons use tools such as claw hammers and sledgehammers, hydraulic jacks, mortar mixers, power saws, and arc welders. Self-employed masons must also be familiar with trade-related software, such as project management systems, and basic word processing suites and programs.

EDUCATION, TRAINING, AND ADVANCEMENT

High School/Secondary

High school students should study industrial arts, including carpentry and construction trades, wood shop, masonry, and similar classes. They should also study math, including geometry and algebra, for help in calculating measurements and proportions. Additionally, subjects that build communication skills are very useful, as are courses in blueprint drafting and mechanical drawing.

Suggested High School Subjects
- Applied Math
- Blueprint Reading
- Building Trades & Carpentry
- Drafting
- English
- Masonry
- Mechanical Drawing
- Shop Math
- Woodshop

Famous First

The first brick building was constructed in 1633, the bricks being imported from Holland. The location of the building was a Dutch fort in New Amsterdam, or New York City, and was used as a residence for the fifth Dutch governor, Wouter Van Twiller. This was only the first of several brick buildings to be built within the fort.

Postsecondary

After graduation from high school, most brickmasons and stonemasons obtain jobs as apprentices, helpers, or laborers, where they can become familiar with the type of work that goes into masonry. An apprenticeship is the best and most recognized path to becoming a mason, combining practical instruction with classroom education, and many unions and contractors sponsor three-year programs. Some technical colleges and community colleges offer courses in masonry, which can improve a candidate's job prospects.

Related College Majors
- Masonry & Tile Setting

Adult Job Seekers

Individuals who are interested in becoming stonemasons and brickmasons should apply to local contractors or unions for apprenticeships. They may also join and network through trade associations such as the Associated General Contractors of America (AGC) or the Brick Industry Association (BIA).

Professional Certification and Licensure

There are no licensing requirements for brickmasons or stonemasons, but many construction unions require masons to pass a test in order to become members.

Additional Requirements

Brickmasons and stonemasons must be at least seventeen years old. They should be able to lift heavy objects and withstand long hours working on their feet or their knees. Masons must have strong math skills and an excellent grasp of construction and mechanical concepts. Those who aim to be self-employed should demonstrate competency in business management.

Fun Fact

Biblical scholars believe it's more likely that Jesus was a stonemason than a carpenter because most things in the region were made from rocks, not wood.

Source: http://christianity.stackexchange.com/questions/4896/what-evidence-is-there-that-jesus-was-a-carpenter and many others

EARNINGS AND ADVANCEMENT

Earnings depend on the geographic location of the employer. Nationally, in 2014, brickmasons and stonemasons earned median annual salaries of $47,650. The lowest ten percent earned less than $29,700, while the highest ten percent earned more than $80,350.

Earnings in these trades may be less because poor weather and downturns in construction activity limit the time brickmasons and stonemasons can work. Union apprentice brickmasons and stonemasons start at fifty percent of a journeyman's rate which increases as experience is gained. Brickmasons and stonemasons are required to purchase their own hand tools.

Brickmasons and stonemasons may receive paid vacations, holidays, and sick days; life and health insurance and retirement benefits. These are usually paid by the employer

Metropolitan Areas with the Highest
Employment Level in this Occupation

Metropolitan area	Employment	Employment per thousand jobs	Hourly mean wage
New York-White Plains-Wayne, NY-NJ	2,670	0.49	$32.47
Chicago-Joliet-Naperville, IL	2,020	0.54	$36.83
Houston-Sugar Land-Baytown, TX	1,480	0.52	$18.67
Washington-Arlington-Alexandria, DC-VA-MD-WV	1,420	0.60	$23.23
Nassau-Suffolk, NY	1,010	0.80	$37.93
Boston-Cambridge-Quincy, MA	930	0.52	$40.83
Baltimore-Towson, MD	920	0.71	$18.81
St. Louis, MO-IL	910	0.70	$31.17
Minneapolis-St. Paul-Bloomington, MN-WI	860	0.47	$30.91
Pittsburgh, PA	770	0.68	$24.16

Source: Bureau of Labor Statistics

EMPLOYMENT AND OUTLOOK

There were approximately 85,000 brickmasons and stonemasons employed nationally in 2012. About one-fourth were self-employed. Employment is expected to grow much faster than the average for all occupations through the year 2022, which means employment is projected to increase 30 percent or more. This is a result of a growing population and more homes, factories, offices, and other buildings being built using brick, which is energy-efficient. Also stimulating the demand will be the restoration of a large number of old brick buildings.

Employment Trend, Projected 2012–22

Brickmasons and blockmasons: 36%

Stonemasons: 29%

Construction trades workers: 22%

Total, all occupations: 11%

Note: "All Occupations" includes all occupations in the U.S. Economy. Source: U.S. Bureau of Labor Statistics, Employment Projections Program

Related Occupations
- Cement Mason
- Construction Laborer
- Plasterer
- Tile & Marble Setter

Conversation With . . .
TIMOTHY SMITH

Owner, T.D. Smith Stonemasonry
Philmont, New York
Stonemason, 40 years

1. What was your individual career path in terms of education/training, entry-level job, or other significant opportunity?

I was a schoolteacher and got a draft deferral to teach social studies in Bellows Falls, Vermont, so that I didn't have to go to Vietnam. When I moved to Vermont, I noticed all this stonework—and I also noticed poverty for the first time. I had grown up in an upper middle class environment in California. These kids had no money at all. So, I started an after-school program teaching kids to rebuild stone walls. I didn't know what I was doing, but these wonderful old Italian stonemasons in Barre, Vermont, taught me. People were paying us to repair these old stone walls, which were everywhere, and I was making so much money that I quit teaching school.

I stayed 10 years in Vermont and then I heard about a project constructing a new south tower at the Cathedral of St. John the Divine in New York City. I went down and applied to work under British master builders. They hired me because of my teaching background. We trained 150 kids from Harlem to do hand-cut Gothic stonework. I was very lucky because I worked on the cathedral for 10 years. There are no cathedrals being built anymore. After that, I settled in the culturally rich Hudson Valley, working for New York State Office of Parks, Recreation and Historic Preservation, and later started my own business. I still hire students as part of a work-based learning program for kids who aren't responding to regular school and teach them to build things like stone waterfalls and fireplaces.

2. What are the most important skills and/or qualities for someone in your profession?

Stonemasonry is a trade that requires a five-year apprenticeship. You don't get it from going to school or reading a book. For middle class kids, they'll need to take five years of their life during which they will actually do physical labor, which can be a whole new experience for many of them. So you have to have a good attitude about new experiences.

3. What do you wish you had known going into this profession?

The first thing a really good stonemason will tell you is forget everything you know. We're taught in school to know things, but in stonemasonry, especially when you're working in different climates, you need to do it and experience it and learn what works. And you learn by your mistakes. A lot of kids today want to hide their mistakes because they're taught to be perfect. I tell the kids working for me, "Be happy you made a mistake because you can learn from it and never make that mistake again."

4. Are there many job opportunities in your profession? In what specific areas?

In the United States, the trades are really flourishing. There's a lot of work in hardscape—in other words, a patio or a stone wall in the backyard. Almost every house has a brick chimney, so you should learn how to work with bricks as well as stone. You can very quickly teach young people to rebuild chimneys. It's a pretty easy skill to learn. There's a big demand for that.

Historic restoration is a fine trade. Most people won't let you do historic restoration until you can prove you have a good command of your trade. There's a tremendous amount of money to be made there.

5. How do you see your profession changing in the next five years? What role will technology play in those changes, and what skills will be required?

In five years, there's going to be more demand. Because of the digital age, there's no such thing as weekenders anymore. People are buying big old houses in the country and restoring them to live in year-round. They don't have to live in New York City or Boston.

Also, cell phone technology really helps a lot. If a young worker on a job has a question, he can text me a picture and say, "What should I do next?"

6. What do you enjoy most about your job? What do you enjoy least about your job?

The thing I like most is teaching young people the trade. I feel like I'm somehow making a contribution to the future. I teach them to teach themselves—I get a thrill out of that. When you build something, at the end of the day, you feel like you're accomplishing something. And you're outside.

I like it least when I have to fire a kid. Some kids are only interested in a job, but they don't want to truly learn the trade.

7. Can you suggest a valuable "try this" for students considering a career in your profession?

Summer jobs are great. Here's my best advice: Go out to building sites and tell them you'll work the first day for free, and then work your butt off. Really rip it up. Show the contractor you're a hard worker. That's a great way to get a job. Also, the National Park Service's Historic Preservation Training Center in Frederick, Maryland, has a masonry section.

MORE INFORMATION

Associated General Contractors of America
Director, Construction Education Services
2300 Wilson Boulevard, Suite 400
Arlington, VA 22201
703.548.3118
www.agc.org

Brick Industry Association
1850 Centennial Park Drive
Suite 301
Reston, VA 20191-1525
703.620.0010
www.gobrick.com/default.aspx

Building Trades Association
16th Street, NW
Washington, DC 20006
800.326.7800
www.buildingtrades.com

International Masonry Institute
The James Brice House
42 East Street
Annapolis, MD 21401
410.280.1305
www.imiweb.org

International Union of Bricklayers and Allied Craftworkers
620 F Street NW
Washington, DC 20004
202.783.3788
www.bacweb.org

Mason Contractors Association of America
1481 Merchant Drive
Algonquin, IL 60102
224.678.9709
www.masoncontractors.org

Masonry Advisory Council
1400 Renaissance Drive, Suite 340
Park Ridge, IL 60068
847.297.6704
www.maconline.org

Masonry Institute of America
22815 Frampton Avenue
Torrance, CA 90501
800.221.4000
www.masonryinstitute.org

Masonry Society
3970 Broadway, Suite 201-D
Boulder, CO 80304
303.939.9700
www.masonrysociety.org

National Association of Home Builders
1201 15th Street, NW
Washington, DC 20005
800.368.5242
www.nahb.com

**National Center for Construction
Education and Research**
13614 Progress Boulevard
Alachua, FL 32615
888.622.3720
www.nccer.org

**National Concrete Masonry
Association**
13750 Sunrise Valley Drive
Herndon, VA 20171-4662
703.713.1900
www.ncma.org

Michael Auerbach/Editor

Bulldozer & Heavy Equipment Operator

Snapshot

Career Cluster(s): Building & Construction, Architecture & Construction

Interests: Managing heavy equipment, working outdoors, working as part of a team

Earnings (Yearly Average): $43,510

Employment & Outlook: Faster Than Average Growth Expected

OVERVIEW

Sphere of Work

A bulldozer and heavy equipment operator works in the construction industry, driving and operating a heavy-duty tractor used to level ground and move large amounts of soil, rocks, sand, and other materials. A bulldozer may also be used to demolish buildings or other structures. Bulldozer operators are responsible for cleaning and maintaining bulldozers to ensure that they work properly

and must at times identify mechanical malfunctions and carry out repairs.

Work Environment

Bulldozer operators work in a large variety of outdoor environments, in all climates and weather conditions. They perform duties at commercial, industrial, residential, and roadside jobsites. When performing roadwork, a bulldozer operator may be required to work on the side of a highway. Bulldozer operators are typically exposed to a high level of noise from the machines themselves as well as the ongoing work and must take precautions to avoid hearing damage and ensure effective communication with other workers. Construction jobsites present a number of additional hazards, so safety measures must always be enforced.

Profile

Working Conditions: Work Outdoors
Physical Strength: Heavy Work
Education Needs: On-The-Job Training, High School Diploma or G.E.D., High School Diploma with Technical Education, Apprenticeship
Licensure/Certification: Usually Not Required
Opportunities For Experience: Apprenticeship, Military Service
Holland Interest Score*: REC

* See Appendix A

Occupation Interest

Work as a bulldozer operator encompasses many tasks, including hauling, leveling, and excavating. Those interested in this profession should be adaptable to the variety of challenging tasks and should enjoy working outdoors and with a team. They also must be able to focus consistently on the job, as bulldozers can be dangerous.

A Day in the Life—Duties and Responsibilities

Prior to beginning any construction or demolition work, a bulldozer operator must first inspect the bulldozer to make sure all of the components are functioning properly. These components include levers, pedals, and the hydraulics that operate the blade. The blade, the large metal plate at the front of the bulldozer, is used to move, haul, or level materials. Depending on the job, a bulldozer may be equipped with a shovel or digging scoop rather than a blade. The bulldozer operator must next go over the day's tasks with the rest of the construction crew. Bulldozers move a large quantity of material and greatly alter the landscape, so significant coordination is required by the entire crew to ensure that nothing is done out of turn or incorrectly.

The bulldozer operator controls the movement of the machine using pedals similar to those of a car. The blade or scooper mechanism is controlled using a lever, also known as a joystick. If a bulldozer is being used to level a surface, the operator will lower the blade to the surface and slowly drive forward. This flattens the surface. For digging jobs, an operator will maneuver the blade or scooper mechanism to dig up and transport the materials to a designated spot. While carrying out these tasks, the operator must consistently meet safety standards.

Duties and Responsibilities

- Moving levers and pushing pedals to move the tractor and manipulate the blade
- Reshaping and distributing earth to raise or lower the ground to grade specifications
- Estimating the depth of cuts by the feel of levers and the stalling action of the engine
- Repairing tractors and attachments

OCCUPATION SPECIALTIES

Scarifier Operators

Scarifier Operators strictly operate a bulldozer for the purpose of loosening soil.

Angledozer Operators

Angledozer Operators drive a bulldozer equipped with a special angled blade attached to the front.

Crawler-Tractor Operators

Crawler-Tractor Operators drive a tractor that is specially equipped to move over rough or muddy ground.

Fine-Grade-Bulldozer Operators

Fine-Grade-Bulldozer Operators grade land to close specification.

Scraper Operators

Scraper Operators operate bulldozers for the purpose of scraping surface clay to determine the existence and types of clay deposits or to gather clay into piles in preparation for its removal to brick-and-tile manufacturing plants.

WORK ENVIRONMENT

Physical Environment

Bulldozer operators most frequently work at construction sites, which can be in commercial, industrial, or residential zones, or along roadways. These sites are often very loud due to the heavy machinery being used and may present additional hazards based on the nature of the construction being carried out.

Relevant Skills and Abilities

Interpersonal/Social Skills
- Working as a member of a team

Technical Skills
- Working with machines, tools or other objects

Unclassified Skills
- Using set methods and standards in your work

Work Environment Skills
- Working outdoors

Human Environment

Because bulldozer operators must coordinate and collaborate with other workers on jobsites in order to complete their work successfully, strong communication skills are essential. Bulldozer operators are usually required to check in with site managers and contractors daily.

Technological Environment

In addition to bulldozers, a bulldozer operator may be required to operate other pieces of heavy machinery. This may include road graders and trench excavators. An operator will also handle light safety equipment such as reflector vests and hardhats.

EDUCATION, TRAINING, AND ADVANCEMENT

High School/Secondary

Most employers require bulldozer operators to have completed high school or an equivalent degree program. Prospective bulldozer operators will benefit from high school courses in subjects such as geology and machine repair.

Suggested High School Subjects
- On-the-Job Training
- Apprenticeship
- High School Diploma or G.E.D.
- High School Diploma with Technical Education
- Junior/Technical/Community College

Famous First

The traditional design of the bulldozer is made up of two parts, the blade and the tracks. The blade was originally pulled behind mules and oxen in order to plow the land, but in the early 1900s, Benjamin Holt of Stockton, CA created the first continuously moving tracks for a tractor known as the Caterpillar. The first real bulldozer, however, was created in the 1920s by James Cummings of Morrowville, KS. Meanwhile, the tracks that Holt had developed were used to create the first military tank!

Postsecondary

A number of schools offer specialized vocational programs in the operation of construction equipment. These courses typically provide students with several weeks of hands-on training by qualified instructors. Students are also instructed in the basics of surveying, project layout, and safety and maintenance. Some of these courses allow students to earn operator credentials from the National Center for Construction Education and Research.

Completion of an operation course at a vocational school may greatly increase an operator's ability to secure a job in the industry. An individual considering enrolling in such a course should research the school's reputation and credibility and consult established workers in the construction industry in regard to the relevance of any particular course.

Related College Majors
- Construction Equipment Operation

Adult Job Seekers

An adult seeking to transition to a career as a bulldozer operator will benefit greatly from prior experience operating construction equipment or other heavy machinery. Adults with no background in the construction industry should consider applying for a specialized program at a vocational school. Such programs can properly train applicants and provide them with an easier transition into the industry.

Professional Certification and Licensure

Many bulldozer operators learn the trade through a formal apprenticeship. These programs commonly last for three to four years. During each year of the program, an apprentice is required to complete at least 144 hours of technical instruction and 2,000 hours of on-the-job training. The technical instruction commonly takes place in a classroom environment and focuses on operating procedures for specific equipment, safety and first aid, and maintenance. Apprentices typically learn to operate a variety of machines in addition to bulldozers.

Once on the job, apprentices perform basic tasks and learn how to use and maintain construction equipment. As they progress, apprentices eventually become able to operate machinery with less supervision. Once the apprenticeship is complete, a bulldozer operator is considered a journeyman worker and may perform duties without any supervision.

Bulldozer operators may be required to hold a commercial driver's license (CDL) in order to transport a bulldozer to a jobsite. A CDL allows an operator to drive a semitruck, a vehicle commonly used to haul construction equipment. Employers may be more likely to hire an operator who can transport as well as drive a bulldozer. The requirements for a CDL differ from state to state. In addition, some states have specific licenses for bulldozer operators.

Additional Requirements

A strong knowledge of mechanics and an ability to handle physically demanding tasks are essential to a bulldozer operator. Problem-solving skills are especially important, as bulldozer operators must at times identify and repair mechanical malfunctions while on-site.

Fun Fact

The Komatsu D575A is the world's largest bulldozer with a 1,150 horsepower engine that can move up to 125 cubic yards of material in a single pass.
Source: http://www.totalequipmentonlinetraining.com/freebies/bulldozer_fun_facts.pdf.

EARNINGS AND ADVANCEMENT

Earnings depend on the type of industry, location of the employer, and the type and size of bulldozer. Pay scales are generally higher in metropolitan areas. Earnings for the year can be lower than the weekly rates would indicate because work time may be limited by bad weather. In 2012, bulldozer operators had median annual earnings of $43,510.

Bulldozer operators may receive paid vacations, holidays, and sick days; life and health insurance; and retirement benefits. The employer and bulldozer operator may jointly contribute to union funds used to pay for these benefits

Metropolitan Areas with the Highest
Employment Level in this Occupation

Metropolitan area	Employment	Employment per thousand jobs	Hourly mean wage
Houston-Sugar Land-Baytown, TX	9,420	3.31	$20.65
Dallas-Plano-Irving, TX	4,720	2.11	$18.25
Minneapolis-St. Paul-Bloomington, MN-WI	4,620	2.53	$29.97
Pittsburgh, PA	4,540	4.02	$22.65
Washington-Arlington-Alexandria, DC-VA-MD-WV	4,470	1.88	$21.83
New York-White Plains-Wayne, NY-NJ	4,330	0.80	$43.51
Chicago-Joliet-Naperville, IL	4,310	1.15	$37.27
Atlanta-Sandy Springs-Marietta, GA	4,230	1.77	$18.10
Phoenix-Mesa-Glendale, AZ	3,820	2.09	$20.85
Denver-Aurora-Broomfield, CO	3,460	2.61	$21.64

Source: Bureau of Labor Statistics

EMPLOYMENT AND OUTLOOK

There were approximately 408,000 bulldozer and heavy equipment operators employed nationally in 2012. Employment is expected to grow faster than the average for all occupations through the year 2022, which means employment is projected to increase 20 percent to 28 percent. Population growth and increased spending on creating new and improving existing roads, bridges, water and sewer systems, in addition to the electronic power grid, will generate jobs. Job openings will also arise from the need to replace experienced workers who transfer to other occupations or leave the labor force.

Employment Trend, Projected 2012–22

Pile-driver operators: 28%

Construction trades workers: 22%

Paving, surfacing, and tamping equipment operators: 20%

Operating engineers and other construction equipment operators: 19%

Total, all occupations: 11%

Note: "All Occupations" includes all occupations in the U.S. Economy. Source: U.S. Bureau of Labor Statistics, Employment Projections Program

Related Occupations
- Construction Laborer
- Forklift Operator
- Freight, Stock & Material Mover
- Heavy Equipment Service Technician
- Highway Maintenance Worker
- Truck Driver

Related Military Occupations
- Combat Engineer
- Construction Equipment Operator

Conversation With . . .
CHRISTOPHER TREML

Director of Construction Training
International Union of Operating Engineers
Washington, DC
Heavy equipment operator, 28 years

1. What was your individual career path in terms of education/training, entry-level job, or other significant opportunity?

My father was training director for the apprentice program at Local 57 in Providence, Rhode Island, when I graduated from high school, so I applied to their three-year program. I trained in the classroom and had 6,000 on-the-job training hours because when you go through your apprenticeship program, you work for a contractor. I ended up working for that same contractor for almost twenty years. I ran all the equipment they had, such as bulldozers, cranes, backhoes, front-end loaders, bobcats, and asphalt paving equipment. I also repaired and maintained the equipment, which is part of an operating engineer's job.

During that time, I was hired by the union local to be a part-time instructor for their apprentice program, and then spent nine years as training director. Eventually I was offered a job at the international union in Washington, D.C. I travel to different locals and supply them with curricula, training materials, and pieces of equipment. I provide the instructors with what they need to run their training programs smoothly. From time to time, I get on different pieces of equipment to demonstrate; there are more than thirty different machines we're responsible for operating and maintaining.

2. What are the most important skills and/or qualities for someone in your profession?

You have to love the outdoors and be willing to do physical labor because this is not just about sitting in machines and pulling levers. You may have your knuckles scratched on a job or be accidentally burned with a torch. You have to have mechanical ability, a willingness to work long hours, and be physically fit. You need to take care of your body—wear hearing and eye protection, don't jump off machines, and pay attention to your doctor's appointments to maintain your health as you get older.

 You have to be a people person, because you're going to be working with a crew of people who come with a lot of different attitudes and at the end of the day, you have to get the job done.

3. What do you wish you had known going into this profession?

I knew what I was getting into because I followed my father into this profession. But one thing I see a lot today is that many young people need to learn how to manage their finances. Maybe 90 percent of operating engineers go from contractor to contractor, getting laid off from one job and moving on to another. The work is definitely seasonal; by Thanksgiving, guys may be laid off until spring. You need to manage your money through the slow times.

4. Are there many job opportunities in your profession? In what specific areas?

Yes, jobs are available because people are retiring. Equipment is computer-based now, so it's easier for young people to come in and troubleshoot because they are computer savvy.

5. How do you see your profession changing in the next five years, what role will technology play in those changes, and what skills will be required?

There will always be a need for operators because at the end of the day, you need someone in the machine to go through the normal paces because you can't have a machine in the middle of a city digging around gas and electrical lines. That said, computers are highly involved. For example, in excavation you have GPS pulling grades off satellites and dictating how much dirt to pull off or pull in. A computer tells you how much a load weighs so you can set up a crane.

6. What do you enjoy most about your job? What do you enjoy least about your job?

I enjoy all the people I've met throughout my career and I still enjoy making friends or picking up new ideas. The most difficult part of the job probably is getting on a new piece of equipment you're unfamiliar with. You can't be afraid to ask questions.

7. Can you suggest a valuable "try this" for students considering a career in your profession?

Different groups hold summer camps for young people so they can learn about the different trades. You should try to spend a day with each trade if you can. As an example of what might happen, you might get on a piece of equipment with us and help dig a hole. The University of Rhode Island holds a Construction Academy; maybe a guidance counselor can help you find one near your home.

MORE INFORMATION

Associated Builders and Contractors
4250 N. Fairfax Drive, 9th Floor
Arlington, VA 22203
703.812.2000
www.abc.org

Associated General Contractors of America
Director, Construction Education Services
2300 Wilson Boulevard, Suite 400
Arlington, VA 22201
703.548.3118
www.agc.org

Building Trades Association
16th Street, NW
Washington, DC 20006
800.326.7800
www.buildingtrades.com

Industrial Truck Association
1750 K Street, NW, Suite 460
Washington, DC 20006
202.296.9880
www.indtrk.org

International Union of Operating Engineers
Director of Research and Education
1125 17th Street, NW
Washington, DC 20036
202.429.9100
www.iuoe.org

Laborers' International Union of North America
905 16th Street NW
Washington, DC 20006
212.737.8320
www.liuna.org

National Center for Construction Education and Research
13614 Progress Boulevard
Alachua, FL 32615
386.518.6500
www.nccer.org

United Construction Workers
3109 Martin Luther King Jr. Avenue SE
Washington, DC 20032
www.unitedconstructionworkers.com

Patrick Cooper/Editor

Carpenter

Snapshot

Career Cluster(s): Building & Construction, Architecture & Construction

Interests: Industrial and creative arts, construction, architecture, working with your hands

Earnings (Yearly Average): $40,820

Employment & Outlook: Faster Than Average Growth Expected

OVERVIEW

Sphere of Work

Carpenters construct the framework of residential and commercial structures. While carpentry traditionally refers to wood construction, modern carpentry has grown to encompass numerous other building materials, from plastic and fiberglass to glass and drywall. Carpenters are traditionally self-employed or employed by construction firms. Depending on the project or employer, carpenters may have supervisory responsibilities over other members of a construction crew, such as laborers and apprentice carpenters. Professional carpenters often transition seamlessly between new construction and renovation projects.

Work Environment

Carpenters work in commercial, industrial, and residential construction sites. Much of their work is performed outdoors, occasionally in inclement conditions. Renovation work can take place in dilapidated or damaged structures. Residential carpenters specialize in constructing walls, floors, stairs, windows, and doors. Commercial carpenters often work in business and professional settings or public facilities to make renovations to damaged or aged infrastructure. Industrial carpenters are often employed in projects related to the construction of large structures such as bridges, dams, stadiums, and highways.

Profile

Working Conditions: Work Indoors, Work both Indoors and Outdoors
Physical Strength: Medium Work, Heavy Work
Education Needs: On-The-Job Training, High School Diploma with Technical Education, Apprenticeship
Licensure/Certification: Required
Opportunities For Experience: Internship, Apprenticeship, Military Service, Part-Time Work
Holland Interest Score*: CRS, REI, RES, RIE

* See Appendix A

Occupation Interest

Carpentry professionals are typically individuals with an interest in industrial and creative arts, architecture, and construction. Carpenters customarily learn their skills through on-the-job experience and immersion into the trade at the apprentice level. Extensive formal education is rarely a prerequisite for the job, and many carpenters get their start in entry-level construction positions.

A Day in the Life—Duties and Responsibilities

Carpentry is an unpredictable field of work that can bring new and unexpected challenges on a daily basis. Carpenters specializing in new construction often begin the day working with architects and engineers to review blueprints and available materials in order to develop a strategy and a list of goals for the day.

Renovation carpenters work on projects of varying size and scope. Large-scale renovations may take several months to complete. However, carpenters specializing in small-scale projects such as window and door repair, decks, and interior finish work may work on and complete several different projects in a single day.

Formwork carpentry tasks, such as the construction and assembly of framework and walls, can be repetitive in nature. Challenging, specialized work is common in several unique fields of carpentry. Luthiers repair and build stringed instruments, while furniture makers create custom cabinets and shelving to unique specifications. Ship carpenters build and repair boats.

Duties and Responsibilities

- Studying blueprints, sketches and building plans
- Ordering building materials
- Preparing materials to prescribed measurements using hand and power tools
- Assembling, fastening and installing materials
- Measuring dimensions and trueness of a structure to verify it is completed
- Installing or replacing panes of glass, ceiling tiles, doors, cabinets and other furniture

WORK ENVIRONMENT

Physical Environment

Carpenters work in new construction sites and in renovation sites. Some carpenters, particularly those working in specialized disciplines, may also work in studio spaces and indoor workshops. The role requires the use of numerous tools and machines that may be harmful if handled improperly, and safety precautions must be observed at all times.

Human Environment

Carpentry work may require extensive collaboration with other workers depending on the scale and scope of a project. Many specialty and renovation carpenters may work alone or in concert with two or three assistants.

Relevant Skills and Abilities

Interpersonal/Social Skills
- Being able to work independently
- Working as a member of a team

Organization & Management Skills
- Following instructions
- Paying attention to and handling details

Technical Skills
- Performing scientific, mathematical and technical work
- Working with machines, tools or other objects
- Working with your hands

Technological Environment

Carpentry requires extensive knowledge of materials, machinery, and tools. The ability to adapt to new technologies quickly is also essential to a carpenter's success.

EDUCATION, TRAINING, AND ADVANCEMENT

High School/Secondary

Students can best prepare for a career in carpentry by taking high school courses in algebra, geometry, trigonometry, chemistry, physics, and industrial arts. Coursework in drafting and art can also prepare students for a future in specialty carpentry. Many vocational high schools throughout the United States offer extensive courses in woodworking.

Many carpenters receive initial exposure to the trade through summer apprenticeships, laborer jobs, or school-sponsored internships. Such on-the-job instruction enables prospective carpenters to develop their knowledge of building methods, troubleshooting, and construction strategy over time.

Suggested High School Subjects
- Applied Math
- Blueprint Reading
- Building Trades & Carpentry
- English
- Machining Technology
- Metals Technology
- Shop Math
- Shop Mechanics
- Welding
- Woodshop

Famous First

Carpenters have existed since Roman times, if not before. The first woodcut, though, was completed in 1669 in the Massachusetts Bay Colony. John Foster was the engraver, and he carved the surface of a wood block in order to leave the design in the raised wood, with the carved areas working as negative space. This technique was popular for many years after.

Postsecondary

Bachelor's degree–level coursework in carpentry is uncommon in the United States. However, many community and technical colleges offer certificate and associate's degree programs in carpentry and woodworking. College-level education in the fine arts is of particular benefit to carpenters who plan to specialize in a niche realm of carpentry, such as furniture construction or nautical carpentry. Certificate programs in carpentry offer instruction in the care and use of tools and machinery, cost estimation, blueprint reading, and the contractor licensing process. Carpenters interested in forming their own companies may benefit from postsecondary programs dedicated to small business management.

Related College Majors
- Carpentry
- Woodworking

Adult Job Seekers

Professional immersion in the field of carpentry at an adult age is somewhat uncommon, given the extensive entry-level experience required to learn the trade. However, many adult job seekers acquire positions in carpentry and remodeling, given the industry's need for workers and its relevance nationwide. Apprenticeships and formal training at a secondary school or vocational training center can considerably improve the chances of adult candidates seeking to obtain a job in carpentry.

Professional Certification and Licensure

Carpenters are required by many states and districts to attain and maintain a carpentry license. Carpenters may also be required to show proof of insurance to protect against any damages incurred during construction.

Additional Requirements

Carpenters must be physically capable of meeting the demands of the job, which can require working long hours in inclement conditions and lifting heavy objects.

Fun Fact

The 17th century Shakers are credited with pioneering modern-day carpentry and inventing the circular saw.

Source: http://www.luotuofushi.net/what-are-some-interesting-facts-about-carpentry-81951881/

EARNINGS AND ADVANCEMENT

Earnings depend on the type of work, union affiliation, and geographic location of the employer. Median annual earnings of carpenters were $40,820 in 2014. The lowest ten percent earned less than $25,640, and the highest ten percent earned more than $74,750. Earnings may be reduced on occasion because carpenters lose work time in bad weather and during recessions when jobs are unavailable. Carpenters may be required to purchase their own hand tools and safety equipment.

Carpenters may receive paid vacations, holidays, and sick days; life and health insurance; and retirement benefits. These are usually paid by the employer.

Metropolitan Areas with the Highest Employment Level in this Occupation

Metropolitan area	Employment	Employment per thousand jobs	Hourly mean wage
New York-White Plains-Wayne, NY-NJ	23,670	4.39	$32.32
Chicago-Joliet-Naperville, IL	12,860	3.43	$30.94
Los Angeles-Long Beach-Glendale, CA	12,810	3.16	$26.08
Nassau-Suffolk, NY	10,720	8.50	$29.71
Washington-Arlington-Alexandria, DC-VA-MD-WV	10,450	4.39	$22.41
Houston-Sugar Land-Baytown, TX	10,260	3.61	$16.69
Seattle-Bellevue-Everett, WA	10,190	6.83	$26.09
Philadelphia, PA	9,750	5.24	$26.27
Riverside-San Bernardino-Ontario, CA	9,430	7.54	$23.01
Pittsburgh, PA	8,650	7.66	$22.79

Source: Bureau of Labor Statistics

EMPLOYMENT AND OUTLOOK

There were approximately one million carpenters employed nationally in 2012. About one-third of all carpenters were self-employed. Employment of carpenters is expected to grow faster than the average for all occupations through the year 2022, which means employment is projected to increase 20 percent to 25 percent. Population growth over the next decade should increase construction activity with demand for new housing. The need to renovate existing buildings, especially to make them more energy efficient, will also encourage job growth. However, the demand for carpenters will be offset somewhat as a result of the increasing use of prefabricated components, such as prehung doors, windows, wall panels and stairs, that can be installed much more quickly.

Employment Trend, Projected 2012–22

Carpenters: 24%

Construction trades workers: 22%

Total, all occupations: 11%

Note: "All Occupations" includes all occupations in the U.S. Economy. Source: U.S. Bureau of Labor Statistics, Employment Projections Program

Related Occupations
- Construction Laborer
- Drywall Installer & Taper
- General Maintenance Mechanic
- Insulation Worker
- Plasterer
- Roofer
- Solar Energy System Installer
- Woodworker

Related Military Occupations
- Combat Engineer
- Construction Specialist

Conversation With . . .
MARIA KLEMPERER-JOHNSON

Owner/Instructor, Hammerstone School
Trumansburg, New York
Carpenter, 13 years

1. What was your individual career path in terms of education/training, entry-level job, or other significant opportunity?

I had no formal education before becoming a carpenter. I had dabbled with woodworking as a kid. In college, I was inspired to build some small furniture. I really loved the Shaker style, so I bought a plan book and built a Shaker bedside table and a side table. I still have and use one of them; the other was a wedding present for a friend. But, aside from woodshop in middle school, I had no previous carpentry schooling. I did go to college to study computer science, and that served me well by training me to think critically, write clearly, and work hard. These traits have helped me as both a carpenter and a business owner.

When I decided to become a carpenter, I interviewed at several cabinet shops and took a job at the one that seemed the best fit and that paid the best. From there, I learned what I know on the job.

In 2013, I started Hammerstone School, which focuses on carpentry for women with the goal of increasing the number of women in the trades. I had been working as a carpenter for eleven years, and was almost always the only woman on a job site. Nationally, fewer than 3 percent of carpenters are women. We organized the first class around the construction of a tiny house for a local woman, and the instant response (we filled the class in only two weeks) demonstrated the need for classes like this. Since then, we have expanded the school and teach year-round. We still teach classes around the building of tiny houses, since they are the perfect size for short classes, but we offer other programs as well.

I always knew that I loved making things, which is part of why I studied computer science. I was able to build things, albeit in the virtual world. After I graduated, I did work for a couple years as a programmer in Seattle. What I realized is that programming only satisfied one part of my creative urge. The act of working with my hands in a physical manner was missing. And I didn't like being stuck indoors all the time. When I became a carpenter, I was able to take beautiful materials and build things that served a useful purpose.

2. What are the most important skills and/or qualities for someone in your profession?

When I'm hiring carpenters, the qualities I look for are the ability to listen well, learn quickly, and work hard no matter what the task. The technical skills can be learned quickly by anyone who's bright and tries hard. It's helpful to be coordinated, have good spatial and math skills, and not be afraid of heights—but all these traits can be developed with patience and exposure. The personal character traits of a good attitude and work ethic are the core traits I look for.

3. What do you wish you had known going into this profession?

I wish I had known how much I was going to love it. I would have become a carpenter sooner!

4. Are there many job opportunities in your profession? In what specific areas?

Opportunities for carpenters are very dependent on the economy. Right now, I know a lot of contractors who are looking for good carpenters and can't find them. Even in slow times, though, carpentry is a sought-after skill. You might end up doing more fix-it work rather than new construction.

5. How do you see your profession changing in the next five years? What role will technology play in those changes, and what skills will be required?

There are huge advances being made in the field of building science, and soon, all builders—not just those specializing in energy-efficient construction—will have to understand the science behind what they build. If you work building homes, you will find that very little of your job involves cutting and nailing wood. You will be working with high tech wraps and tapes and insulation, and will have to understand the principles of building science to install them correctly.

6. What do you enjoy most about your job? What do you enjoy least about your job?

I enjoy working with my mind and body in equal measure. I enjoy working outside, even in marginal weather. The part of my job I enjoy the least is estimating the cost of a job.

7. Can you suggest a valuable "try this" for students considering a career in your profession?

If you know of a house being built, ask if you can watch. Talk to someone from the crew to learn more about their job. You could get a summer job as a carpenter's assistant or volunteer with Habitat for Humanity. Take woodshop or a carpentry course at your local vocational school and tackle carpentry projects of your own.

MORE INFORMATION

Associated Builders and Contractors
4250 N. Fairfax Drive, 9th Floor
Arlington, VA 22203
703.812.2000
www.abc.org

Associated General Contractors of America
Director, Construction Education Services
2300 Wilson Boulevard, Suite 400
Arlington, VA 22201
703.548.3118
www.agc.org

Building Trades Association
16th Street, NW
Washington, DC 20006
800.326.7800
www.buildingtrades.com

National Association of Home Builders
1201 15th Street, NW
Washington, DC 20005
800.368.5242
www.nahb.com

National Association of the Remodeling Industry
P.O. Box 4250
Des Plaines, Illinois 60016
847.298.9200
www.nari.org

National Center for Construction Education and Research
13614 Progress Boulevard
Alachua, FL 32615
888.622.3720
www.nccer.org

United Brotherhood of Carpenters
101 Constitution Avenue NW
Washington, DC 20001
www.carpenters.org

John Pritchard/Editor

Carpet Installer

Snapshot

Career Cluster(s): Building & Construction, Architecture & Construction
Interests: Working with your hands, mathematics, customer service
Earnings (Yearly Average): $35,880
Employment & Outlook: Average Growth Expected

OVERVIEW

Sphere of Work

Carpet installers install flooring materials in residences and commercial buildings. In addition to preparing surfaces for new carpet, they may remove old carpets and flooring materials as part of a complete floor-covering overhaul. Carpet installers are skilled at determining the type of floor covering that is best suited for a particular space or application. Unlike most trade positions, carpet installers have a relatively high amount of interaction with clients, making customer service an integral part of the job.

Work Environment

Carpet installers work in residences, businesses, and industrial buildings where carpeted surfaces are needed. Nearly all carpet installations take place indoors. Much of the work of carpet-installation professionals is done close to the ground, in a kneeling or crouching position.

Profile

Working Conditions: Work Indoors
Physical Strength: Heavy Work
Education Needs: On-The-Job Training, High School Diploma or G.E.D., High School Diploma with Technical Education, Apprenticeship
Licensure/Certification: Usually Not Required
Opportunities For Experience: Apprenticeship, Part-Time Work
Holland Interest Score*: REI, RES

* See Appendix A

Occupation Interest

Carpet installation attracts professionals who have some background in other trades, such as carpentry and construction, and enjoy working with their hands. Many people are attracted to the field of carpet installation because of their desire to be self-employed, as many small-scale carpeting jobs can be completed by individuals or small teams of workers. Since the trade is learned through on-the-job training, carpet installation is a common job for transitioning construction-labor professionals, students, and other workers who are biding their time for career transitions or vacancies in their desired field.

A Day in the Life—Duties and Responsibilities

Carpet installers begin projects by consulting with clients about the type of carpet they need. Assisting clients in selecting the type of carpet that is best suited to a particular space is one of the major aspects of the position. This is often achieved through the presentation of sample carpet pieces, discussion about the intended use and everyday foot traffic in a particular space, and consideration of texture, style, color, and durability.

Carpet installers may also be called upon to remove old carpets that are old or have been damaged by water or other substances. Carpet removal is a somewhat intricate process that involves removing floor coverings without causing extensive damage to subfloors. Removal of old carpet adhesives may require the use of certain chemicals.

The measurement and analysis of the floor space is another major facet of the job. Carpet installers need to make and record accurate measurements to ensure that the right amount of material is ordered for a particular job. Appropriately managing floor-covering materials and eliminating the possibility of waste is one of the key responsibilities of carpet-installation professionals .

Duties and Responsibilities

- Studying blueprints or floor sketches to determine amount of material needed
- Removing old carpeting where necessary
- Measuring, cutting and installing tackless strips along baseboard or wall
- Measuring and cutting carpet to fit along wall edges, openings and projections
- Sewing or taping sections of carpeting together and seaming edges where necessary
- Pressing carpet in place over tackless strips
- Using metal pins to fasten carpet or using adhesive to fasten carpet tiles to floor

WORK ENVIRONMENT

Physical Environment

Carpet installers work anywhere carpets are used, from homes and businesses to commercial and public buildings, including schools, libraries, theaters, retail stores, and showrooms.

Relevant Skills and Abilities

Organization & Management Skills
- Making decisions
- Paying attention to and handling details
- Performing routine work

Technical Skills
- Performing scientific, mathematical and technical work
- Working with your hands

Unclassified Skills
- Using set methods and standards in your work

Human Environment

Carpet installation requires strong collaboration and customer-service skills, as there is a high degree of customer interaction. In addition, carpet installers must also be able to work effectively in small work groups on occasion to ensure projects are completed on budget and in a timely and organized manner.

Technological Environment

Carpet installers use a variety of different technologies and tools. Computer software is an increasingly common component in helping clients choose carpet color, texture, and style. Common hand tools for carpet installation include cutters, rollers, utility knifes, shears, and adhesive applicators. Use of chalking and measurement tools is also commonplace.

EDUCATION, TRAINING, AND ADVANCEMENT

High School/Secondary

High school students can best prepare for a career in carpet installation with courses in algebra, geometry, chemistry, physics, and computers. Advanced placement (AP) classes in these subjects are especially recommended. Course work in foundational arts and industrial arts can also provide an effective foundation for future work in construction and design.

Suggested High School Subjects
- Applied Math
- Blueprint Reading
- English
- Industrial Arts

- Shop Math
- Woodshop

Famous First

William Peter Sprague of Philadelphia, PA founded the first carpet mill in 1791. He mostly manufactured Axminster carpets, which were made on handlooms, and many of his designs reflected the patriot atmosphere surrounding the creation of the newly formed republic of the United States of America. By 1810, the handloom was modified in order to create more product more efficiently.

Postsecondary

Postsecondary course work is not a prerequisite for a career in the carpet-installation industry. An individual interested in establishing his or her own small business concentrating on carpet and flooring installation will benefit from an associate or bachelor's degree in small-business management, business finance, or small industry.

Adult Job Seekers

Carpet installers tend to work varied hours. While carpet installation in new construction sites can take place during regular business hours, renovations or carpet alterations undertaken in public and commercial buildings often take place when the tenants of such establishments are not present, meaning many jobs can take place in the evening, on weekends, or overnight. Carpet installers traditionally have major holidays off.

Professional Certification and Licensure

While no licensure is required to become a carpet installer, necessary insurance and other contractor certification is required in most states for small businesses and tradespeople.

Additional Requirements

Carpet installers must possess the flexibility and strength required to move heavy materials. The physical nature of the job can require long hours of movement close to the ground. Workers must also familiarize themselves with the safety requirements of the position, as they often use potentially hazardous adhesives and other chemicals.

Fun Fact

Carpets of twisted grass or animal hair found in prehistoric caves were primarily for decoration.
Source: http://visual.ly/fun-facts-flooring

EARNINGS AND ADVANCEMENT

Earnings may be affected by the employer's size, geographic location, and union affiliation, and the individual's experience and skill. Carpet installers are paid hourly or according to the amount of carpet installed.

In 2014, median annual earnings for carpet installers were $35,880. The lowest ten percent earned less than $20,580, and the highest ten percent earned more than $73,560. Apprentices and other trainees usually start out earning about half of what an experienced worker earns, though their wage rate increases as they advance through the training program.

Carpet installers may receive paid vacations, holidays, and sick days; life and health insurance; and retirement benefits. These are usually paid by the employer.

Metropolitan Areas with the Highest
Employment Level in this Occupation

Metropolitan area	Employment	Employment per thousand jobs	Hourly mean wage
New York-White Plains-Wayne, NY-NJ	1,280	0.24	$22.87
Santa Ana-Anaheim-Irvine, CA	1,210	0.81	$20.06
Chicago-Joliet-Naperville, IL	1,110	0.29	$31.90
St. Louis, MO-IL	680	0.52	$24.86
San Jose-Sunnyvale-Santa Clara, CA	650	0.66	$27.20
Pittsburgh, PA	640	0.57	$21.86
Oakland-Fremont-Hayward, CA	540	0.53	$30.43
Atlanta-Sandy Springs-Marietta, GA	530	0.22	$15.90
San Diego-Carlsbad-San Marcos, CA	500	0.38	$19.47
Baltimore-Towson, MD	480	0.37	$17.63

Source: Bureau of Labor Statistics

EMPLOYMENT AND OUTLOOK

There were approximately 35,000 carpet installers employed nationally in 2012. Many carpet installers worked for flooring contractors or floor covering retailers. About 48 percent were self-employed. Employment of carpet installers is expected to grow about as fast as the average for all occupations through the year 2022, which means employment is projected to increase 7 percent to 12 percent.

There is less demand for carpet as more homeowners are choosing hardwood and tile flooring, so job opportunities are likely to be best for workers able to install both carpeting and resilient flooring. Because much of their work is done in existing buildings, employment generally remains stable even when construction activity declines.

Employment Trend, Projected 2012–22

Flooring Installers (all): 13%

Carpet Installers: 12%

Total, all occupations: 11%

Note: "All Occupations" includes all occupations in the U.S. Economy. Source: U.S. Bureau of Labor Statistics, Employment Projections Program

Related Occupations
- Tile & Marble Setter
- Upholsterer

Conversation With . . .
E. C. "BILL" DEARING

President
North American Laminate Flooring Association (NALFA)
Flooring Business Consultant, TORLYS, Inc.
Mississaugua, Ontario
Flooring industry, 22 years

1. What is a typical career path in your industry and, if you have specialized, how did you go about doing so?

My experience was in bringing consumer goods into the U.S. Twenty years into my career, I was asked, through a relationship with an executive in Sweden, to assist a small team to bring laminate flooring into the United States. This was two decades ago and the company was Pergo. They were established in the Scandinavian countries and had been exported to Germany and France. My background is in sales and, as I rose through the ranks, I learned to work closely with marketing and then, more broadly, in finance. My passion always has been to bring a new consumer product to market.

Launching Pergo in North America took a year of preparation and market research. When I first met with my colleague to discuss the prospects, I associated flooring with non-branded sales and was skeptical. By the time we got to launch—and I had been in every country where Pergo was sold, including Asian countries—we knew everything. Our success was significant; people still think of Pergo and laminate flooring as the same thing, the way people say "Coca Cola" when they want a cola soda.

I stayed with Pergo for over twelve years, and then got involved with TORLYS, a company that produces all types of flooring, not just laminate. They produce specialty floors such as leather and even cork.

The beauty of flooring is that everybody has a floor. Much of the business depends on the overall economy and housing growth. That said, even in a down market, people nest and fix up their house. Flooring is one of the few products that has a specialty marketplace and that isn't entirely sold through national chains.

2. What are the most important skills and/or qualities for someone in your profession?

You must be a good listener to succeed in all aspects of our business. Consider installation and inspection services: both involve close interaction with companies and consumers. After listening comes the need to communicate effectively, whether through letters, e-mail, text, or talking.

Finally, perseverance—intelligent perseverance, I call it. That means that if you're constantly hitting a wall and not breaking through, you need to realize there's probably an end to the wall you can slip around. Find it.

3. What do you wish you had known before going into this business?

The critical importance of design and architectural interaction. Many designers have a direct influence on flooring. Builders, for instance, are influenced by designers. If you influence the designer, you double your chance to influence the new home construction market, for example.

4. Are there many job opportunities in your profession? In what specific areas?

Unless the world goes back to dirt as a preferred floor covering, there always will be opportunities in development, retail, commercial, sales, marketing, and technical fields. For example, because installation companies are in high demand, competent installation service is a sure win. The hands-on aspects can be learned at many community colleges or through on-the-job training. The business aspects of installation are also taught through college-level business courses. Installation can be tedious and physically hard, which is why a good education is important in order to advance.

5. How do you see your profession changing in the next five years, what role will technology play in those changes, and what skills will be required?

Computer-generated flooring plans, developed onsite, can instantly show the consumer, architect, or designer their measurements and design choices. This is already available on the commercial side of the business. Retail, manufacturing, or distributing companies that aren't investing in this area will be left behind. In addition, installers are aligning with businesses that have sub-specialties such as insurance replacement for flooring.

6. What do you enjoy most about your job? What do you enjoy the least?

I love the thrill of bringing a new product to market. You are creating ripples for other people to get good, gainful employment from something that wasn't there before, as we did when we brought laminate to this country.

I least enjoy the travel and time away from home. I'm a family man.

7. Can you suggest a valuable "try this" for students considering a career in your profession?

If you are interested the flooring business, look at trade publications, which are quick and easy to review, such as "Floor Covering Weekly" or "Floor Covering News;" these cover products and personalities. "Floor Focus" does product studies. In addition, trade associations can be very helpful. These include the North American Laminate Association, National Wood Flooring Association, Carpet and Rug Institute, and the American Floorcovering Alliance.

MORE INFORMATION

Certified Floorcovering Installers
CFI National Office
2400 East Truman Road
Kansas City, MO 64127
816.231.4646
www.cfiinstallers.com

Floor Covering Installation Contractors Association
7439 Millwood Drive
West Bloomfield, MI 48322-1234
248.661.5015
www.fcica.com

International Union of Painters & Allied Trades
7234 Parkway Drive
Hanover, MD 21076
410.564.5900
www.iupat.org

National Association of Home Builders
1201 15th Street, NW
Washington, DC 20005
800.368.5242
www.nahb.com

National Center for Construction Education and Research
13614 Progress Boulevard
Alachua, FL 32615
888.622.3720
www.nccer.org

Resilient Floor Covering Institute
115 Broad Street, Suite 201
LaGrange, GA 30240
www.rfci.com

United Brotherhood of Carpenters
101 Constitution Avenue, NW
Washington, DC 20001
202.546.6206
www.carpenters.org

John Pritchard/Editor

Cement Mason

Snapshot

Career Cluster(s): Building & Construction, Architecture & Construction

Interests: Working with machinery, working with your hands

Earnings (Yearly Average): $36,760

Employment & Outlook: Faster Than Average Growth Expected

OVERVIEW

Sphere of Work

Cement masons perform a large variety of construction tasks. They pour and smooth concrete and other cement mixtures to create and repair sidewalks, walkways, roads, and other surfaces. Cement masons work with engineers and construction workers to properly set the frames that hold concrete in place while it is drying. Reinforcing rebar or mesh wires are placed within these frames by cement masons to further strengthen the concrete. Once the concrete is poured, cement masons spread, level, and smooth the composite.

Work Environment

Cement masons work in a variety of environments, both indoors and outdoors and in all kinds of weather. Cement masons will often work within a construction site, but they can also perform jobs at commercial buildings and residential locations.

Depending on the job location, a cement mason could work in an environment that is dusty or muddy, so proper protective gear is recommended. Like all construction jobs, a cement mason's work environment has hazards to be aware of.

Profile

Working Conditions: Work both Indoors and Outdoors
Physical Strength: Medium Work, Heavy Work
Education Needs: On-The-Job Training, High School Diploma with Technical Education, Apprenticeship
Licensure/Certification: Usually Not Required
Opportunities For Experience: Apprenticeship, Military Service
Holland Interest Score*: RES

* See Appendix A

Occupation Interest

A cement mason's job covers a diverse range of construction tasks. This job attracts professionals who enjoy working with their hands outside of an office environment and can adapt to different work environments. Cement masons use a variety of tools to complete their jobs, so the ability to handle heavy and light machinery is recommended.

A Day in the Life—Duties and Responsibilities

After assessing a particular job, a cement mason will set the frames and reinforcing materials that hold the concrete in place. Concrete is made through a mixture of cement, sand, and water inside a concrete mixing machine. The frames need to be set at the proper pitch and depth and aligned correctly. Concrete is then poured into the frames. The concrete can be poured from a truck, by hand, or via a wheelbarrow. The cement mason needs to watch and make sure that the concrete is poured evenly in the correct places. Throughout the process, a cement mason must ensure the job is in compliance with certain laws, regulations, and standards.

While the concrete is still wet, a cement mason will spread, level, and smooth the concrete using a variety of hand tools, including rakes, shovels, trowels, and screeds. The edges of the concrete are smoothed and straightened with tools such as jointers and straightedges. After the concrete has dried, a cement mason will determine if the surface requires any hardening, sealing, or waterproofing compounds. A cement mason can also use colored powder to create a predetermined finish on the concrete.

If the cement mason is performing a repair job, different tools and tasks are required. In order to repair concrete that has already been set and dried, a cement mason will chip, grind, and remove areas using pneumatic chisels, power grinders, or a variety of hand tools.

Duties and Responsibilities

- Spreading concrete to specified depth and consistency
- Leveling and shaping surfaces of freshly poured concrete
- Finishing surfaces by wetting concrete and rubbing with abrasive stone
- Removing rough or defective spots from surfaces, patching holes with fresh concrete or epoxy compound
- Molding expansion joints and edges
- Operating machines to smooth concrete surfaces
- Coloring and texturing concrete to prescribed finish
- Mixing cement, using hoes or concrete mixing machines
- Setting forms

OCCUPATION SPECIALTIES

Step Finishers

Step Finishers are cement masons who specialize in finishing steps and stairways.

Maintenance Cement Masons

Maintenance Cement Masons break up and repair old concrete surfaces using pneumatic tools.

Cementers

Cementers may spread premixed cement over the deck, inner surfaces, joints, and crevices of ships.

Terrazzo Workers

Terrazzo Workers apply cement, sand, coloring materials and marble chips to floors, stairways and cabinet fixtures to create durable and decorative surfaces.

WORK ENVIRONMENT

Physical Environment

Construction sites are the most common environments that cement masons will work in, but they can also work in and around commercial and residential locations. While the job is being assessed and during the planning stages, a cement mason may work in an office environment with other construction workers and contractors.

Human Environment

Cement masons collaborate and interact with a variety of professionals in the construction business, including engineers, site managers, contractors, and other masons.

Relevant Skills and Abilities

Organization & Management Skills
- Following instructions
- Meeting goals and deadlines

Organization & Management Skills
- Paying attention to and handling details
- Performing routine work
- Working quickly when necessary

Technical Skills
- Performing scientific, mathematical and technical work
- Working with data or numbers
- Working with machines, tools or other objects

Unclassified Skills
- Performing work that produces tangible results

Technological Environment

Cement masons use a variety of technologies, ranging from power tools such as power drills and grinders to hand tools such as chisels and straightedges. They also have to wear a variety of safety gear, including helmets, gloves, and goggles.

EDUCATION, TRAINING, AND ADVANCEMENT

High School/Secondary

There are no specific education requirements to become a cement mason, but masons most commonly have a high-school diploma or the equivalent. Cement masons should be adept in a variety of subjects that may be taught in high school, including mathematics, mechanical drawing, and how to read blueprints.

Suggested High School Subjects
- Applied Math
- Blueprint Reading
- English
- Machining Technology
- Masonry
- Mechanical Drawing

- Metals Technology
- Shop Math
- Woodshop

Famous First

While cement was originally invented in England in the second half of the nineteenth century, American David Oliver Saylor of Allentown, PA, bettered the process in 1871. Even though his hydraulic cement received a patent, the prevailing idea was that English cement was better and continued to be brought to America on ballast ships because it was so heavy. In 1897, American cement usage outstripped European usage for the first time.

Postsecondary

Cement masons are usually not required to have a college degree, but it is a great help if they have a strong background in a variety of subjects. Since the job often requires the ability to read and modify blueprints, knowledge of mechanical drawing and mathematics is important. Many technical colleges offer appropriate courses for a cement mason.

Knowledge of administration and management is also helpful for a cement mason. Management courses can help a mason understand the strategic planning, resource allocation, and human resource aspects of the construction business. Many community colleges offer such courses.

Related College Majors
- Masonry & Tile Setting

Adult Job Seekers

Adults who are interested in becoming cement masons should first research forecasted job opportunities and annual income to make sure this position matches their needs. Being a cement mason requires a lot of communication and collaboration with others in the construction trade, so a potential mason should be very outgoing and possess great interpersonal and communication skills. A cement mason should be in excellent physical condition, as the job requires constant kneeling, bending over, and using power tools. Job seekers should also be mindful that a cement mason works in a large variety of environments that can be hazardous.

Professional Certification and Licensure

Cement masons will often be trained in a three-year apprenticeship under an experienced mason. Cement masons in training must receive 144 hours of technical instruction and 2,000 hours of paid training every year during their apprenticeship. Cement masons are instructed in a variety of construction basics, such as safety practices, first aid, and blueprint reading. Once cement masons complete their apprentice programs, they are considered to be journeymen, which will allow them to complete tasks without supervision.

Additional Requirements

Becoming a cement mason requires a lot of on-the-job training. Many cement masons begin their career as a laborer or helper on a construction site. This is when a lot of the basics of construction are learned. On-the-job training programs for cement masons are typically informal. Experienced cement masons and others in the construction trade will train new masons to use the tools, machines, and materials required of them. Training commonly begins with the use of tools and how to edge, joint, and modify wet concrete after it has been poured. Training will then progress to more complex tasks such as framing, reinforcing, and pouring.

After completing an apprenticeship, a cement mason can apply to join a local construction union. Once a cement mason has been accepted into a local union, he or she can contact the local union contractor or business agent to ask about joining the Laborers' International Union of North America (LIUNA), which is one of the largest unions in the United States. Joining any union requires proof of hours worked, such as pay stubs or W-2 tax forms. There are initiation fees to be paid while joining a union and yearly fees after the cement mason has become a member.

Fun Fact

The English quarried a natural deposit of cement rock in 1796, sold as Roman Cement. In 1874, a bricklayer created a powdered cement he named Portland Cement because its color was similar to quarried stone from the Isle of Portland.

Source: http://sciencewithkids.com/science-facts/facts-about-concrete.html

EARNINGS AND ADVANCEMENT

Cement masons are usually paid an hourly rate that is governed by the union contract covering the job site. Non-union wages are usually lower than those of union workers. Earnings of cement masons may occasionally be reduced because bad weather and downturns in construction activity can limit the time they can work. In 2014, cement masons had median annual earnings of $36,760. The lowest ten percent earned less than $24,810, and the highest ten percent earned more than $64,250.

Apprentices usually start at fifty to sixty percent of the rate paid to experienced workers. Cement masons may travel to different job sites at their own expense and are usually required to purchase their own tools.

Cement masons may receive paid vacations, holidays, and sick days; life and health insurance; and retirement benefits. These are usually paid by the employer

Metropolitan Areas with the Highest
Employment Level in this Occupation

Metropolitan area	Employment	Employment per thousand jobs	Hourly mean wage
Houston-Sugar Land-Baytown, TX	4,420	1.56	$14.84
Phoenix-Mesa-Glendale, AZ	3,460	1.90	$18.25
Washington-Arlington-Alexandria, DC-VA-MD-WV	3,270	1.37	$20.43
Chicago-Joliet-Naperville, IL	3,060	0.81	$30.65
Dallas-Plano-Irving, TX	2,980	1.33	$14.75
Los Angeles-Long Beach-Glendale, CA	2,750	0.68	$25.23
Santa Ana-Anaheim-Irvine, CA	2,410	1.63	$25.14
Minneapolis-St. Paul-Bloomington, MN-WI	2,380	1.30	$23.11
Riverside-San Bernardino-Ontario, CA	2,360	1.89	$22.55
New York-White Plains-Wayne, NY-NJ	2,290	0.43	$33.89

Source: Bureau of Labor Statistics

EMPLOYMENT AND OUTLOOK

There were about 145,000 cement masons employed nationally in 2012. Employment is expected to grow much faster than the average for all occupations through the year 2022, which means employment is projected to increase up to 29 percent. These workers will be needed to build highways, bridges, subways, factories, office buildings, hotels, shopping centers, schools, hospitals and other structures to accommodate the growing population. In addition, the increasing use of concrete as a building material will add to the demand. Job openings will also arise from the need to replace workers transferring to other occupations or leaving the labor force.

Employment Trend, Projected 2012–22

Cement masons and concrete finishers: 29%

Construction trades workers: 22%

Terrazzo workers and finishers: 20%

Total, all occupations: 11%

Note: "All Occupations" includes all occupations in the U.S. Economy. Source: U.S. Bureau of Labor Statistics, Employment Projections Program

Related Occupations
- Brickmason/Stonemason
- Construction Laborer
- Drywall Installer & Taper
- Plasterer
- Tile & Marble Setter

Conversation With . . .
MICHELLE WILSON

Director of Concrete Technology
Portland Cement Association, Skokie, Illinois
Cement industry, 22 years

1. What was your individual career path in terms of education/training, entry-level job, or other significant opportunity?

Growing up, I wanted to be an architect and was obsessed with structures. I have a bachelor's degree in architectural engineering with an emphasis in structural engineering and concrete materials from the Milwaukee School of Engineering. One of my first structural engineering courses was in concrete design and I loved it. It was partly due to a great professor, as well as the subject. My professor did a hands-on demonstration about reinforced concrete. I was mesmerized by how different materials handle stress, and how the component materials of concrete and steel worked together.

After receiving my bachelor's degree, I continued researching concrete materials while taking graduate classes at University of Wisconsin-Milwaukee. I also worked full-time as a field inspector performing quality control and laboratory testing of concrete and other construction materials for STS Consultants in Milwaukee. While working at STS, I subcontracted with Construction Technology Laboratories (now CTLGroup) on a restoration project. That led to a full time position with CTL as an assistant engineer, troubleshooting concrete and inspecting repair projects all over North America. It was an exciting time in my career. My only regret was leaving graduate school without completing my master's degree.

In 1999, I was offered a position in the education and training department at the Portland Cement Association (PCA), educating members and other industry professionals through literature, e-learning, and in-house training. It was a big change from field work, so I was hesitant at first to accept, but it has been a perfect fit. My role has expanded into a job that blends university research with industry needs. It's essential that I keep up with trends, technologies, and other matters affecting the industry.

Now, as Director of Concrete Technology, in addition to teaching courses and writing about concrete technology, I help develop industry standards through committee involvement with the American Concrete Institute (ACI) and the American Society of Testing and Materials (ASTM).

2. What are the most important skills and/or qualities for someone in your profession?

You'll need math, chemistry, geology, problem-solving, and hands-on laboratory and testing skills.

You'll also need strong communication skills, enthusiasm for the materials, motivation, attention to detail, a good work ethic, time-management skills, and the ability to work as a team player.

3. What do you wish you had known going into this profession?

I wish, as a student, I had been more involved with professional associations such as the American Concrete Institute. I would have gained a much broader perspective of the jobs available in the concrete industry earlier in my career if I'd attended chapter meetings and conventions as a student. Mentors are available to students. Both PCA and ACI have education foundations that provide scholarships for students who study concrete-related research topics.

4. Are there many job opportunities in your profession? In what specific areas?

Yes, many. We have a high demand for a skilled labor force. Certifications in this area are often required, and very desirable, whether you're a driver working at a ready-mix plant, field laborer, or testing technician.

The cement industry employs many engineers—ceramics, chemical, civil, electrical, environmental, geological, materials, and mechanical; analytical, organic, and inorganic chemists; geologists; and computer scientists. In addition to people who can manage companies, we need researchers to develop new technologies. Educators, promoters, and technical sales and marketing are also needed.

5. How do you see your profession changing in the next five years, what role will technology play in those changes, and what skills will be required?

Concrete is a highly technical field that is ever-changing. Recent innovations include translucent, smog-eating, bendable, and self-consolidating concretes. Yes, you can throw some water in with cement and gravel and install a fencepost. But concrete used for commercial structures is very technical. There are minimum code requirements and science behind changing the mixture to meet the end performance, such as setting faster, gaining higher strengths, and resisting different types of weather.

6. What do you enjoy most about your job? What do you enjoy least about your job?

I love the subject matter. I still get excited when talking and writing about concrete. I also love the interaction and collaboration with leaders and experts in the industry. The relationships I have built with my colleagues over the past 20 years mean the most to me. On the downside, there can be long meetings and late nights reviewing reports and ballots.

7. Can you suggest a valuable "try this" for students considering a career in your profession?

Take a tour of a local ready-mix or cement plant and attend a chapter meeting of a concrete-related organization such as the American Concrete Institute. Volunteer for Habitat for Humanity. Take a class on geology.

MORE INFORMATION

ACI International
P.O. Box 9094
Farmington Hills, MI 48333
248.848.3700
www.aci-int.org

American Concrete Pavement Association
9450 Bryn Mawr, Suite 150
Rosemont, IL 60018
847.966.2272
www.pavement.com

Associated General Contractors of America
Director, Construction Education Services
2300 Wilson Boulevard, Suite 400
Arlington, VA 22201
703.548.3118
www.agc.org

Building Trades Association
16th Street, NW
Washington, DC 20006
800.326.7800
www.buildingtrades.com

International Masonry Institute
The James Brice House
42 East Street
Annapolis, MD 21401
410.280.1305
www.imiweb.org

International Union of Bricklayers and Allied Craftworkers
620 F Street NW
Washington, DC 20004
202.783.3788
www.bacweb.org

Laborers' International Union of North America
905 Sixteenth Street NW
Washington, DC 20006
212.737.8320
www.liuna.org

National Association of Home Builders
1201 15th Street, NW
Washington, DC 20005
800.368.5242
www.nahb.com

National Center for Construction Education and Research
13614 Progress Boulevard
Alachua, FL 32615
888.622.3720
www.nccer.org

National Concrete Masonry Association
13750 Sunrise Valley Drive
Herndon, VA 20171-4662
703.713.1900
www.ncma.org

National Terrazzo & Mosaic Association
P.O. Box 2605
Fredericksburg, TX 78624
800.323.9736
www.ntma.com

Operative Plasterers' & Cement Masons' Intl. Association
11720 Beltsville Drive, Suite 700
Beltsville, MD 20705
301.623.1000
www.opcmia.org

Portland Cement Association
5420 Old Orchard Road
Skokie, IL 60077
847.966.6200
www.cement.org

United Brotherhood of Carpenters
101 Constitution Avenue, NW
Washington, DC 20001
202.546.6206
www.carpenters.org

Patrick Cooper/Editor

Civil Engineer

Snapshot

Career Cluster: Building & Construction; Science, Technology, Engineering & Mathematics

Interests: Infrastructure, construction, solving problems

Earnings (Yearly Average): $87,130

Employment & Outlook: Faster Than Average Growth Expected

OVERVIEW

Sphere of Work

Civil engineers plan and oversee infrastructure construction projects such as bridges, dams, roads and highways, sewer systems, power plants, and buildings. They assess costs, durability of building materials, and the physical environments in which the project is being constructed. Civil engineers direct and help survey sites, analyze all blueprints, drawings, and photographs, test soil and other materials, and write and present important reports. They work for federal, state, and local governments as well as engineering and architectural firms. Most

civil engineers specialize in a subfield such as sanitation engineering, structural engineering, or transportation engineering.

Work Environment

Civil engineers work in government offices, architectural firms, engineering consultant groups, utility companies, and other office environments where meetings are conducted, plans are drafted, and reports are filed. Civil engineers also spend a great deal of time at project sites, which include building renovation and construction projects, active roadways and highways, along sewer and water lines, and other parts of a region's infrastructure. Many civil engineers spend the majority of their time on site. Although most civil engineers work a standard forty-hour workweek, they may work extra hours as deadlines approach or emergencies occur.

Profile

Working Conditions: Work both Indoors and Outdoors
Physical Strength: Light Work
Education Needs: Bachelor's Degree, Master's Degree, Doctoral Degree
Licensure/Certification: Required
Opportunities For Experience: Internship, Apprenticeship, Military Service, Part-Time Work
Holland Interest Score*: IRE

* See Appendix A

Occupation Interest

Civil engineering is essential to all developed communities—civil engineers help build roads, water and sewer systems, waste management units, and irrigation networks. As they are responsible for public safety, civil engineers must be attentive to detail, demonstrate sound judgment, work well under pressure, and adhere to a strict code of ethics. They also need to be innovative and have strong reasoning skills. The demand for civil engineers remains high, and the number of open jobs is expected to increase dramatically over the next decade. Civil engineering salaries are competitive, and civil engineers typically receive strong benefits.

A Day in the Life—Duties and Responsibilities

Civil engineers' daily responsibilities and duties vary based on their place of employment and specialty. A civil engineer employed by a city government may focus on only one or two major projects per year, while a civil engineer employed by a major architectural firm may be involved in a greater number of projects. Some civil engineers conduct thorough soil studies in addition to structural integrity and strength tests on building materials. Many civil engineers are also supervisors, overseeing construction crews and other engineers at work sites. Civil engineers occasionally act as consultants, providing technical advice and studies to the client as needed.

In general, civil engineers conduct studies and evaluations of existing engineering issues, such as traffic flow studies for roadway construction projects or flow rate analyses for water system upgrades. They prepare public reports, such as environmental impact assessments, bid proposals for contractors, and detailed descriptions of the proposed project site or sites. Civil engineers write feasibility studies in which they estimate the costs and quantities of building materials, equipment, and labor required for a given project. Using drafting tools and software, they create designs for new or improved infrastructure. During the construction phase, civil engineers visit and inspect work sites regularly, monitoring progress and ensuring compliance with government safety standards and the client's wishes. These inspections also entail testing the strength and integrity of the materials used as well as the environment in which they are being used.

Duties and Responsibilities

- Preparing plans and specifications
- Estimating costs and requirements of projects
- Testing materials to be used
- Determining solutions to problems
- Supervising construction and maintenance
- Inspecting existing or newly constructed projects and recommending repairs
- Performing technical research
- Determining the impact of construction on the environment

OCCUPATION SPECIALTIES

Transportation Engineers

Transportation Engineers design and prepare plans, estimates and specifications for the construction and operation of surface transportation projects. Transportation engineers may specialize in a particular phase of the work such as making surveys of roads, improving road signs or lighting, or directing and coordinating construction or maintenance activity.

Structural Engineers

Structural Engineers plan, design and oversee the erection of steel and other structural materials in buildings, bridges and other structures that require a stress analysis.

Hydraulic Engineers

Hydraulic Engineers design and direct the construction of power and other hydraulic engineering projects for the control and use of water.

Construction Engineers

Construction Engineers manage construction projects to ensure that they are built according to plan and completed on schedule.

Geotechnical Engineers

Geotechnical Engineers are concerned primarily with foundations and how structures interact with the earth (i.e., soil, rock).

WORK ENVIRONMENT

Physical Environment

Civil engineers work in office environments, where they conduct meetings with clients and government officials, prepare public reports, design systems and structures, and organize all documentation pertaining to projects. They also spend a great deal of time at project sites, conducting inspections and overseeing personnel. Some civil engineers also teach at colleges and universities.

Relevant Skills and Abilities

Communication Skills
- Speaking effectively
- Writing concisely

Organization & Management Skills
- Coordinating tasks
- Demonstrating leadership
- Managing people/groups
- Paying attention to and handling details

Research & Planning Skills
- Analyzing information
- Solving problems

Technical Skills
- Performing scientific, mathematical and technical work

Human Environment

Depending on their areas of specialty, civil engineers interact and collaborate with government officials, architects, construction crews, materials and equipment suppliers, business executives, and other engineers. Civil engineering professors also work with students, other professors, and school administrators.

Technological Environment

Civil engineers work with a wide range of technologies and tools during the course of their work. In the office, they use computer-aided design (CAD) and other design software, cartography software, project management systems and databases, and other analytical and scientific programs. At a project site, they use soil collection equipment, electronic distance-measuring devices, levels, compasses, pressure gauges, and scales.

EDUCATION, TRAINING, AND ADVANCEMENT

High School/Secondary

High school students should study physics, chemistry, and biology. Mathematics, including algebra, geometry, trigonometry, and calculus, are also essential courses. Furthermore, high school students should take computer science courses and hone their writing and public speaking skills through English and communications classes. Courses that help students understand blueprints and architecture, such as drafting and industrial arts, are also highly useful.

Suggested High School Subjects
- Algebra
- Applied Communication
- Applied Math
- Applied Physics
- Biology
- Blueprint Reading
- Calculus
- Chemistry
- College Preparatory
- Composition
- Computer Science
- Drafting
- Economics
- English
- Geometry
- Mathematics
- Mechanical Drawing
- Physics
- Science
- Trigonometry

Famous First

The first bridge with piers sunk in the open sea, thus forming the foundation for its towers, was the Golden Gate Bridge in San Francisco, pictured. It was the first bridge to be built across the outer mouth of a major ocean harbor—in this case, San Francisco Bay, opening out to the Pacific Ocean. Construction took from 1933 to 1937.

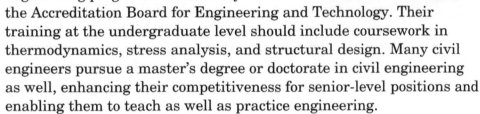

College/Postsecondary

Civil engineers must receive a bachelor's degree in civil engineering from an engineering program accredited by the Accreditation Board for Engineering and Technology. Their training at the undergraduate level should include coursework in thermodynamics, stress analysis, and structural design. Many civil engineers pursue a master's degree or doctorate in civil engineering as well, enhancing their competitiveness for senior-level positions and enabling them to teach as well as practice engineering.

Related College Majors
- Architectural Engineering
- Civil Engineering
- Civil Engineering/Civil Technology
- Engineering Design

Adult Job Seekers

Qualified civil engineers may apply directly to government agencies, architectural firms, and other employers with open positions. Many universities have placement programs that can help recent civil engineering graduates find work. Additionally, civil engineers may join and network through professional associations and societies, such as the American Society of Civil Engineers (ASCE).

Professional Certification and Licensure

Civil engineers who work with the public must be licensed as a Professional Engineer (PE) in the state or states in which they seek to practice. The licensure process includes a written examination, a specified amount of education, and at least four years of work experience. Continuing education is a common requirement for ongoing licensure.

Some professional civil engineering associations, like the American Society of Civil Engineers, the Academy of Geo-Professionals, and the American Academy of Water Resources Engineers, offer specialty certification programs as well. Leadership in Energy and Environmental Design (LEED) certification may be necessary for some projects.

Additional Requirements

 Civil engineers must be able to analyze and comprehend complex systems. In addition to acquiring a strong understanding of the engineering field and their area of specialty, civil engineers must be excellent communicators, as they often work with others in a team environment or in a supervisory capacity. Successful completion of a civil service exam may be required for employment by a government agency.

Fun Facts

Civil engineers do more that build roads and bridges . . . a civil engineer created the slippery part of a water slide by designing a pumping system to circulate the proper amount of water to the flume, along with the proper design to hold the rider's weight, the water, and the wind force!
Source: www.nspe.org/resources/media/resources/ten-fun-and-exciting-facts-about-engineering#sthash.Q4ova3Js.dpuf

In the 18th century, people started using the new term "civil engineering" to describe non-military work by civilians. Before then, "architect" and "engineer" often described the same person.
Source: http://www.onlineengineeringdegree.org/35-fundamental-facts-about-civil-engineering

EARNINGS AND ADVANCEMENT

Earnings depend on the size and geographic location of the employer and the employee's qualifications. In 2012, the average salary offer to college graduates with a bachelor's degree in civil engineering was $56,874 per year, according to the National Association of Colleges and Employers. Civil engineers with a master's degree were offered first year-salaries averaging $65,931, while those with a Ph.D. were offered $70,090 annually.

Mean annual earnings of civil engineers were $87,130 in 2014. The lowest ten percent earned less than $52,570, and the highest ten percent earned more than $128,110.

Civil engineers may receive paid vacations, holidays, and sick days; life and health insurance; and retirement benefits. These are usually paid by the employer.

Metropolitan Areas with the Highest
Employment Level in this Occupation

Metropolitan area	Employment [1]	Employment per thousand jobs	Annual mean wage
Houston-Sugar Land-Baytown, TX	10,850	3.81	$112,480
New York-White Plains-Wayne, NY-NJ	8,210	1.52	$97,680
Los Angeles-Long Beach-Glendale, CA	6,880	1.70	$97,980
Chicago-Joliet-Naperville, IL	6,640	1.77	$90,550
Seattle-Bellevue-Everett, WA	5,970	4.00	$86,100
Washington-Arlington-Alexandria, DC-VA-MD-WV	5,730	2.41	$93,710
Sacramento--Arden-Arcade--Roseville, CA	4,660	5.43	$97,870
Santa Ana-Anaheim-Irvine, CA	4,400	2.97	$97,410
Atlanta-Sandy Springs-Marietta, GA	4,320	1.81	$93,080
Oakland-Fremont-Hayward, CA	4,290	4.18	$107,990

[1]Does not include self-employed. Source: Bureau of Labor Statistics

EMPLOYMENT AND OUTLOOK

There were approximately 273,000 civil engineers employed nationally in 2012. Most were employed by firms providing architectural and engineering services, primarily developing designs for new construction projects. Employment of civil engineers is expected to grow faster than the average for all occupations through the year 2022, which means employment is projected to increase up to 20 percent or more.

As a result of growth in the population and an increased emphasis on security, more civil engineers will be needed to design and construct safe and higher capacity transportation, water supply and pollution control systems, in addition to large buildings and building complexes. They also will be needed to repair or replace existing roads, bridges and other public structures. Job openings will also result from the need to replace civil engineers who transfer to other occupations or leave the labor force

Employment Trend, Projected 2012–22

Civil engineers: 20%

Total, all occupations: 11%

Engineers (all): 9%

Note: "All Occupations" includes all occupations in the U.S. Economy. Source: U.S. Bureau of Labor Statistics, Employment Projections Program

Related Occupations
- Architect
- Construction & Building Inspector
- Energy Engineer
- Environmental Science Technician
- Mechanical Engineer
- Surveyor & Cartographer
- Urban & Regional Planner
- Water & Wastewater Engineer
- Wind Energy Engineer

Related Occupations
- Civil Engineer
- Environmental Health & Safety Officer
- Surveying & Mapping Manager

Conversation With . . .
JAMES W. BLAKE, P.E., P.L.S.

Owner, Blake Consulting Services, LLC
Civil Engineer, 35 years

1. What was your individual career path in terms of education/training, entry-level job, or other significant opportunity ?

My father was a civil engineer, and although I wasn't quite sure what I wanted to do, I knew if I had that degree, I'd have options. I earned a B.S. in civil engineering from the University of Maryland, and considered becoming a pilot. Unfortunately, my vision wasn't good enough. So I went to work as a civil/structural engineer, then went right back to school and earned a B.S. in business and accounting because I was interested in management and the business of engineering. My first job was a lot of sitting at a desk and crunching numbers and I wanted more variety, so I moved into transportation and general civil engineering, which allowed me to interact with clients, politicians and a greater variety of projects. I got into management about eight to 10 years out of college. My specialty is roadway design and construction management. A lot of what I do now is business development related and involves competing for and winning consulting contracts from federal, state, and local governmental agencies.

2. What are the most important skills and/or qualities for someone in your profession?

The ability to communicate technical ideas in plain language is critical. You also need to be organized, and to have the ability to analyze a complex problem quickly, break it down into its various parts and then come up with a practical and economical solution that serves the client's best interests.

3. What do you wish you had known going into this profession?

Construction and civil engineering can be cyclical, and it's very much tied to the economy. So that means my workload can be cyclical. The politics of winning work through public agencies is also more involved and complex than I'd imagined it to be. Someone who wants to win public sector work must be very visible and involved with a particular governmental agency and those who oversee it.

4. Are there many job opportunities in your profession? In what specific areas?

I'd say very many. Job opportunities are excellent in transportation, structural, civil, environmental and geotechnical engineering, as well as construction inspection. Civil engineering is a very broad and diverse field, and there are some great challenges and opportunities.

5. How do you see your profession changing in the next five years, what role will technology play in those changes, and what skills will be required?

Technical advances are being adapted to complete projects more efficiently and expeditiously. If you need to do a technical analysis of a building—for example, an unusually-shaped building or structure—software analysis and document production programs allow you to do a more elaborate analysis more quickly and cheaply. Aerial drones are being used for inspection work on tall buildings and bridges; you just fly your drone over the area you wish to observe and it takes video as well as pictures of the subject area. An engineer on the ground can then confirm that construction is in fact proceeding in accordance with the construction documents. GPS is relatively old news; it's being programmed into black boxes on earthwork machines so they automatically excavate and grade areas; the machine will then drive itself and make all the cuts and fills using GPS and lasers for elevations. Other construction-related uses for GPS have continued to become more common.

6. What do you enjoy most about your job? What do you enjoy least about your job?

I most enjoy the variety of projects and my ability to interact with various people who have different roles in the development and completion of a project. As with any industry, there are difficult people you have to deal with and that's probably the hardest part.

7. Can you suggest a valuable "try this" for students considering a career in your profession?

Find an engineering company and see if they sponsor a student mentor day. Some professional organizations do that, such as the American Society of Civil Engineers or the Society of American Military Engineers. You could also intern or work part-time. There are also many good books on the topic, as well as YouTube videos, of different types of construction projects.

SELECTED SCHOOLS

Most colleges and universities offer programs in engineering; a variety of them also have concentrations in civil engineering. Some of the more prominent schools in this field are listed below.

Carnegie Mellon University
5000 Forbes Ave
Pittsburgh, PA 15213
Phone: (412) 256-2000
http://www.cmu.edu

Cornell University
242 Carpenter Hall
Ithaca, NY 14850
Phone: (607) 254-4636
https://www.cornell.edu

Georgia Institute of Technology
225 North Avenue
Atlanta, GA 30332
Phone: (404) 894-2000
http://www.gatech.edu

Massachusetts Institute of Technology
77 Massachusetts Avenue
Room 1-206
Cambridge, MA 02139
Phone: (617) 253-1000
http://web.mit.edu

Purdue University, West Lafayette
701 W. Stadium Avenue
Suite 3000 ARMS
West Lafayette, IN 47907
Phone: (765) 494-4600
http://www.purdue.edu

Stanford University
Huang Engineering Center Suite 226
450 Serra Mall
Stanford, CA 94305-4121
Phone: (650) 723-2300
https://www.stanford.edu

University of California, Berkeley
320 McLaughlin Hall #1700
Berkeley, CA 94720-1700
Phone: (510) 642-6000
http://www.berkeley.edu/

University of Illinois, Urbana, Champaign
1398 West Green
Urbana, IL 061801
Phone: (217) 333-1000
http://illinois.edu

University of Michigan, Ann Arbor
Robert H. Lurie Engineering Center
Ann Arbor, MI 48109
Phone: (734) 764-1817
https://www.umich.edu

University of Texas, Austin (Cockrell)
301 E. Dean Keeton St.
Stop C2100
Austin, TX 78712
Phone: (512) 471-1166
http://www.engr.utexas.edu

MORE INFORMATION

Academy of Geo-Professionals
1801 Alexander Bell Drive
Reston, VA 20191
703.295.6314
www.geoprofessionals.org

**Accreditation Board for
Engineering and Technology**
111 Market Place, Suite 1050
Baltimore, MD 21202-4012
410.347.7700
www.abet.org

**American Academy of Water
Resources Engineers**
1801 Alexander Bell Drive
Reston, VA 20191
703.295.6414
www.aawre.org

**American Society of Civil
Engineers**
1801 Alexander Bell Drive
Reston, VA 21091-4400
800.548.2723
www.asce.org

**National Action Council for
Minorities in Engineering**
440 Hamilton Avenue, Suite 302
White Plains, NY 10601-1813
914.539.4010
www.nacme.org

**National Council of Structural
Engineers Associations**
645 North Michigan Avenue, Suite 540
Chicago, IL 60611
312.649.4600
www.ncsea.com

**National Society of Black
Engineers**
205 Daingerfield Road
Alexandria, VA 22314
703.549.2207
www.nsbe.org

**National Society of Professional
Engineers**
1420 King Street
Alexandria, VA 22314-2794
703.684.2800
www.nspe.org

**Society of Hispanic Professional
Engineers**
13181 Crossroads Parkway North,
Suite 450
City of Industry, CA 91746-3497
323.725.3970
www.shpe.org

Society of Women Engineers
203 N. La Salle Street, Suite 1675
Chicago, IL 60601
877.793.4636
www.swe.org

Technology Student Association
1914 Association Drive
Reston, VA 20191-1540
703.860.9000
www.tsaweb.org

Michael Auerbach/Editor

Construction & Building Inspector

Snapshot

Career Cluster(s): Building & Construction, Architecture & Construction, Government & Public Administration, Manufacturing
Interests: Engineering, physical science, architecture, civic planning
Earnings (Yearly Average): $56,040
Employment & Outlook: Average Growth Expected

OVERVIEW

Sphere of Work

Construction and building inspectors survey construction and remodeling sites to ensure the safety of the surrounding community, site workers, and future tenants. While building inspectors may also survey existing structures, construction inspectors focus primarily on new building sites. Many building inspectors are employed by local, state, and national governments. Construction inspectors are privately employed by contracting companies, engineering firms, and commercial developers.

Construction inspection is a multidisciplinary field that requires an extensive knowledge of architecture and construction. In addition to possessing a sound knowledge of the effects of physical exposure on infrastructure, many contemporary building inspectors are also well versed in green engineering practices and energy-efficient building practices.

Work Environment

Building inspectors work primarily on construction sites. Depending on an inspector's specialty, such sites can range from large-scale civic engineering projects such as bridges, highways, and transportation hubs to smaller-scale projects such as residential work sites, antique home restorations, or new housing developments. Building inspectors must be comfortable working in potentially hazardous construction sites as well as with exposure to subterranean spaces, harsh natural elements, and high altitudes.

Profile

Working Conditions: Work both Indoors and Outdoors
Physical Strength: Light Work
Education Needs: On-The-Job Training, High School Diploma with Technical Education, Junior/Technical/Community College, Apprenticeship
Licensure/Certification: Required
Opportunities For Experience: Apprenticeship, Part-Time Work
Holland Interest Score*: RCS, REC

* See Appendix A

Occupation Interest

The field of building inspection often attracts those with backgrounds in engineering, physical science, architecture, and civic planning. Many inspectors arrive at the position after several years in the private construction industry, either as skilled laborers or as engineering consultants, project managers, or architects.

Construction is a multifaceted discipline that requires knowledge of an array of logistics and systematic infrastructure, including architecture, HVAC, plumbing, electrical circuitry, weatherproofing, load-bearing metrics, and aerodynamics. Inspectors must also be very well versed in local, state, and national building regulations.

A Day in the Life—Duties and Responsibilities

Much of the day-to-day responsibilities of building inspectors involve traveling to and inspecting construction sites. The scale, location, and breadth of site surveys will depend on the specialty of the inspector.

Civic building inspectors survey all new construction sites and renovation projects within their particular jurisdictions to ensure that the projects fall within the parameters of regional, state, and federal building codes.

Construction inspectors spend much of their noninspection time educating themselves about alterations to existing codes as well as new building codes, which are traditionally issued on an annual basis. In many cases, inspectors are required to attend conferences and seminars where new building codes or code-friendly building techniques are taught.

Civic inspectors possess the capacity to halt construction projects that are in violation of building codes. Reasons for a building inspector to shut down construction can range from the use of illegal materials to improper site waste management, hazardous work conditions, improper implementation of safety equipment, or repetition of a combination of such offenses. Construction projects that are halted by inspectors are required to reapply for building certificates and often must pass thorough inspections prior to being allowed to proceed. Building inspectors are often called upon to interpret construction laws and building codes for project managers eager to preempt a disruption of progress.

Duties and Responsibilities

- Inspecting buildings, dams, highways or bridges
- Inspecting wiring, fixtures, plumbing, sewer systems and fire sprinklers for safety
- Preparing reports concerning violations not corrected
- Interpreting blueprints and specifications
- Verifying levels, alignment and elevation of installations
- Reviewing requests for and issuing building permits

OCCUPATION SPECIALTIES

Electrical Inspectors

Electrical Inspectors check electrical installations to verify safety laws and ordinances.

Plumbing Inspectors

Plumbing Inspectors check plumbing installations for conformance to governmental codes, sanitation standards and construction specifications.

Construction Inspectors

Construction Inspectors examine and oversee the construction of bridges, dams, highways and other types of construction work to insure that procedures and materials comply with specifications.

Elevator Inspectors

Elevator Inspectors examine the safety of lifting and conveying devices such as elevators, escalators, ski lifts and amusement rides.

Mechanical Inspectors

Mechanical Inspectors examine the installation of kitchen appliances, heating and air conditioning equipment and gasoline tanks to insure that they comply with safety standards.

WORK ENVIRONMENT

Physical Environment

Building inspectors work primarily on job sites of varying scales and across all climates and weather conditions. Many environments require the use of safety equipment such as hard hats and safety goggles. Comfort with construction environments, including both underground sites and sites at high altitudes, is a necessity of the role.

Relevant Skills and Abilities

Communication Skills
- Speaking effectively
- Writing concisely

Interpersonal/Social Skills
- Cooperating with others
- Working as a member of a team

Organization & Management Skills
- Organizing information or materials
- Paying attention to and handling details

Technical Skills
- Performing scientific, mathematical and technical work

Human Environment

Construction and building inspectors must be effective interpersonal communicators who can explain complicated technical and legal parameters with relative ease. Conflict-resolution strategies and relationship-building techniques also benefit those in the profession.

Technological Environment

Construction inspectors must be well-versed in a variety of measurement systems and analytical tools measuring corrosion, exposure, and temperature. Advanced mathematic skills are also highly beneficial.

EDUCATION, TRAINING, AND ADVANCEMENT

High School/Secondary

High school students can best prepare to enter the field of building inspection by completing courses in algebra, calculus, geometry, industrial arts, trigonometry, chemistry, physics, and computer science. Coursework related to drafting and architecture can also be beneficial to those interested in the field. Exposure to the construction industry via summer employment, school internships, or administrative volunteer work can be especially beneficial to students who are interested in building inspection.

Suggested High School Subjects
- Applied Communication
- Applied Math
- Blueprint Reading
- Building Trades & Carpentry
- Drafting
- English
- Shop Math
- Woodshop

Famous First

Not until 1799 were there laws in place to ensure that buildings housing workers were safe to operate in. That year, Massachusetts made a law to create the Massachusetts Fire Insurance Company and created the first requirement for construction and building inspectors. Thenceforth, companies had to submit to an examination of their affairs and take an oath. Further, they had to be approved to continue to run their businesses.

Postsecondary

A postsecondary degree is not typically required but may be preferred by some employers. Construction and building inspectors often arrive at the profession after postsecondary study in related fields such as architecture, engineering, and civic planning. Beneficial postsecondary coursework can include surveys of building and home inspection, drafting, blueprint reading, construction safety, and inspection techniques and reporting methods.

Many aspiring building inspectors use their undergraduate years both to learn the fundamental aspects of construction engineering and to gain experience in the field through internships with private construction, engineering, or building inspection firms.

Related College Majors
- Architectural Engineering Technology
- Construction/Building Inspection
- Construction/Building Technology
- Electrical, Electronic & Communication Engineering Technology
- Electrician Training
- Heating, Air Conditioning & Refrigeration Mechanics & Repair
- Plumbing & Pipefitting

Adult Job Seekers

Adult job seekers can prepare for a career in building inspection by gaining sustained experience in the engineering field, particularly at the supervisory level. Leadership and managerial experience in construction management is also desirable. Many inspectors have several years of experience working as carpenters, systems engineers, or electricians. Sound collaborative and communication skills are also paramount for those seeking careers in the field. Candidates with multidisciplinary backgrounds in construction often have broadened opportunities.

Professional Certification and Licensure

Local, state, and national certification is required for all professional building inspectors. Most certificates and licenses are issued on an annual basis, so inspection professionals must stay up to date with developments in the field. Inspectors working in specialized fields of construction may also receive on-the-job training specific to a particular firm's needs.

Additional Requirements

Aspiring construction and building inspectors must be committed to mastering a broad array of constantly changing building codes and legal requirements. While the knowledge base of each inspector is grounded in basic construction principles, the ability to survey, interpret, and adapt to constantly changing regulations is just as important, as is the ability to convey complex technical concepts in an informative manner.

Fun Fact

The American Society of Home Inspectors reports these three deal-breakers for home buyers: a fixer-upper with too many problems; expensive repairs to large systems like a roof; and problems lurking inside the walls.

Source: http://www.homeinspector.org/HomeInspectionNews/top-3-deal-breaking-problems-in-home-inspections.10-8-2015.1163/Details/Story

EARNINGS AND ADVANCEMENT

Earnings of construction and building inspectors depend on job specialty, geographic location and the amount and nature of an individual's work experience. Salaries are usually set by local governments, according to civil service regulations. Generally, building examiners, including plan examiners, earn the highest salaries. Salaries in large metropolitan areas are substantially higher than those in smaller areas.

Median annual earnings of construction and building inspectors were $56,040 in 2014. The lowest ten percent earned less than $33,970, and the highest ten percent earned more than $88,830.

Construction and building inspectors may receive paid vacations, holidays, and sick days; life and health insurance; and retirement benefits. These are usually paid by the employer. Some employers may provide a company car.

Metropolitan Areas with the Highest Employment Level in this Occupation

Metropolitan area	Employment	Employment per thousand jobs	Hourly mean wage
New York-White Plains-Wayne, NY-NJ	3,930	0.73	$33.06
Washington-Arlington-Alexandria, DC-VA-MD-WV	2,060	0.87	$31.12
Chicago-Joliet-Naperville, IL	2,010	0.54	$32.76
Los Angeles-Long Beach-Glendale, CA	1,910	0.47	$37.90
Houston-Sugar Land-Baytown, TX	1,890	0.67	$32.03
Philadelphia, PA	1,650	0.89	$25.08
Phoenix-Mesa-Glendale, AZ	1,540	0.84	$26.32
Pittsburgh, PA	1,430	1.26	$25.00
Baltimore-Towson, MD	1,360	1.05	$26.81
Dallas-Plano-Irving, TX	1,350	0.60	$25.43

Source: Bureau of Labor Statistics

EMPLOYMENT AND OUTLOOK

There were approximately 102,000 construction and building inspectors employed nationally in 2012. Employment is expected to grow about as fast as the average for all occupations through the year 2022, which means employment is projected to increase 10 percent to 19 percent. Growing concern for public safety and improvements in the quality of construction should continue to stimulate demand for construction and building inspectors. Opportunities are best for highly experienced supervisors and craft workers who have some college education, some engineering or architectural training, or who are certified as inspectors or plan examiners.

Employment Trend, Projected 2012–22

Other construction and related workers: 12%

Construction and building inspectorss: 12%

Total, all occupations: 11%

Note: "All Occupations" includes all occupations in the U.S. Economy. Source: U.S. Bureau of Labor Statistics, Employment Projections Program

Related Occupations
- Civil Engineer
- Construction Manager
- Customs Inspector
- Inspector & Compliance Officer
- Inspector & Tester
- Quality Control Inspector
- Real Estate Appraiser

Conversation With . . .
AUDREY CLINE

Code Official
Town of Stratham Building/Codes Department
Stratham, New Hampshire
Building inspector, 10 years

1. What was your individual career path in terms of education/training, entry-level job, or other significant opportunity?

Like many (if not most) building inspectors, code enforcement officers, and code officials, I landed in this field as a mid-career change. I graduated from Boston University with a degree in business administration. A handful of years later, I developed an interest in architecture and attended the architectural engineering program at New Hampshire Technical Institute. After graduation, I worked as a self-employed residential designer. After a decade or so, the work began to feel mundane and I starting casting about for another situation where I could use my skills and training.

I "discovered" the field of building codes when I saw an ad in my local paper for an employment opportunity with the Town of Wolfeboro, N.H. As the town's building official, I managed the building department's processes, which included reviewing plans for compliance with the New Hampshire State Building Code and local zoning ordinances and collaborating with local fire officials for compliance with the New Hampshire State Fire Code. I enjoy the legal aspects of code administration and property rights. My favorite projects are redevelopment or so-called "infill" projects that rejuvenate older buildings and neighborhoods while bringing them up to code to meet structural strength and safety regulations.

2. What are the most important skills and/or qualities for someone in your profession?

It's important to realize that the decisions you make may have a significant effect on personal property rights. It's critical to develop an approach based on the desire to be part of the solution, while fulfilling your responsibility to the public health, safety, and welfare. This is not a career for the faint-of-heart. In the end, credibility is the goal. With credibility, even difficult decisions can be understood as being necessary and fair.

3. What do you wish you had known going into this profession?

There isn't anything I regret about making this career move. What I didn't know, and what was most surprising to me, is that public service is very different from working in the private sector. I had to re-evaluate my basic decision-making and judgment processes in order to accommodate the notion of the public good rather than the good of an individual, or indeed, my own preference.

4. Are there many job opportunities in your profession? In what specific areas?

In New Hampshire as well as many other states, the next five to ten years will see a major shortage of people entering this field. In response to the expected shortage, New Hampshire Technical Institute has begun a certificate program designed to attract people to the industry. The program can lead to immediate employment after six courses or can be the foundation for stepping into an associate's or bachelor's degree program in a related field like construction management or architecture/engineering.

While building inspectors and code officials typically work for a city or town, there are home inspection jobs in private industry. When people buy a home, the bank typically requires a home inspection that covers the condition of the home from the foundation to the roof: heating and a/c systems, plumbing and electrical systems, attic/insulation, ceiling, windows and floors. Home inspectors inspect these systems and write up a report for the buyer.

5. How do you see your profession changing in the next five years? What role will technology play in those changes, and what skills will be required?

Just as in fields like medicine and technology, there will be distinct sub-specialties. There will be a need for management personnel who have a thorough grasp of technical codes, as well as the education (such as a degree in public administration) to manage a municipal office. Most building offices are instituting electronic applications, plan review, and inspection protocols.

6. What do you enjoy most about your job? What do you enjoy least about your job?

As the town's building official, I am just as apt to be outside on a job site as in the plan review room or attending a policy committee meeting. I love the variety. Being a resource for builders and potentially saving a project from an expensive or time-consuming retrofit is very satisfying. It can be discouraging to see a project that has derailed because of lack of proper design, planning or implementation. But after ten years, I am still waiting to learn what I least like about my job!

7. Can you suggest a valuable "try this" for students considering a career in your profession?

I would urge interested students to contact the association of building officials in their state. If you're in New Hampshire or nearby, contact the New Hampshire Building Officials Association (www.nhboa.net). The association has the ability to set up a shadowing program and will reserve a seat for a curious student at one of our monthly training meetings. I'm sure other state organizations have similar programs.

MORE INFORMATION

International Association of Electrical Inspectors
P.O. Box 830848
Richardson, TX 75803-0848
972.235.1455
www.iaei.org

International City/County Management Association
Member Services Department
777 N. Capitol Street NE, Suite 500
Washington, DC 20002
202.289.4262
www1.icma.org

International Code Council
500 New Jersey Avenue NW
6th Floor
Washington, DC 20001
888.422.7233
www.iccsafe.org

National Association of Commercial Building Inspectors and Thermographers
10599 E Betony Drive
Scottsdale, AZ 85255
480.308.4967
www.nacbi.org

National Association of Home Builders
1201 15th Street, NW
Washington, DC 20005
800.368.5242
www.nahb.com

National Center for Construction Education and Research
13614 Progress Boulevard
Alachua, FL 32615
888.622.3720
www.nccer.org

National Conference of States on Building Codes & Standards
505 Huntmar Park Drive, Suite 210
Herndon, VA 20170
703.437.0100
www.ncsbcs.org

National Institute of Building Inspectors
2 N Main Street, Suite 203
Medford, NJ 08055
www.nibi.com

John Pritchard/Editor

Construction Laborer

Snapshot

Career Cluster(s): Building & Construction, Architecture & Construction

Interests: Working with your hands, working alone or with a team, working outdoors

Earnings (Yearly Average): $31,090

Employment & Outlook: Faster Than Average Growth Expected

OVERVIEW

Sphere of Work

Construction laborers assist skilled workers and project supervisors on construction sites. Unlike workers who are trained in a specific facet of construction, such as carpentry, plumbing, or electricity, laborers are traditionally workers who have yet to attain a particular skill and are thus responsible for a diverse array of tasks.

The responsibilities of a laborer evolve on a daily basis, and they can range from menial tasks to more difficult contributions. Laborers work in all facets of the construction industry, from early site development to demolition and materials removal.

Work Environment

Construction laborers work almost exclusively outdoors or in partially constructed structures. The nature of the work environment varies by project type, what phase of the process the project is in, and where it is geographically located. Laborers may assist with the removal of tiles from a roof one day and prepare a foundation for concrete the next. Laborers may also work in shop environments, preparing materials for transportation or later use.

Profile

Working Conditions: Work both Indoors and Outdoors
Physical Strength: Heavy Work
Education Needs: No High School Diploma, On-The-Job Training, High School Diploma with Technical Education, Apprenticeship
Licensure/Certification: Usually Not Required
Opportunities For Experience: Apprenticeship, Military Service, Part-Time Work
Holland Interest Score*: RES, RIE

* See Appendix A

Occupation Interest

The field of construction labor attracts a diverse array of candidates. Some laborers are students who hold positions during breaks from study. Others are workers who are eager to gain experience across a variety of different trades as preparation for careers in the construction industry.

Since construction labor positions are primarily entry level, they attract workers from a variety of backgrounds and with diverse skill sets. Many possess entry-level experience in other trades, such as woodworking, metalworking, farming, landscaping, or product manufacturing.

A Day in the Life—Duties and Responsibilities

The day-to-day responsibilities of a construction laborer vary significantly based on the nature of the project and the particular trade of employment. Demolition laborers spend a large majority of their time removing secondary building features, such as lighting fixtures, windows, walls, old plumbing, electrical systems, and floor work. Such workers are responsible for the proper removal and disposal of debris into on-site waste containers.

Laborers employed by companies specializing in new construction may begin their day off-loading materials and distributing them throughout the construction site for skilled workers such as carpenters or plumbers to use. Laborers are often also called upon to complete basic but time-consuming tasks such as digging holes and trenches, applying paint primer, or removing a site's antiquated infrastructure. They also maintain the cleanliness of work sites by removing debris and packaging.

Some laborers work as apprentices to licensed electricians or plumbers and may be responsible for gathering and transporting the necessary tools and materials, running lengths of pipe or wiring, and testing systems to make sure they are functional. Many licensed professionals in trades such as plumbing began their careers as construction laborers.

Duties and Responsibilities

- Hauling and hoisting materials
- Digging ditches for foundations
- Operating jackhammers, earth tampers and cement mixers to align and grade ditches and tunnels
- Mixing, pouring and spreading concrete, asphalt or gravel
- Erecting and dismantling scaffolds
- Laying sewer and water pipes
- Grinding, sanding and polishing surfaces
- Loading and unloading trucks
- Cleaning tools and equipment
- Cleaning the construction site

OCCUPATION SPECIALTIES

Hod Carriers or Masons' Helpers

Hod Carriers or Masons' Helpers work as bricklayers' or plasterers' helpers by preparing and carrying materials, setting up and taking down scaffolds and performing other services.

WORK ENVIRONMENT

Physical Environment

Laborers work inside and outside, in varying weather conditions, at demolition or construction sites. Some tasks require working at significant heights, while other projects may necessitate working underground.

Relevant Skills and Abilities

Organization & Management Skills
- Following instructions
- Paying attention to and handling details
- Performing duties which change frequently
- Performing routine work

Technical Skills
- Working with machines, tools or other objects
- Working with your hands

Work Environment Skills
- Working outdoors

Human Environment

Construction laborers interact with numerous professionals on a daily basis. These include fellow site workers, material deliverers, and waste disposal professionals. A strong work ethic and willingness to work collaboratively with several different people each day is necessary.

Technological Environment

Construction laborers may be called upon to use several different forms of technology, from simple tools such as sledgehammers and shovels to more complex tools such as mechanical drills, electrical testing equipment, and skid-steer loaders.

EDUCATION, TRAINING, AND ADVANCEMENT

High School/Secondary

Basic coursework in mathematics, English, and industrial arts can best prepare high school students to enter the field of construction labor. Ancillary chemistry and physics coursework can also be beneficial.

Suggested High School Subjects
- Building Trades & Carpentry
- English
- Industrial Arts
- Shop Math
- Woodshop

Famous First

In 1938, construction was completed on a building, with five rooms and a garage, built entirely inside a factory. It was also the first building floated across a river and towed down the Illinois River from Peoria. Laborers also installed a furnace, a cooling system, laundry, and plumbing in to the house which also contained some furniture. In total, it weighed 41 tons, or 82,000 pounds.

Postsecondary

Postsecondary education is not a traditional requirement for construction laborer positions. However, additional education may be required in order to move into supervisory or skilled positions.

Adult Job Seekers

As most construction laborer positions are entry level, the role may serve as an appropriate starting point for adults seeking to transition into a career in construction. Previous experience with operating construction equipment may be beneficial.

Professional Certification and Licensure

Construction laborers are not traditionally required to hold a certificate or license, although for young workers, a work permit may be required. A driver's license is often preferred but not necessary.

Additional Requirements

Candidates for positions in construction labor must be able to handle the physical requirements of the role, which typically include lifting heavy objects and standing or walking for long periods of time. Individuals must also be willing to comply with safety regulations particular to each project.

Fun Fact

One World Trade Center is 1776 feet high to symbolize the year the U.S. Declaration of Independence was signed.

Source: http://fieldlens.com/blog/building-better/facts-didnt-know-5-famous-construction-projects/

EARNINGS AND ADVANCEMENT

Earnings depend on the geographic location of the employer, the type of work performed and unionization. Median annual earnings for construction laborers were $31,090 in 2014. Earnings for construction laborers can be reduced by poor weather or by downturns in construction activity, which sometimes result in layoffs. Apprentices usually start at about fifty percent of the wage paid to experienced workers. Construction laborers may be required to purchase protective clothing such as steel-toed shoes, protective glasses, and hard hats. They may also have to furnish their own hand tools.

Construction laborers may receive paid vacations, holidays, and sick days; life and health insurance; and retirement benefits. These are usually paid by the employer. In some cases, employers and employees may jointly contribute to union funds used to pay certain benefits

Metropolitan Areas with the Highest
Employment Level in this Occupation

Metropolitan area	Employment	Employment per thousand jobs	Hourly mean wage
Houston-Sugar Land-Baytown, TX	33,380	11.74	$14.46
New York-White Plains-Wayne, NY-NJ	28,380	5.27	$25.40
Chicago-Joliet-Naperville, IL	19,600	5.22	$27.46
Los Angeles-Long Beach-Glendale, CA	18,030	4.45	$20.30
Atlanta-Sandy Springs-Marietta, GA	17,930	7.51	$13.38
Dallas-Plano-Irving, TX	15,470	6.91	$12.92
Phoenix-Mesa-Glendale, AZ	15,010	8.22	$14.76
Washington-Arlington-Alexandria, DC-VA-MD-WV	13,460	5.66	$16.07
Riverside-San Bernardino-Ontario, CA	10,760	8.61	$20.01
Denver-Aurora-Broomfield, CO	10,510	7.93	$15.80

Source: Bureau of Labor Statistics

EMPLOYMENT AND OUTLOOK

There were approximately 1.3 million construction laborers employed nationally in 2012. About one-quarter were self-employed. Employment is expected to grow faster than the average for all occupations through the year 2022, which means employment is projected to increase 20 percent to 28 percent. Job growth will occur as government funding for repairing roads, bridges, water lines and public buildings continues to increase, and as the emphasis on green construction projects will often require additional workers. Opportunities will be best for well-trained laborers who are willing to relocate to different worksites.

Employment Trend, Projected 2012–22

Helpers, construction trades: 31%

Construction laborers: 24%

Construction trades workers: 22%

Total, all occupations: 11%

Note: "All Occupations" includes all occupations in the U.S. Economy. Source: U.S. Bureau of Labor Statistics, Employment Projections Program

Related Occupations
- Brickmason/Stonemason
- Bulldozer Operator
- Carpenter
- Cement Mason
- Construction Manager
- Drywall Installer & Taper
- Freight, Stock & Material Mover
- Highway Maintenance Worker
- Oil & Gas Drilling Operator
- Roofer
- Roustabout

Related Occupations
- Combat Engineer

Conversation With . . .
CURT BOYD

Co-Owner, Academy Roofing
Denver, Colorado
Roofing professional, 35 years

1. What was your individual career path in terms of education/training, entry-level job, or other significant opportunity?

I started roofing part-time in high school, but at the University of Wyoming, I played football and wanted to teach and coach. Because I was playing football, I did not graduate until December of my fifth year in college. There were no teaching jobs available at that time of year, so I found a job with a local roofing contractor until I could get a teaching job. That next summer they offered me a position managing their field crews. I was making a good bit more than I would have been teaching and coaching. I worked for that company just short of four years. My wife, Suzie, came onboard to help in accounting part-time. Eventually I felt I knew everything about the roofing business, and it was time to open our own business. Thinking back, there should have been more discussion between my wife and me—we had three kids, 1, 3, and 5, and I had a salaried position, a company vehicle, and health insurance. But she said OK and joined me. She took care of everything in the office; I took care of everything in the field.

We've grown to 125 employees with commercial and residential sales, service, and installation and repairs of all types of roofs, including solar. Most of our work, even today, is by referral. When people ask me about starting their own company, I always ask: Why do you want to do it? If it's to make money, that's the wrong reason. What's right is to take care of the customer, because if you do that, the profit will come. Patience isn't a virtue that is valued in our society, but success doesn't come overnight.

2. What are the most important skills and/or qualities for someone in your profession?

You have to understand a roof. You need an understanding of how the roofing systems go together, like a mechanic needs to know how a car works. A lot of companies, especially smaller residential companies, are more like labor brokers than knowledgeable roofing contractors. You need to appreciate what you're doing. For instance, we recently had a job where we couldn't get the dumpster close to the house. That meant we had to tear the roof off, drop the trash on the ground, drag it to the street, and put it in the dumpster. If you're bidding the work, you have to understand how long it can take.

You also need a mental toughness. Our work can be routine but it's dangerous. When you daydream, that's how people get hurt.

3. What do you wish you had known going into this profession?

My wife and I joke that we wish we'd had more of a business background. It sounds crazy, but I graduated with a four-year degree and took only one business class: entry-level accounting. It took us a long time to understand the value we brought to our clients —including those who were general contractors—and that they needed to pay us for that.

4. Are there many job opportunities in your profession? In what specific areas?

From top to bottom, our industry is crying out for good, ambitious young people. We have jobs in installation, field management, and project management. We are always looking for estimators.

There's a market for new construction as well as replacement roofs. Everybody has a roof and sooner or later they're going to need a new one. Even when the economy is slow, if the roof is leaking, that becomes a priority. There are always bad roofs being put on, and roofs that need to be repaired.

5. How do you see your profession changing in the next five years, what role will technology play in those changes, and what skills will be required?

We're at a huge deficit for technicians, and we're going to have to get more creative about attracting those people or I see the price of a roof going up. Technology won't change the roofing industry much in the field. There will be new materials to work with, but the labor to remove, repair or install a roof will probably stay the same.

6. What do you enjoy most about your job? What do you enjoy least about your job?

I like walking away from a job and knowing that it's a job well done. I like teaching guys who don't know which end of a hammer to hold and watching them grow. That's the player-development part of the coach in me coming through.

I dislike the danger we work with. Injuries happen. I also dislike when employees we have invested in, training-wise, leave without discussing their futures here with me.

7. Can you suggest a valuable "try this" for students considering a career in your profession?

A summer job will be good steady work and give you an understanding of roofing and the whole construction industry.

MORE INFORMATION

Associated General Contractors of America
Director, Construction Education Services
2300 Wilson Boulevard, Suite 400
Arlington, VA 22201
703.548.3118
www.agc.org

Building Trades Association
16th Street, NW
Washington, DC 20006
800.326.7800
www.buildingtrades.com

Laborers' International Union of North America
905 16th Street NW
Washington, DC 20006
202.737.8320
www.liuna.org

National Association of Home Builders
1201 15th Street, NW
Washington, DC 20005
800.368.5242
www.nahb.com

National Center for Construction Education and Research
13614 Progress Boulevard
Alachua, FL 32615
888.622.3720
www.nccer.org

John Pritchard/Editor

Construction Manager

Snapshot

Career Cluster(s): Building & Construction, Architecture & Construction

Interests: Architecture, design, managing others, problem-solving

Earnings (Yearly Average): $85,630

Employment & Outlook: Faster Than Average Growth Expected

OVERVIEW

Sphere of Work

Construction managers are responsible for overseeing a construction project from start to finish. They hire and fire employees, create and carry out budgets, design projects, and coordinate with the property owner, developer, and other key individuals. Construction managers ensure that the project is operating on time, that employees perform their assigned tasks, that the project stays within the budget, and that it meets the standards of the client. Construction managers may oversee the entire project or a section of that project, setting worker schedules, purchasing

materials and tools, and conducting periodic inspections of the site. A large number of construction managers are self-employed, although many are also employees of a larger construction company.

Work Environment

Construction managers work in offices and at construction sites, working with a large number of people and employees. In many cases, the construction site is far away from the construction manager's home base. In light of this fact, they may have to travel to sites for months at a time until the project is completed. Construction managers should be able to stand for long periods, lift heavy objects, and work in a wide range of weather conditions on sites at which personal safety is a concern. These managers often work long hours and are on call at all times.

Profile

Working Conditions: Work both Indoors and Outdoors
Physical Strength: Light Work
Education Needs: On-The-Job Training, Junior/Technical/Community College, Bachelor's Degree
Licensure/Certification: Recommended
Opportunities For Experience: Part-Time Work
Holland Interest Score*: ERS

* See Appendix A

Occupation Interest

Construction managers have a great deal of prior construction experience and use this experience effectively to oversee the progress of others. These individuals are in charge of virtually every aspect of either the entire project or a section of it. This means that construction managers have a great deal of control over how the job is carried out. Although construction managers should expect to be involved in some on-site work, the higher risk work tends to be delegated to the manager's subordinates.

A Day in the Life—Duties and Responsibilities

Because a construction manager's job encompasses so many different functions, and the building process can be unpredictable, there tends to be great variation in daily tasks. A construction manager plans and directs a project from start to finish, troubleshooting issues that arise throughout. He or she schedules and coordinates each of the project's stages, ensuring that the work will be completed in a reasonable amount of time. Additionally, the construction manager selects and oversees the employees and personnel for each phase of the project; this includes selecting general contractors and subcontractors who will perform certain tasks, such as plumbing and electrical installation. The manager works to ensure that each worker is performing the tasks required, adhering to safety requirements, and operating according to schedule.

Besides overseeing the construction site, the construction manager works with the client to plan the project according to his or her needs. The construction manager must create and implement the project budget and monitor the costs incurred throughout the process. The manager coordinates with architects, developers, and suppliers to verify that the project is proceeding according to plan. The manager must order building materials and equipment and obtain all permits and licenses before the workers can perform their tasks. He or she is responsible for establishing quality control and safety standards for the project, completing the project according to building and safety codes, and monitoring workers' safety on the job site. Although time is spent interacting with clients in an office, much of each day may be spent outside at the building site.

Duties and Responsibilities

- Supervising the hiring and firing of workers
- Monitoring each part of the construction, including preparation before construction begins
- Assuring construction conforms to safety codes, and with labor and union regulations
- Preparing daily reports on labor and materials
- Meeting with owners and suppliers concerning projects

OCCUPATION SPECIALTIES

Energy Systems Managers

Energy Systems Managers make changes to existing buildings to upgrade them to new environmental standards.

WORK ENVIRONMENT

Physical Environment

Construction managers sometimes work in office environments as part of their job responsibilities. These offices may be located at the company's headquarters, where managers meet with clients, developers, and architects during the earliest stages of the project. Managers may also work in field offices located on the construction site itself. A significant part of the workday is usually spent on-site coordinating with workers and contractors, monitoring progress, and performing routine inspections. Some construction managers even purchase the land on which the project will be built.

Relevant Skills and Abilities

Interpersonal/Social Skills
- Being able to remain calm
- Being flexible
- Cooperating with others
- Working as a member of a team

Organization & Management Skills
- Coordinating tasks
- Handling challenging situations

Technical Skills
- Working with your hands

Human Environment

Construction managers must coordinate with a wide range of people in order to bring projects to successful completion. They work with clients, developers, architects, and suppliers. They must also work with the public, including local officials, in order to secure permits and licenses. Finally, construction managers hire, oversee, and when necessary, fire employees, contractors, and subcontractors.

Technological Environment

A construction manager should have experience with and be knowledgeable about construction tools and equipment. He or she must work in close proximity to heavy equipment like backhoes, bulldozers, and cranes as well as smaller equipment like nail guns and saws.

EDUCATION, TRAINING, AND ADVANCEMENT

High School/Secondary

High school students interested in becoming construction managers should study math and geometry as well as shop classes, such as carpentry and the building trades. Since business management, budget oversight, and communications are other important aspects of the manager's job, courses such as business and English are useful.

Suggested High School Subjects
- Applied Math
- Applied Physics
- Blueprint Reading
- Building Trades & Carpentry
- Business Law
- Drafting
- English
- Geometry
- Mathematics

Famous First

Managers are in charge of keeping everything on schedule, such as erecting the first building with a large-scale, clear dome in 1901. Indiana's Colonel Lee Sinclair, businessman and owner of the local sulfur springs, hired architect Harrison Albright and engineer Oliver J. Westcott to build a hotel with a clear dome 130 feet high and 400 feet across. The hotel was opened on September 1, 1902 and held the record for largest freestanding dome structure in the world. Its record was eclipsed in 1965 with the opening of the Houston Astrodome.

Postsecondary

Many construction managers obtain a bachelor's degree in such fields as civil engineering, building science, or construction management. Such training may include courses in cost evaluation, site planning, and business management. Because of the enormous value placed on prior experience in the industry, other managers supplement their years of experience in construction with an associate's degree in a related field and are able to advance that way.

Related College Majors

• Construction/Building Technology

Adult Job Seekers

Experience is critical for construction managers. In light of this, most construction managers join a construction company and work their way through the firm's ranks. Many, though not all, construction managers are self-employed, working as general contractors, hiring their own personnel, and pursuing their own new business.

Professional Certification and Licensure

Although there are no requirements for individuals to be certified to work in the construction industry, such certification is increasingly in demand, particularly for complex projects, and can provide a competitive edge. The American Institute of Constructors and the Construction Management

Association of America both provide such certification programs, which include technical competency exams. Consult credible professional associations within the field and follow professional debate as to the relevancy and value of any certification program.

Additional Requirements

Construction managers should be able to work long hours on their feet. They should also be strong communicators, able to resolve conflicts and coordinate between clients and employees. The ability to plan and organize complex projects is necessary. One of the most important requirements for construction managers is hands-on experience – these individuals should have a great deal of experience in the building and construction industry, including extensive knowledge of building codes, permit requirements, building materials, and equipment.

Fun Fact

Construction Manager is 46th on CNN's list of 100 careers for "big growth, great pay and satisfying work."

Source: http://money.cnn.com/gallery/pf/2015/01/27/best-jobs-2015/46.html

EARNINGS AND ADVANCEMENT

According to a salary survey by the National Association of Colleges and Employers, graduates with a bachelor's degree in construction science/management earned starting annual salaries of $58,132 in 2012. Median annual earnings of construction managers were $85,630 in 2014. The lowest ten percent earned less than $50,990, and the highest ten percent earned more than $150,250.

Construction managers may receive paid vacations, holidays, and sick days; life and health insurance; and retirement benefits. These are usually paid by the employer. Construction managers who are self-employed may have to provide these benefits on their own.

Metropolitan Areas with the Highest Employment Level in this Occupation

Metropolitan area	Employment	Employment per thousand jobs	Hourly mean wage
Houston-Sugar Land-Baytown, TX	9,360	3.29	$42.88
New York-White Plains-Wayne, NY-NJ	9,160	1.70	$57.78
Dallas-Plano-Irving, TX	5,470	2.44	$41.39
Los Angeles-Long Beach-Glendale, CA	5,150	1.27	$49.15
Chicago-Joliet-Naperville, IL	5,120	1.37	$46.41
Washington-Arlington-Alexandria, DC-VA-MD-WV	3,740	1.57	$52.30
Phoenix-Mesa-Glendale, AZ	3,700	2.02	$47.04
Denver-Aurora-Broomfield, CO	3,560	2.68	$43.57
Boston-Cambridge-Quincy, MA	3,290	1.83	$52.68
Portland-Vancouver-Hillsboro, OR-WA	3,090	2.92	$44.96

Source: Bureau of Labor Statistics

EMPLOYMENT AND OUTLOOK

Construction managers held about 485,000 jobs nationally in 2012. About two-thirds were self-employed. Employment is expected to grow about as fast as the average for all occupations through the year 2022, which means employment is projected to increase 10 percent to 19 percent. This is a result of the level of construction activity and complexity of construction projects continuing to grow. Increased spending on the nation's highways, bridges, dams, water and sewage systems, and electric power generation and transmission facilities will result in greater demand for construction managers, as will the need to build more residential housing, commercial and office buildings and factories. In addition, continuing maintenance on existing structures will also contribute to the demand for these workers.

Employment Trend, Projected 2012–22

Construction managers: 16%

Total, all occupations: 11%

Management occupations: 7%

Note: "All Occupations" includes all occupations in the U.S. Economy. Source: U.S. Bureau of Labor Statistics, Employment Projections Program

Related Occupations
- Architect
- Construction & Building Inspector
- Construction Laborer
- Supervisor
- Urban & Regional Planner

Conversation With . . .
CHRISTIAN AMORELLO

Construction Project Manager
J. Cougler, Inc., West Harwich, Massachusetts
General contracting, 19 years

1. What was your individual career path in terms of education/training, entry-level job, or other significant opportunity?

When I was sixteen, I started as a "go-fer" for a construction crew working on a sewer rehabilitation project. It was my job to get whatever the pipe layers needed from the truck and drop it to them in the trench: fittings, tools, pipe lubricant, chains and, of course, coffee for the crew. Eventually, they started sending me out to pick up materials. I got good at making lists, figuring out the quickest route, and even the best place to buy supplies. This was my logistics training, most of which was before mobile phones. The more they told me to buy, the more I focused on all the pieces needed and the costs involved. This was my estimating training. I eventually started managing a crew, which allowed me to put all the pieces of my training together. This company primarily did underground utility work.

In college, I pursued a Bachelor of Arts in architectural studies at Hobart and William Smith Colleges. After I graduated, I realized that I wanted to work above ground and preferred the construction end of architecture. I moved to New York City to work for a general contractor in residential construction. There I focused on project management, contracting with subcontractors and pricing $10 million projects for competitive bids.

2. What are the most important skills and/or qualities for someone in your profession?

Accountability is a quality expected in any profession; construction management is no different. You also need the skill to size up a situation, evaluate the variables, address the risk, come up with steps to work through it and communicate this to others. This can be applied to massive projects that take years or a problem you encounter in the morning and resolve by the afternoon.

I traveled around the world for a few years after college and had to ask a lot of questions of a lot of people, whether it was directions to where I was going or directions on how to eat their native food or maneuver their transportation system. Project management for construction is pretty similar. I don't know everything about construction so I need to ask a lot of people, like subcontractors, a lot of questions about what they do, how they do it, and how much it costs.

3. What do you wish you had known going into this profession?

I wish I had learned to speak a few languages before going into this profession. A construction job site is usually a very culturally diverse place.

4. Are there many job opportunities in your profession? In what specific areas?

There are many opportunities because project management is not limited to just construction. Most businesses have a need for someone who can recognize the steps required to accomplish something and communicate that to others.

5. How do you see your profession changing in the next five years? What role will technology play in those changes, and what skills will be required?

The construction field has changed enormously with the use of mobile technology. With mobile phones, managers can talk to an individual performing work in the field and the worker can do the same, asking questions to make sure they're doing what they're supposed to. I can see what's going on in the field without leaving my office. I get photos of work progress and real-time videos of installations. I can video-conference with workers in the field who can show me what they're having in issue with by pointing the camera at it. This puts more responsibility on me, and it increases our ability to get work done more accurately and faster.

6. What do you enjoy most about your job? What do you enjoy least about your job?

Construction projects have a start and finish. You're always moving on to the next project at the next location, and most every project is unique. I most enjoy this aspect of what I do.

What I enjoy least is working on a project for someone whose goals for the project don't align with the reality of the project.

7. Can you suggest a valuable "try this" for students considering a career in your profession?

I worked as a line cook in New York City while I was in college. I found it to be invaluable training. I learned how to make a deadline every five minutes by getting a dish to the window; to precisely meet someone else's standards over and over again; to understand and follow a process for assembly (a recipe); to accept both criticism and praise for my work; and to get along with lots of different people in hot, cramped areas.

It isn't easy to get a job in construction with no experience, but restaurant kitchens are always hiring. I started at a burger joint that needed someone that very night, and eventually, I worked in some of the best restaurants on the East Coast and as a chef on private luxury yachts.

MORE INFORMATION

American Institute of Constructors and Constructor Certification Commission
700 North Fairfax Street, Suite 510
Alexandria, VA 22314
703.683.4999
www.professionalconstructor.org

Associated General Contractors of America
2300 Wilson Boulevard, Suite 400
Arlington, VA 22201
703.548.3118
www.agc.org

Construction Management Association of America
7926 Jones Branch Drive, Suite 800
McLean, VA 22102-3303
703.356.2622
www.cmaanet.org

International Code Council
500 New Jersey Avenue, NW
6th Floor
Washington, DC 20001
888.422.7233
www.iccsafe.org

National Association of Home Builders
1201 15th Street, NW
Washington, DC 20005
800.368.5242
www.nahb.com

National Center for Construction Education and Research
13614 Progress Boulevard
Alachua, FL 32615
888.622.3720
www.nccer.org

National Conference of States on Building Codes & Standards
505 Huntmar Park Drive, Suite 210
Herndon, VA 20170
703.437.0100
www.ncsbcs.org

Michael Auerbach/Editor

Drafter

Snapshot

Career Cluster(s): Building & Construction, Architecture & Construction, Science, Technology, Engineering & Mathematics

Interests: Mathematics, engineering, drawing

Earnings (Yearly Average): $49,970

Employment & Outlook: Slower Than Average Growth Expected

OVERVIEW

Sphere of Work

Drafting is the process of translating or converting designs into technical schematics and diagrams. Most modern drafting is done using computer-aided drafting and design (CADD) software, and drafters are sometimes called CADD operators. Drafting can be used to design a variety of objects, ranging from architectural projects to small components for electronics. Drafters are also responsible for adding dimensions and other technical elements to designs to specify construction parameters. They may specialize in specific types of drafting, including architectural, civil engineering, and electronics drafting.

Work Environment

Drafters usually work in an indoor office environment, supervised by engineers or architects. In small offices, there may be only one drafter present, while larger engineering or architectural firms may hire multiple drafters to work on various projects.

Drafters may work alongside other office workers who manage accounting, customer service, advertising, marketing, and other aspects of the business. They must be able to communicate effectively with other members of the team working within an engineering or architectural office.

Profile

Working Conditions: Work Indoors
Physical Strength: Light Work
Education Needs: High School Diploma with Technical Education, Junior/Technical/Community College, Apprenticeship
Licensure/Certification: Recommended
Opportunities For Experience: Part-Internship, Apprenticeship, Military Service, Part-Time Work
Holland Interest Score*: IRC, IRE, ISE, RCI

* See Appendix A

Occupation Interest

Individuals attracted to careers in drafting tend to be detail oriented and have a strong background in mathematics or engineering. Drafting is a skill that is learned by a variety of engineering and architectural professionals, and many people who work as drafters do so in order to advance within these fields.

Visual acuity and technical aptitude are among the most important traits for a drafter to have, and individuals who are drawn to the field tend to enjoy drawing and have skill in judging perspective and dimension. Drafters must also be able to work under tight deadlines and therefore must have the time-management skills necessary to complete their work within the parameters of a given project.

A Day in the Life—Duties and Responsibilities

Drafters typically work as part of a design-and-development team that translates the ideas of engineers into designs for construction or manufacturing. They generally work during regular business hours, and the set of tasks for any given day may vary considerably.

Typically, drafters consult with project managers, engineers, and architects during a typical business day to plan and schedule projects.

Drafters may spend part of a business day translating paper drawings to CADD format, or they may work directly in CADD to design a new schematic. A certain amount of time must also be spent updating or refining existing CADD designs following a review and incorporating additional requirements determined by the engineers. Some time might be spent conducting office work, such as sending schematics or design templates to clients or customers and communicating with others in the office about ongoing and future projects.

Duties and Responsibilities

- Preparing complete and accurate working plans and detailed drawings from rough or detailed sketches or notes
- Preparing final sketches and checking dimensions of parts and materials to be used
- Preparing charts of statistical data
- Drawing finished designs from sketches
- Using computer-aided drafting systems to prepare drawings

OCCUPATION SPECIALTIES

Architectural Drafters

Architectural Drafters produce architectural and structural working drawings of any type of building or other structure to comply with building codes.

Electrical Drafters

Electrical Drafters prepare wiring diagrams and drawings of electrical equipment for use by construction and repair workers who build, install and repair electrical equipment and wiring.

Civil Drafters

Civil Drafters prepare detailed construction drawings, topographical profiles and related maps, and specification sheets used in the planning and construction of highways, in flood control, drainage and other projects.

Mechanical Drafters

Mechanical Drafters prepare detailed working drawings of machinery and mechanical devices.

Marine Drafters

Marine Drafters make drawings of ships, docks and other marine structures and equipment.

Commercial Drafters

Commercial Drafters perform general duties in all-around drafting such as laying out building locations, planning arrangements, and preparing charts, forms and records.

WORK ENVIRONMENT

Physical Environment

Most drafters work within professional engineering or architectural offices, which may or may not be cubicle-type office environments. Typically, drafters use a large work desk that holds their computer and also allows sufficient space to lay out paper designs for reference and examination.

Plant Environment

Drafters may occasionally work in engineering plant environments in order to closely monitor where the parts are manufactured using drafted designs.

Relevant Skills and Abilities

Organization & Management Skills
- Managing time
- Meeting goals and deadlines
- Paying attention to and handling details
- Performing routine work

Research & Planning Skills
- Analyzing information
- Developing evaluation strategies

Technical Skills
- Applying the technology to a task
- Performing scientific, mathematical and technical work
- Working with machines, tools or other objects

Human Environment

Drafters work under the supervision of engineers or architects and must communicate effectively to complete collaborative projects. In addition, they may work alongside a variety of office workers who assist in preparing, presenting, and marketing various products.

Technological Environment

Professional drafters utilize some form of CADD software and may use a variety of other programs depending on the nature of their work. They occasionally use three-dimensional modeling software to create designs for various products or component parts. There are also project-management software programs that allow drafters, engineers, and other specialists to collaborate on designs through a computer network.

EDUCATION, TRAINING, AND ADVANCEMENT

High School/Secondary

Some high schools offer courses in drafting, which may include traditional pen-and-paper design methods as well as basic CADD courses. In addition, high school students looking to pursue a career in drafting can benefit from technical drawing and art classes, as well as geometry and basic mathematics. Students can also engage in computer-literacy programs in high school that will enable them to better learn the various types of software used in drafting.

Suggested High School Subjects
- Algebra
- Applied Math
- Computer Science
- Drafting
- English
- Geometry
- Graphic Communications
- Mechanical Drawing
- Trade/Industrial Education
- Trigonometry

Related Career Pathways/Majors

Architecture & Construction Cluster
- Design/Pre-Construction Pathway

Science, Technology, Engineering & Mathematics Cluster
- Engineering & Technology Pathway
- Science & Mathematics Pathway

Famous First

Drafters create the technical specifications for the ideas and plans of architects and engineers, but some are more outlandish than others—such as when James V. Lafferty decided, in 1882, to erect a building called "the Elephant." This was a building covered in tin and painted to resemble the hide of an elephant, with a spiral staircase hidden in a hind leg leading to Lafferty's office. The purpose of the building was to attract potential buyers to Lafferty's real estate holdings.

Postsecondary

Most drafting specialists have at least an associate's degree in a related field before being hired for professional projects. Community colleges sometimes offer drafting classes as well as programs in industrial and technical design. The community-college environment also allows students to pursue classes in related areas, including mathematics, engineering, computer science, and architecture. By contrast, technical institutes may offer more specific classes aimed at those pursuing a career in drafting. Technical institutes are more likely than community colleges or four-year postsecondary institutions to offer classes in specific types of drafting, as well as classes focused on using CADD programs and other types of software used in technical design.

Though many drafting positions require only an associate's degree, those with bachelor's degrees or higher may have an advantage in seeking employment. Some professionals work as drafters while serving as interns in an engineering or architecture firm and use the position as a stepping stone toward a career as a professional engineer or architect. In addition, advanced training in mathematics, engineering, and architecture can help drafters to advance in their careers by being involved in other aspects of the production process.

Related College Majors
- Architectural Drafting
- Construction/Building Technology
- Drafting, General
- Mechanical Drafting

Adult Job Seekers

Adults attempting to transition to drafting from other fields are advised to pursue classes at a technical institute or community college. For some adults, classes in basic computer skills may be necessary, depending on the individual's level of familiarity with digital design programs. Some retired or former architects and engineers may choose to work as drafters on a contract basis.

Professional Certification and Licensure

Technical institutes offer certificate training programs in specific types of drafting and in the operation of technical design software. For instance, some technical training institutes offer AutoCAD, a software series designed by the Autodesk company that allows for 2-D and 3-D drafting projects. There are a variety of other software options for professional drafting, and technical institutes often provide students with certificates proving their proficiency on specific programs.

Additional Requirements

Drafters must be strongly motivated to work independently on projects while also having the communication skills necessary to work closely with engineers and architects. There are a variety of different subfields within the drafting profession, and individuals tend to specialize in one area, learning the software and techniques specific to that subset of drafting.

Fun Fact

Leonard da Vinci was a draftsman, as well as a painter and sculptor. Read more in a book published by Metropolitan Museum of Art: "Leonard da Vinci: Master Draftsman."
Source: www.metmuseum.org/research/metpublications/Leonardo_da_Vinci_Master_Draftsman

EARNINGS AND ADVANCEMENT

Earnings depend on the specialty and level of responsibility of the employee and the type and geographic location of the employer. Median annual earnings of drafters in 2014 were $49,970. The lowest ten percent earned less than $32,820, and the highest ten percent earned more than $75,650.

Drafters may receive paid vacations, holidays, and sick days; life and health insurance; and retirement benefits. These are usually paid by the employer.

Metropolitan Areas with the Highest Employment Level in this Occupation

Metropolitan area	Employment	Employment per thousand jobs	Hourly mean wage
New York-White Plains-Wayne, NY-NJ	560	0.10	$30.07
Houston-Sugar Land-Baytown, TX	530	0.19	$31.67
Seattle-Bellevue-Everett, WA	490	0.33	$27.19
Phoenix-Mesa-Glendale, AZ	370	0.20	$24.84
Chicago-Joliet-Naperville, IL	370	0.10	$31.14
Portland-Vancouver-Hillsboro, OR-WA	300	0.28	$28.85
Los Angeles-Long Beach-Glendale, CA	290	0.07	$27.34
Oakland-Fremont-Hayward, CA	240	0.24	$28.17
Minneapolis-St. Paul-Bloomington, MN-WI	220	0.12	$27.81
New Orleans-Metairie-Kenner, LA	210	0.38	$38.13

Source: Bureau of Labor Statistics

EMPLOYMENT AND OUTLOOK

Drafters held about 200,000 jobs in 2012. About one-half of all jobs were in architectural and civil drafting; another one-third were in mechanical drafting; and most of the rest were in electrical and electronics drafting. Employment is expected to grow slower than the average for all occupations through the year 2022, which means employment is projected to increase only 1 percent. CADD systems that are more advanced and easier to use will allow more tasks to be done by other technical professionals, thus limiting demand for drafters.

Drafters are highly concentrated in industries that are sensitive to cyclical swings in the economy, such as engineering, architectural services and durable goods manufacturing. During recessions, when fewer buildings are designed, drafters may be laid off. Opportunities should be best for individuals who have at least two years of postsecondary training in a drafting program that provides strong technical skills and who have considerable skill and experience using CADD equipment and drafting software programs.

Employment Trend, Projected 2012–22

Total, all occupations: 11%

Drafters, engineering technicians, and mapping technicians: 2%

Drafters: 1%

Note: "All Occupations" includes all occupations in the U.S. Economy. Source: U.S. Bureau of Labor Statistics, Employment Projections Program

Related Occupations
- Architect
- Engineering Technology

Related Military Occupations
- Surveying, Drafting & Mapping Technician

Conversation With . . .
KIM PRITCHARD

Mechanical Drafter/Designer
Bard Medical, Salt Lake City, Utah
Drafting and design, 10 years

1. What was your individual career path in terms of education/training, entry-level job, or other significant opportunity?

I got my Associate of Applied Science in engineering graphics and design technology from Utah Valley University. My first career-related job was as a part-time drafter using SolidWorks software while I was still in school. From there, I bounced through a few drafting jobs until I got into the medical device industry as a mechanical drafter/designer. I've been in that field ever since and am now finishing up my bachelor's in technology management. If you can, get a bachelor's degree. I didn't have to pay for mine because my employers have all had tuition reimbursement policies.

2. What are the most important skills and/or qualities for someone in your profession?

You need to be a visual person. You need to be organized, clean, and precise. Your drawings must leave nothing to the imagination; they must have every piece of needed information so that those who use them to build, write quotes, etc., won't have to call you about some important detail that's missing. You need to be able to work with others, particularly engineers. They will ask for something and often, you'll need to press them for more information. They sometimes provide vague details expecting you to fill in the blanks. You won't be able to fill in the blanks on your own; you'll need them to help you.

It helps to be open-minded and willing to learn new things, especially when it comes to design. As you get more experience, you'll learn how to design as engineers do. That is where your value increases, so don't be afraid to push yourself into taking on new roles. Some drafters are just that, drafters. They come to work, take orders, churn out simple drawings, and go home. Learn to grow your skills, learn new CAD programs, and learn engineering concepts. Most importantly, evolve into a designer, which will earn you more respect and money. You can be making as much as an engineer, with half the schooling!

3. What do you wish you had known going into this profession?

You will not be recognized as a full-blown engineer. Engineers go to school for four to eight years and earn the recognition and responsibility of that title. In school, I thought that drafters evolved into engineers with experience—this is false. You may gain experience over time that will make it seem like you're an engineer, but without that bachelor's degree in engineering, you're not one.

A big goal for me was making lots of money, so I pressed people on which drafting fields made the most money. Architectural? Mechanical? Structural? From what I've seen, electrical drafters make the most money. Electrical is ingrained in high technology and construction, which are both lucrative industries. A friend who has the same degree as I do makes over $100,000 a year doing electrical building information modeling (BIM) work. Structural steel drafters also do well.

4. Are there many job opportunities in your profession? In what specific areas?

As long as the world needs drawings, there will be a need for drafters. There are opportunities everywhere, in any field you can think of. A basic 2D drafter can find a job almost anywhere for about $18 an hour. If you want to make more, you need to specialize and become a designer. Then your value goes up, because you're no longer just putting basic lines on paper; you are designing components, systems, layouts, and the like.

5. How do you see your profession changing in the next five years? What role will technology play in those changes, and what skills will be required?

The world is moving into 3D and beyond; 2D is dead. Learn to think in 3D. Learn parametric software programs like SolidWorks, Creo, Inventor, and Revit. AutoCAD, which is 2D, is still around, but it's becoming a relic. Rarely will you find a high-paying, complex job that uses AutoCAD.

6. What do you enjoy most about your job? What do you enjoy least about your job?

What I enjoy most is creating and drawing. You don't have the responsibilities of engineers, but you can make as much money. In my experience, drafters are rarely on the hot seat. People tend to leave you alone. The engineers have to deal with all the difficult stuff. The downside is drafters often can be overlooked. When it comes time for accolades and awards, prepare to never see your name come up. You can often feel undervalued and under-appreciated.

7. Can you suggest a "try this" for students considering a career in your profession?

If you like to draw and create, drafting and design is for you. If you decide to pursue this field, get a drafting degree; drafting certificates are worthless. In your last year of school, get a part-time job as a drafter. I made $16 an hour as a part-time drafter in college, which, at the time, was excellent money!

MORE INFORMATION

American Council of Engineering Companies
1015 15th Street NW, 8th Floor
Washington, DC 20005
202.347.7474
www.acec.org

American Design Drafting Association
105 E. Main Street
Newbern, TN 38059
731.627.0802
www.adda.org

American Institute of Architects
1735 New York Avenue, NW
Washington, DC 20006-5292
800.242.3837
www.aia.org

Association of Collegiate Schools of Architecture
1735 New York Avenue, NW
Washington, DC 20006
202.785.2324
www.acsa-arch.org

Society of American Registered Architects
14 E. 38th Street
New York, NY 10016
888.385.7272
www.sara-national.org

Technology Student Association
1914 Association Drive
Reston, VA 20191-1540
703.860.9000
www.tsaweb.org

Micah Issitt/Editor

Drywall Installer & Taper

Snapshot

Career Cluster(s): Building & Construction, Architecture & Construction

Interests: Solving problems, working with your hands, communicating with others

Earnings (Yearly Average): $38,100

Employment & Outlook: Faster Than Average Growth Expected

OVERVIEW

Sphere of Work

A drywall installer applies drywall wallboards to the interior of buildings. Drywall installers, also known as drywallers, work with a variety of wallboard materials. They use different tools to cut, fit, and fasten wallboards. A taper readies the wallboards for painting with tape and other materials. Drywall installers and tapers are considered part of the construction and building industry.

Work Environment

Drywall installers and tapers work indoors in a variety of commercial and residential buildings. They spend most of the day on their feet, bending, climbing, or stretching. Workers use a variety of tools to get the job done, typically simple hand tools such as utility knives and hammers. They also work with scaffoldings and ladders and will often have to handle large, heavy wallboards.

Working with drywall and other materials can make the workplace dusty. Because of these conditions, drywall installers and tapers should wear protective gear such as goggles and face masks.

Profile

Working Conditions: Work Indoors
Physical Strength: Medium Work, Heavy Work
Education Needs: On-The-Job Training, High School Diploma or G.E.D., High School Diploma with Technical Education, Apprenticeship
Licensure/Certification: Usually Not Required
Opportunities For Experience: Apprenticeship
Holland Interest Score*: RCS, RES, RIE

* See Appendix A

Occupation Interest

Since drywall installers and tapers work in all different types of buildings, no two jobs are the same. Those interested in the profession should be able to adapt to various tasks and should have good problem-solving skills. Drywall installers and tapers should enjoy building things with their hands. They should also be capable of working as part of a team as well as by themselves.

A Day in the Life—Duties and Responsibilities

When drywall installers and tapers are hired for a job, they must first go over the design plans, either at the actual jobsite or by examining blueprints. They have to take into account the location of windows, electrical outlets, and other obstructions. Measuring as precisely as possible will cut down on the amount of drywall and time wasted.

Once the measurements are done, a drywall installer will cut the appropriate amount of wallboard using utility knives or power saws, depending on the job. Using nails, screws, or sealing compounds, he or she then fastens the drywall in place. The edges of the drywall are then evenly smoothed and trimmed and all nail holes are patched up by a taper. Depending on the size of the job, a worker may complete it alone or with a team of people. Drywall installers and tapers use trowels to spread and smooth spackling paste over nail holes, cracks, or any other flaws. If there is any existing drywall at the site where the worker must install new wallboards, it is removed using crowbars or hammers.

Duties and Responsibilities

- Cutting and fitting wallboard to studding and joists
- Trimming rough edges or wallboard to obtain an even joint
- Installing metal corners and stop beads
- Scribing measurements on wallboard
- Cutting out openings in the wall panels for electrical outlets, air conditioning units and plumbing connections
- Mixing and sealing compound and spreading it over the joint between boards

WORK ENVIRONMENT

Physical Environment

Drywall installers and tapers commonly work indoors at commercial and residential sites. They work at buildings that are under construction or undergoing renovations. Sometimes a person must work atop a ladder or on scaffolding. Working with drywall creates a dusty and dirty environment.

Human Environment

A lot of collaboration with clients and other workers in the construction trade is required of drywall installers and tapers. Therefore, a drywaller and taper should be outgoing and possess great interpersonal communication skills. Less experienced workers will have to frequently check in with their supervisors.

Relevant Skills and Abilities

Organization & Management Skills
- Coordinating tasks
- Making decisions
- Managing people/groups

Organization & Management Skills
- Paying attention to and handling details
- Performing routine work

Research & Planning Skills
- Developing evaluation strategies

Technical Skills
- Performing scientific, mathematical and technical work
- Working with machines, tools or other objects

Unclassified Skills
- Performing work that produces tangible results
- Using set methods and standards in your work

Technological Environment

Drywall installers and tapers work with a large variety of tools, including utility knives, power saws, hammers, screwdrivers, and more. They work with different sealing compounds as well, the most common being plaster. For some jobs, a ladder or scaffolding is required. Safety equipment worn by workers includes goggles, masks, and sometimes hardhats.

EDUCATION, TRAINING, AND ADVANCEMENT

High School/Secondary

Most employers require drywall installers and tapers to have a high school diploma or GED certificate. There are some common high school courses that would benefit a potential drywall installer and taper, including wood shop, mathematics, and mechanical drawing.

Suggested High School Subjects
- Applied Math
- Building Trades & Carpentry
- English

- Industrial Arts
- Shop Math
- Woodshop

Famous First

Drywall, or gypsum board, emerged in the early twentieth century based on an earlier plaster-based product called Sackett board. In 1917 United States Gypsum Corporation came out with a product they called Sheetrock. Sheetrock is a trademarked term, although it is sometimes used in a generic sense to refer to drywall. Later versions of Sheetrock improved fire resistance and made the panels lighter and less brittle.

Postsecondary

While most employers do not require a drywall installer and taper to have a college education, many workers can benefit from courses offered at trade and vocational schools. Many community colleges also offer courses that potential drywall installers and tapers will find useful in the industry. Courses in construction and carpentry will train a worker in the basics of the job, such as tools, safety, and blueprint reading. Most schools offer hands-on training, which will prove useful when applying for jobs. Employers are more likely to hire someone who has completed a formal course in the industry.

Related College Majors
- Carpentry

Adult Job Seekers

Drywall installers and tapers commonly work forty hours per week, but they may be required to work overtime for larger, more urgent jobs. Since the job is physically demanding, a potential worker should be in good physical shape and be able to perform the required tasks. If a person has no background in the drywall trade, he or she should consider taking construction and carpentry courses at a trade or vocational school.

Professional Certification and Licensure

Workers can learn drywalling on the job or through a formal apprenticeship. Those who learn on the job undergo informal training by helping those more experienced in the trade. This type of training usually lasts up to one year.

Those who go through a formal apprenticeship can expect to be working without supervision after three to four years. During each year of the apprenticeship, a worker must complete 144 hours of instruction and 2,000 hours of on-the-job training. This instruction will cover construction and carpentry basics such as tools, reading and modifying blueprints, and building-code laws. On the job, apprentices will help more experienced workers until they gradually become more skillful and can work on their own. At the end of the apprenticeship, a drywall installer and taper is considered a journeyworker and may perform jobs on his or her own.

A drywall installer and taper may join a local or national union. Joining a union ensures that a worker receives benefits, proper training, and a pension. Many unions sponsor apprenticeships.

Additional Requirements

Drywall installers and tapers should be physically able to do the job. While most tools used are not that heavy, a panel of drywall can weigh up to one hundred pounds, and a drywall installer needs to be able to lift and maneuver these panels. Drywall installers and tapers should have great attention to detail, especially when it comes to accurately measuring the amount of panels needed. A strong understanding of basic mathematics is also helpful.

EARNINGS AND ADVANCEMENT

Earnings for drywall installers and tapers depend on the employer, union affiliation, economic factors and whether they are self-employed. Median earnings of drywall installers and tapers were $38,100 in 2014. The lowest ten percent earned less than $25,360, and the highest ten percent earned more than $75,570.

Drywall installers and tapers often work independently and may be paid at a rate according to the number of panels installed or on an hourly basis. Apprentices started at fifty percent of journeymen scale and received wage increases as they gained experience.

Drywall installers and tapers may receive paid vacations, holidays, and sick days; life and health insurance; and retirement benefits. These are usually paid by the employer.

Metropolitan Areas with the Highest
Employment Level in this Occupation

Metropolitan area	Employment	Employment per thousand jobs	Hourly mean wage
Santa Ana-Anaheim-Irvine, CA	3,710	2.50	$25.68
Los Angeles-Long Beach-Glendale, CA	3,410	0.84	$27.54
Houston-Sugar Land-Baytown, TX	2,870	1.01	$15.27
Riverside-San Bernardino-Ontario, CA	2,660	2.13	$24.90
Phoenix-Mesa-Glendale, AZ	2,180	1.19	$17.64
San Diego-Carlsbad-San Marcos, CA	2,170	1.65	$25.58
Dallas-Plano-Irving, TX	2,130	0.95	$15.33
Washington-Arlington-Alexandria, DC-VA-MD-WV	2,120	0.89	$18.82
New York-White Plains-Wayne, NY-NJ	1,530	0.28	$31.38
Oakland-Fremont-Hayward, CA	1,490	1.46	$33.76

Source: Bureau of Labor Statistics

EMPLOYMENT AND OUTLOOK

There were approximately 114,000 drywall installers & tapers employed nationally in 2012. Employment is expected to grow much faster than the average for all occupations through the year 2022, which means employment is projected to increase 12 percent to 19 percent. New building construction and home improvement and remodeling projects will create demand. Most drywall installation and finishing is done indoors. Therefore, drywall installers and tapers lose less worktime because of inclement weather than do some other construction workers. Nevertheless, they may be unemployed between construction projects and during downturns in construction activity.

Employment Trend, Projected 2012–22

Construction trades workers: 22%

Drywall and ceiling tile installers: 16%

Tapers: 15%

Total, all occupations: 11%

Note: "All Occupations" includes all occupations in the U.S. Economy. Source: U.S. Bureau of Labor Statistics, Employment Projections Program

Related Occupations
- Carpenter
- Cement Mason
- Construction Laborer
- Insulation Worker
- Plasterer

Conversation With . . .
MARGARITA ARNOLD

Drywall Finisher
Anning-Johnson, Melrose Park, Illinois
Drywall Finisher/Taper, 7 years

1. What was your individual career path in terms of education/training, entry-level job, or other significant opportunity?

I used to clean people's homes and I wasn't getting a lot of work. They only gave me one house to clean and it was super far from the city. I was a single mom with two kids; my youngest was only 10 months old. I decided I needed a little help so I could find another job. I had no choice, so I went to the state Department of Human Services to apply for assistance. I sat in the office for five hours and I was bored so I started to walk around. I saw this board with a picture of a woman in a hardhat. It said, "Would you like to earn $19 an hour as a construction worker?" and I said, "What?!" As luck would have it, the orientation was to be held that same day in two hours. I just went for it. It was the Technical Opportunities Program (TOP) offered by Chicago Women in Trades. I was always interested in the trades. Some of my relatives did painting, but in my culture—I'm Mexican—females are not supposed to work in male fields, so I was always shot down.

I'm not an office type of person. I don't think I could handle sitting at a computer all day. I like being able to stand back and see what I've done. But in the end, it was really about the money—the pay and great benefits. I make $43 an hour, and with benefits, it's worth $65 an hour. I now have a chance to help put my kids through college thanks to this trade.

2. What are the most important skills and/or qualities for someone in your profession?

Handwork is the most important skill. It takes a long time to perfect, but it comes with practice. Also, you have to be a good stilt walker, because you'll be walking on stilts a lot. It only took me about a month to learn that.

3. What do you wish you had known going into this profession?

I wish I had the handwork skills. It was frustrating and I was hard on myself. I didn't have a mentor to tell me it would come eventually.

Being a woman in this field is definitely difficult. Men dominate the field and there's still discrimination against us. I believe the men get intimidated when they see a woman on the job. The hardest part is listening to some of the things they say.

4. Are there many job opportunities in your profession? In what specific areas?

There are. The company I work for is international. I usually work in commercial buildings in Chicago, on new high rises or remodels of existing buildings. If it gets slow, they let you go, but being a member of the International Union of Painters and Allied Trades, I can always call the next company.

You have to start at the bottom and work your way up to foreman or superintendent. If you'd make a good advocate for workers in the field, you should get involved in the "local" of your union. A good opportunity to consider is to be an officer of the local union. That's a paid job.

5. How do you see your profession changing in the next five years? What role will technology play in those changes, and what skills will be required?

We're looking at a compound that will be like a paint that you spray on instead of using a roller and once it's sprayed, it will set up like the final "level five" finish. You won't have to skim and sand over it again and again. We will have to be trained in how to use the sprayer, especially safety measures.

6. What do you enjoy most about your job? What do you enjoy least about your job?

Working by hand. I love it. I actually consider myself—and I've heard it from many people—that I'm very good at it. And working on stilts is so cool! The day goes by quickly because we're so productive. I consider my trade as a marathon. It's a run every day.

What I don't enjoy is the discrimination. Sexual harassment is still out there. Also, I don't like the inconvenience of not having a restroom available. That's pretty tough. Even the men complain about it sometimes.

7. Can you suggest a valuable "try this" for students considering a career in your profession?

A pre-apprenticeship program is the surest way to get a feel for what the trades are about. It's a 12-week program. You don't have to do it before an apprenticeship, but I highly recommend it. I did it through the Chicago Women in Trades Technical Opportunities Program. Boys can contact the union about similar programs. Drywall finishing is a sure career. There's nothing like having an education, but after a two-year apprenticeship, you're not going to have college debt.

MORE INFORMATION

Associated Builders and Contractors
4250 N. Fairfax Drive, 9th Floor
Arlington, VA 22203
703.812.2000
www.abc.org

Association of the Wall and Ceiling Industries, International
513 West Broad Street, Suite 210
Falls Church, VA 22046
703.538.1600
www.awci.org

Building Trades Association
16th Street, NW
Washington, DC 20006
800.326.7800
www.buildingtrades.com

Drywallers and Acoustical Contractors Association
P.O. Box 743484
Dallas, TX 75374-3484
877.356.7700
www.dacadfw.org

Finishing Trades Institute
7230 Parkway Drive
Hanover, MD 21076
800.276.7289
www.finishingtradesinstitute.org

International Union of Painters & Allied Trades
7234 Parkway Drive
Hanover, MD 21076
410.564.5900
www.iupat.org

National Association of Home Builders
1201 15th Street, NW
Washington, DC 20005
800.368.5242
www.nahb.com

National Center for Construction Education and Research
13614 Progress Boulevard
Alachua, FL 32615
888.622.3720
www.nccer.org

United Brotherhood of Carpenters
101 Constitution Avenue, NW
Washington, DC 20001
202.546.6206
www.carpenters.org

Patrick Cooper/Editor

Electrician

Snapshot

Career Cluster(s): Building & Construction, Architecture & Construction, Manufacturing, Transportation, Distribution & Logistics
Interests: Construction, working with your hands, solving problems
Earnings (Yearly Average): $51,110
Employment & Outlook: Faster Than Average Growth Expected

OVERVIEW

Sphere of Work

Electricians install, repair, maintain, and modify electrical systems in homes and businesses. Some electricians work as general contractors in the home repair and improvement fields. Others specialize in specific types of electrical systems for industrial or corporate applications. Electricians must work within a variety of state, local, and national guidelines that regulate the use of electricity.

Work Environment

Electricians work both indoors and outdoors on internal and external systems for homes and businesses. In order to ensure safe working conditions, they tend to avoid working outdoors during inclement weather. Most electricians work full time during regular business hours, though evening, late-night, and weekend hours are common during emergency situations or when essential electrical systems require overnight maintenance. An electrician's work environment will vary from job to job, or even during a single job; it is common to spend time working in a basement or utility room, move through a variety of other rooms, and then complete outside installations on external walls and the roof.

Profile

Working Conditions: Work both Indoors and Outdoors
Physical Strength: Medium Work
Education Needs: On-The-Job Training, High School Diploma with Technical Education, Apprenticeship
Licensure/Certification: Required
Opportunities For Experience: Apprenticeship, Military Service
Holland Interest Score*: RIE

* See Appendix A

Occupation Interest

Those seeking to pursue a career in electrical work should be detail oriented and comfortable with physically demanding work. Since many electrical projects require working with other subcontractors, electricians also benefit from an interest in home or business remodeling and construction. Electrical work is a hands-on field that requires individuals to be on their feet or in a crouched position most of the day, so individuals with muscular, joint, or other physical problems may have difficulty.

A Day in the Life—Duties and Responsibilities

In a typical day, an electrician may spend time planning for a future project, installing wiring or specialized equipment to draw or distribute electricity, or examining wiring or equipment to detect and fix problems in an electrical system. While many homes and businesses often hire local electricians, in some cases, electricians may have to commute to remote areas to work on projects.

Before an electrical installation, diagrams of the electrical system are prepared by either an electrician or another home-construction specialist. The diagrams include integration of the electrical systems with the other components of the building.

Installing electrical systems generally requires two components: the equipment used to harness and distribute electricity, which may include transformers, generators, and fuse or power boxes, and the electrical wiring that will be used to provide access to the building's electrical supply. In some cases, electricians complete different aspects of a job on different days, while other projects are small enough in scope to be completed in a single workday.

Many electricians, especially independent contractors, spend time trying to find faults in preexisting electrical systems. The ability to detect problems and repair electrical systems is one of the most important skills for any electrician. In many cases, electricians are called in to diagnose problems in systems they did not install, which may require a painstaking examination of wires and other equipment. Once the fault in the system has been located, however, repairs can be completed quickly and efficiently.

Duties and Responsibilities

- **Planning installations, specifications and local electrical codes**
- **Preparing sketches showing the location of wiring and equipment, and installing electrical conduits**
- **Pulling wires through conduits and connecting them to fixtures and equipment**
- **Installing switches, relays and circuit-breaker panels**
- **Connecting power cables to equipment and installing ground leads**
- **Locating the cause of breakdowns and making repairs**
- **Installing fiber optic cable and equipment for computers and other telecommunications equipment**

OCCUPATION SPECIALTIES

Commercial and Industrial Electricians

Commercial and Industrial Electricians maintain and repair large motors, equipment, and control systems in businesses and factories. They use their knowledge of electrical systems to help these facilities run safely and efficiently. Some also install the wiring for businesses and factories that are being built..

Residential Electricians

Residential Electricians install wiring and troubleshoot electrical problems in peoples' homes. Those who work in new-home construction install outlets and provide access to power where needed. Those who work in maintenance and remodeling typically repair and replace faulty equipment

WORK ENVIRONMENT

Physical Environment

Electricians work in a wide variety of environments, including homes, offices, factories, plants, and isolated or rural locations. They may be required to work in any and all parts of a building, including rooftops and outdoor areas. Electricians sometimes specialize in one or more subsets of the electrical industry, which may determine the type of daily environment they encounter in the course of their work.

Electricians suffer from a higher rate of on-the-job injuries than many other occupations, largely because of the danger posed by working with high-voltage electrical systems. In addition, electricians regularly exert themselves during the course of their work, and injuries caused by repetitive stress and strain are common.

Relevant Skills and Abilities

Organization & Management Skills
- Following instructions
- Making decisions

Research & Planning Skills
- Developing evaluation strategies
- Using logical reasoning

Technical Skills
- Performing scientific, · mathematical and technical work
- Working with machines, tools or other objects

Unclassified Skills
- Performing work that produces tangible results

Plant Environment

Electrical plants hire electrical engineers and electricians to maintain the equipment and wiring used to transmit electricity from the generator facility to customers. Electricians working in these plants use a specialized set of skills and often work with equipment that is vastly different from equipment used in consumer electrical systems.

Human Environment

Electricians work either independently, handling all aspects of a job on their own, or as part of a team. They may work as general contractors, installing wiring and equipment as part of a larger home repair or construction project, or they may work closely with other home repair or improvement specialists to integrate electrical design and installation into an overall structural design. Electricians also interact directly with clients, such as homeowners and building managers.

Technological Environment

Electricians use various hand and power tools, such as pliers, wire strippers, saws, and drills. They also use testing equipment, such as voltage or current meters, and basic electrical equipment, including circuits, electrical panels, and other peripheral equipment. In addition, electricians may use analytical and computer-aided design (CAD) software.

EDUCATION, TRAINING, AND ADVANCEMENT

High School/Secondary

Many electricians begin work in their field out of high school, and most electrical education or apprenticeship programs require that applicants have a high school diploma or the equivalent. In addition, apprenticeship programs often require that applicants have completed at least one year of high school algebra. To prepare for a career as an electrician, high school students should study basic mathematics, engineering, and physics. Computer literacy is also important, since technical diagrams and electrical wiring specifications are typically computer generated.

Suggested High School Subjects
- Applied Math
- Blueprint Reading
- Building & Grounds Maintenance
- Drafting
- Electricity & Electronics
- English
- First Aid Training
- Machining Technology
- Mathematics
- Mechanical Drawing
- Science
- Shop Math
- Trade/Industrial Education
- Welding

Famous First

The first electric cooking experiment was performed by Benjamin Franklin in 1749, when he killed and cooked a turkey for dinner. But the first electric stove would not be introduced to households everywhere until 1896, over 100 years later. William S. Hadaway, Jr. from New York City invented a one-ring, spiral-coiled conductor stove which allowed for uniform heat distribution. This much improved technology spread quickly.

Postsecondary

The traditional route to becoming an electrician is to complete an apprenticeship course offered through a state-licensed program. Local and state unions regularly offer apprenticeship programs. Utility companies and private companies that regularly employ electricians will sometimes offer apprenticeship training.

In general, an apprentice must complete a minimum of 144 hours of classroom training and 2,000 hours of on-the-job training before he or she is qualified to take tests for certification. In the classroom, students learn the details of reading and creating electrical blueprints, the basics of electrical theory, and the physics of electrical systems, as well as specific skills such as soldering, wiring, and safety procedures that will be used on the job.

Some electricians begin by attending technical or trade schools, which provide certificate programs and two-year degree programs that can help students satisfy some of the requirements for completing an apprenticeship. In many cases, technical institutes work directly with apprenticeship programs, helping students get into the appropriate programs and obtain the education needed to pass licensing tests.

Related College Majors
- Electrical & Electronics Equipment Installation & Repair
- Electrical, Electronics & Communications Engineering
- Electrician Training

Adult Job Seekers

Adults with a background in home repair or general contracting work who are interested in becoming electricians should seek out local apprenticeship organizations and inquire about special programs available to help adult workers transition into the electrical field. They may also attend continuing-education or introductory courses through a community college or technical school.

Professional Certification and Licensure

Most states have specific requirements for electrical certification and licensure, and the process of obtaining local licenses varies from state to state. The National Electrical Code (NEC) is a set of guidelines that most states have adopted regarding safety and security in electrical-systems wiring and installation. Most apprenticeships tailor their programs to meet specific local and state requirements.

Additional Requirements

Electricians frequently work directly with customers, so customer-service skills are important. They should also have strong critical-thinking skills. Electrical work can be physically exhausting and demanding, and electricians must take care to protect their bodies from potential harm. Because electricians frequently identify wires by color, individuals with certain types of visual impairments, including color blindness and poor color vision, might be unable to perform some forms of electrical work.

Fun Fact

A Master Electrician has to crack the books and work hard—for at least eight years. That's how long it takes to earn the rank, via classroom instruction and hands-on experience.

Source: http://www.trade-certificates.com/electrician/5-surprising-facts-about-electricians/

EARNINGS AND ADVANCEMENT

Hourly wages for electricians are among the highest in the building trades. They may vary by type, size, and geographic location of the employer, area of specialization of the employee and union affiliation. Electricians had median annual earnings of $51,110 in 2014. The lowest ten percent earned less than $31,170, and the highest ten percent earned more than $85,590.

Depending on experience, apprentices usually start at between 30 and 50 percent of the rate of skilled electricians. Increases are given as they gain skills and experience.

Electricians may receive paid vacations, holidays, and sick days; life and health insurance; and retirement benefits. These are usually paid by the employer.

Metropolitan Areas with the Highest Employment Level in this Occupation

Metropolitan area	Employment	Employment per thousand jobs	Hourly mean wage
New York-White Plains-Wayne, NY-NJ	23,630	4.38	$36.31
Houston-Sugar Land-Baytown, TX	16,850	5.92	$23.54
Chicago-Joliet-Naperville, IL	15,250	4.06	$35.99
Los Angeles-Long Beach-Glendale, CA	10,830	2.67	$28.71
Phoenix-Mesa-Glendale, AZ	10,530	5.77	$21.77
Atlanta-Sandy Springs-Marietta, GA	10,440	4.37	$22.92
Washington-Arlington-Alexandria, DC-VA-MD-WV	9,770	4.11	$27.07
Dallas-Plano-Irving, TX	9,340	4.17	$19.95
Denver-Aurora-Broomfield, CO	8,160	6.16	$23.46
Boston-Cambridge-Quincy, MA	6,980	3.89	$32.26

Source: Bureau of Labor Statistics

EMPLOYMENT AND OUTLOOK

Electricians held about 583,000 jobs in 2012. Employment of electricians is expected to grow faster than the average for all occupations through the year 2022, which means employment is projected to increase 18 percent to 25 percent. As the population grows, more electricians will be needed to install and maintain electrical devices and wiring in homes, schools, offices, restaurants and other structures. Installation of automated manufacturing systems and robots in factories will create demand for electricians. Job growth will also result from the trend to install more energy efficient items in buildings, such as solar panels and motions sensors for lighting.

Employment Trend, Projected 2012–22

Construction trades workers: 22%

Electricians: 20%

Total, all occupations: 11%

Note: "All Occupations" includes all occupations in the U.S. Economy. Source: U.S. Bureau of Labor Statistics, Employment Projections Program

Related Occupations
- Aircraft Mechanic
- Electrical & Electronics Engineer
- Electrical Line Installer & Repairer
- General Maintenance Mechanic
- Maintenance Supervisor
- Robotics Technician
- Telecommunications Equipment Repairer

Related Occupations
- Building Electrician
- Communications Equipment Repairer
- Electrical Products Repairer
- Power Plant Electrician
- Power Plant Operator
- Powerhouse Mechanic
- Ship Electrician

Conversation With . . .
JEFF KELJIK

Education Director
Minnesota Electrical Association, Minneapolis, Minnesota
Electrician and electrical field, 41 years

1. What was your individual career path in terms of education/training, entry-level job, or other significant opportunity?

My uncle really knew how and why to put things together and make them work. From the time I was little, I liked that idea. So I started taking things apart and figuring out how to make them work. Even now, I like that capability of making things work, or at least analyzing why they don't.

I enrolled in a technical college for a two-year program because I knew I wanted to work in the electrical field but wasn't sure in what capacity. While I was in school, I worked a part-time job doing electrical maintenance while attending the University of Minnesota for engineering classes. I stopped after three years because I knew I wanted to work toward my journeyman's electrical license. I knew I wanted to work with tools and not spend time at a desk. I went on to get my master electrician's license, then teach at my alma mater, Dunwoody College of Technology. Although I went on to become department chair for the electrical training program, I was also the master electrician of record for the campus, so I regularly got my tools out and had apprentices.

I eventually earned a bachelor's in business communications and a post-secondary teaching degree. Now, I'm the director of education for a large electrical association of contractors in Minnesota. I am still licensed and still use my skills and tools in electrical work.

In addition, I've authored five textbooks on electricity, as well as their subsequent editions.

2. What are the most important skills and/or qualities for someone in your profession?

The ability to think conceptually but work concretely. You cannot see electricity, so you need to understand the theory of electrical fundamentals, and then apply those principles to building a safe and efficient system. You need a genuine interest in doing an important job that many people will not do. To keep yourself safe and provide your customer with a safe installation, you must always be thinking.

3. What do you wish you had known going into this profession?

I wish I had known the electrical industry had so many facets, allowing you to work in planning, managing, finance, sales, engineering, or as an electrician.

4. Are there many job opportunities in your profession? In what specific areas?

The field can include electrical generation and utility work, from engineering to managing the daily electrical load; planning electrical needs; managing resources for environmental requirements; sales and account management; product development; distribution of tools and supplies; construction projects from small residential to large commercial or industrial projects; and maintenance of electrical systems ranging from systems in homes to highly automated and sophisticated manufacturing plants. All these endeavors require different skills and backgrounds to support the practicing electricians who make the plans come to life.

5. How do you see your profession changing in the next five years, what role will technology play in those changes, and what skills will be required?

The next five years will require more skills from the electrical worker. Not only will they need to maintain the older systems that still provide service, but they will have to deal with more computer-controlled equipment. The speed of data will require them to be very skilled at design software, drawing software, and building information systems that allow design changes to happen immediately. Electricians will need more diagnostic skills using laptop or smart phone applications.

6. What do you enjoy most about your job? What do you enjoy least about your job?

I really enjoy the variety and the challenges of the work. I'm always learning new electrical code requirements, new ways to do old jobs, and new technologies. I enjoy being able to help people solve complex problems or answer questions from my friends about how something works.

The only drawback to this type of work—for me—is that I am always thinking about how to solve problems or how to be creative and achieve a desired outcome within budget and on time. The challenge sometimes keeps me awake at night.

7. Can you suggest a valuable "try this" for students considering a career in your profession?

Ask an electrical professional if they can explain to you what they do on a daily basis. How dangerous is it? How physically and mentally demanding? Do you need to be at work every day or can you work from home? How do you keep up with current information? Explore various occupations within the electrical field, ask about union and non-union electrician benefits, and ask about the licensure requirements in your state

MORE INFORMATION

Associated Builders and Contractors
4250 N. Fairfax Drive, 9th Floor
Arlington, VA 22203
703.812.2000
www.abc.org

Independent Electrical Contractors
4401 Ford Avenue, Suite 1100
Alexandria, VA 22302
703.549.7351
www.ieci.org

International Brotherhood of Electrical Workers
900 Seventh Street, NW
Washington, DC 20001
202.833.7000
www.ibew.org

National Association of Home Builders
1201 15th Street, NW
Washington, DC 20005
800.368.5242
www.nahb.com

National Electrical Contractors Association (NECA)
3 Bethesda Metro Center, Suite 1100
Bethesda, MD 20814
301.657.3110
www.necanet.org

National Joint Apprenticeship and Training Committee
301 Prince George's Boulevard
Suite D
Upper Marlboro, MD 20774
301.715.2300
www.njatc.org

National Labor-Management Cooperation Committee
3 Bethesda Metro Center, Suite 1100
Bethesda, MD 20814-5372
www.nlmcc.org

Micah Issitt/Editor

Elevator Installer/ Repairer

Snapshot

Career Cluster(s): Building & Construction, Architecture & Construction, Manufacturing

Interests: Mechanics, solving problems, analyzing information, working with your hands

Earnings (Yearly Average): $78,620

Employment & Outlook: Faster Than Average Growth Expected

OVERVIEW

Sphere of Work

Elevator technicians install, troubleshoot, and repair elevator systems. Professional elevator technicians are licensed mechanical professionals who install building transport systems to the design specifications of both government and industry safety standards.

Elevator repair professionals are trained in diagnosing and repairing routine and emergency elevator problems such as faulty electrical wiring, sensors, control panels, and ventilation. They sometimes help trapped passengers and are responsible for repairing any damage to the elevator or

elevator system as a result of a fire. They also perform annual testing and replace and update older equipment and systems. In addition, elevator technicians often install and repair escalators and moving walkways.

Work Environment

Elevator technicians work in a variety of multi-floor buildings, including commercial buildings, factories, and residences. Because elevators are often accessed through public areas of a building, many elevator-repair tasks are conducted in lobbies and common areas. Work on control panels and similar components is usually completed in building substructures or utility rooms. Inspection and repair of elevator pulleys and weight systems may require accessing elevator shafts. Header tanks, which house much of the technological infrastructure of elevator systems, are traditionally kept on building rooftops.

Profile

Working Conditions: Work Indoors
Physical Strength: Medium Work, Heavy Work
Education Needs: On-The-Job Training, High School Diploma or G.E.D., High School Diploma with Technical Education, Apprenticeship
Licensure/Certification: Required
Opportunities For Experience: Apprenticeship, Military Service
Holland Interest Score*: RIS

* See Appendix A

Occupation Interest

Elevator installation and repair attracts a wide variety of candidates from different educational and professional backgrounds. The majority are technologically savvy individuals who possess analytical problem-solving skills, manual dexterity, and high inductive-reasoning capabilities. Elevator installations are intricate processes that require large teams of contractors. Routine elevator maintenance usually requires one or two mechanics, making the trade suitable for those who enjoy working either alone or in teams.

A Day in the Life—Duties and Responsibilities

Elevator installers and repairers usually specialize in installation, repair, or maintenance. Installers work with building architects and construction engineers and review architectural blueprints to determine the scope of work and type of tools and supplies needed to complete the installation. Installers work on scaffolding and platforms to bolt and weld the elevator walls to the elevator shaft. Elevator technicians must ensure that each elevator is installed to specific safety regulations and legal requirements. Depending on the size and number of elevators required for a particular project, installations can take anywhere from several weeks to several months.

Installers and maintenance workers generally need a greater knowledge of electricity, electrical systems, and electronics, as a significant portion of their work involves maintaining elevators and troubleshooting problems. Common tasks related to routine maintenance include lubricating parts and replacing lighting and damaged safety signage. Other maintenance tasks include fixing malfunctioning control panels and general cosmetic repairs.

Elevator, escalator, and automated-walkway maintenance can expose technicians to potentially hazardous conditions and environments. Technicians often come in contact with dangerous equipment, so adherence to safety protocol and use of protective equipment is a major part of the job.

Elevator technicians must also maintain logs that carefully document any routine maintenance conducted, replacement parts issued, and any other pertinent information that will be of use to future maintenance mechanics. Such information is also required by law for elevators to pass annual license certification.

Duties and Responsibilities

- Studying blueprints and laying out necessary parts
- Installing cables, counterweights, pumps, motor foundations, elevator cars, escalator drives and control panels
- Positioning electric motors and equipment on top of elevator shafts
- Verifying alignments
- Connecting electrical wiring to control panels and electric motors
- Testing and adjusting the elevators for maximum performance

OCCUPATION SPECIALTIES

Elevator Constructors

Elevator Constructors specialize in installation, maintenance or repair work. They may be designated according to the type of equipment which they install.

Elevator Repairers

Elevator Repairers are also called maintenance mechanics. They do preventive maintenance on elevators, escalators and similar equipment to meet safety regulations and building codes.

WORK ENVIRONMENT

Relevant Skills and Abilities

Interpersonal/Social Skills
- Working as a member of a team

Organization & Management Skills
- Paying attention to and handling details

Technical Skills
- Performing scientific, mathematical and technical work
- Working with machines, tools or other objects

Physical Environment

Elevator technicians work in and around elevator cars, shafts, and physical plant locations and control rooms. Installers and repairers often work in tight, cramped indoor spaces within buildings or in buildings under construction, including residential, commercial, and industrial structures.

Human Environment

Much of the technical and mechanical aspects of elevator repair are conducted individually or with small groups of fellow technicians.

Elevator technicians may be required to interact with other members of a building's maintenance staff.

Technological Environment

Elevator technicians possess a strong technical aptitude and familiarity with both the technical and nontechnical aspects of elevator systems. Elevator company employees are often required to undergo ongoing training in order to stay knowledgeable of new technologies and repair methods.

EDUCATION, TRAINING, AND ADVANCEMENT

High School/Secondary

High school students can best prepare for a career as an elevator technician with course work in algebra, calculus, geometry, trigonometry, physics, and computers. English and composition classes can prepare students for the communication and problem-solving aspects of the job. Courses in industrial arts and any physics-related courses are also beneficial to students interested in a career in mechanical maintenance, as these aid in their understanding of physical principles, material dynamics, and mechanical processes.

Suggested High School Subjects
- Applied Math
- Blueprint Reading
- Building & Grounds Maintenance
- Electricity & Electronics
- English
- Mathematics
- Shop Mechanics
- Welding

Famous First

The first elevator was created in 1850 by Henry Waterman and was a simple platform, without enclosing walls. It was first used in a milling building in order to hoist barrels upstairs, not transport human passengers. The first passenger elevator was created seven years later in 1857 by Elisha Graves Otis. It was installed in E. V. Haughwout's store on the corner of Broadway and Broome Street in New York City. Otis-brand elevators still operate today.

Postsecondary

Postsecondary education is not traditionally a prerequisite for employment as an elevator technician. Most elevator installers and repairers enroll in an apprenticeship program. Programs are offered by local unions, employers, or independent contractors.

Related College Majors
• Electrical & Electronics Equipment Installation & Repair

Adult Job Seekers

Elevator technicians traditionally work forty-hour weeks during regular business hours, unless they are employed by a firm that provides emergency repair services. In such cases, technicians may work on-call shifts, sometimes on weekends and holidays.

The field of elevator repair can also be a transitional field. It is often explored by mechanics who are phasing out of previous employment in another area of system repair, such as automobile or small-machinery repair. It is also a field utilized as temporary employment for mechanics and engineers eager to move on to managerial roles in systems maintenance or to positions as mechanics in other larger and more complex mechanical systems, such those found in transportation and energy.

Professional Certification and Licensure

Depending on their state of employment, elevator technicians may be required to complete professional apprenticeships before becoming certified. Nearly all states require licensure or certification of some kind.

Additional Requirements

In addition to state-issued certification, the National Association of Elevator Contractors (NAEC) also offers certification courses for professionals in the field. While NAEC certification is not required to become an elevator technician, it can often be advantageous when applying to open positions.

Fun Fact

The Kingdom Tower in Saudi Arabi, projected to be the worlds tallest skyscraper, will have the world's fastest elevator, capable of traveling 32 feet a second, when it is completed in 2019.

Source: http://www.dailymail.co.uk/sciencetech/article-2650663/Dont-look-Worlds-tallest-tower-feature-lift-travels-32-feet-SECOND-opens-2018.html and others

EARNINGS AND ADVANCEMENT

Elevator installers and repairers are among the highest paid of all construction trades workers. Earnings of elevator installers and repairers depend on the individual's experience and training, and the type, size, geographic location and extent of unionization of the employer. Median annual earnings of elevator installers and repairers were $78,620 in 2014. The lowest ten percent earned less than $41,930, and the highest ten percent earned more than $109,450.

Union members generally receive their benefits through insurance, pension, and vacation funds established by union contracts. These are usually paid by the employer.

Metropolitan Areas with the Highest Employment Level in this Occupation

Metropolitan area	Employment	Employment per thousand jobs	Hourly mean wage
New York-White Plains-Wayne, NY-NJ	3,120	0.58	$39.20
Chicago-Joliet-Naperville, IL	1,450	0.39	$41.10
Washington-Arlington-Alexandria, DC-VA-MD-WV	930	0.39	$39.07
Houston-Sugar Land-Baytown, TX	870	0.31	$30.70
Minneapolis-St. Paul-Bloomington, MN-WI	740	0.41	$38.69
Dallas-Plano-Irving, TX	660	0.29	$34.04
Atlanta-Sandy Springs-Marietta, GA	520	0.22	$29.07
Los Angeles-Long Beach-Glendale, CA	440	0.11	$41.37
Boston-Cambridge-Quincy, MA	390	0.22	$42.06
Fort Lauderdale-Pompano Beach-Deerfield Beach, FL	310	0.41	$37.26

Source: Bureau of Labor Statistics

EMPLOYMENT AND OUTLOOK

Elevator installers and repairers held about 20,000 jobs nationally in 2012. Employment is expected to grow about as fast as the average for all occupations through the year 2022, which means employment is projected to increase about 25 percent. Job growth is related to an increase in nonresidential construction, such as commercial office buildings and stores that have elevators and escalators. The need to continually update and modernize old equipment, improve appearance and install sophisticated equipment and computerized controls also should add to the demand for elevator installers and repairers.

Relatively few new job openings will be generated because this occupation is small. Replacement needs, which are another source of jobs, will also be relatively low, in part because a substantial amount of time is invested in specialized training that yields high earnings, and workers tend to remain in this field. Job prospects should be best for those with postsecondary training in electronics or more advanced formal education.

Employment Trend, Projected 2012–22

Elevator installers and repairers: 25%

Other construction and related workers: 12%

Total, all occupations: 11%

Note: "All Occupations" includes all occupations in the U.S. Economy. Source: U.S. Bureau of Labor Statistics, Employment Projections Program

Related Occupations
- Boilermaker
- Millwright

Related Occupations
- Automotive & Heavy Equipment Mechanic

Conversation With . . .
GERALDINE SCHINZEL

Elevator Safety Inspector
State of Illinois Elevator Safety Division, Chicago, Illinois
Elevator mechanic, 31 years

1. What was your individual career path in terms of education/training, entry-level job, or other significant opportunity?

Out of high school, I worked for General Motors in Detroit. I worked for GM for 4½ years and then the plant closed. I got $4,400 in Trade Readjustment Assistance. I took that money and went to MoTech Industrial Mechanics Education Center to learn about hydraulics, solid state electronics, and mechanics. Two weeks before I graduated, a business agent for the International Union of Elevator Contractors Local 36 came and spoke to the class. Basically, we were studying hi-lows, forklifts—things that go up and down. We all said, "Oh, I never really thought about elevators." I started as a probationary apprentice. I went on to get the three licenses required in Michigan. One day the chief of the state Elevator Safety Division asked if I'd be interested in pursuing a career as a state elevator inspector. I did that for 6½ years, which was great because I learned the back side of the industry. Then I was offered a job with Otis Elevator Company installing a tram at the Detroit Metro Airport. I got my journeyman's license and went back to work for Otis. I retired in 2014 and went into real estate, but recently I decided to go back to work as a state inspector.

2. What are the most important skills and/or qualities for someone in your profession?

You really have to like to get dirty, especially if you're servicing elevators. Make sure you're not afraid of heights. If you don't like to stand on top of your car, it's probably not for you. And, especially if you're working in elevator construction, you need to work out and be strong. Don't be afraid of electrical work. Don't be afraid of hard work, and I mean *hard* work.

3. What do you wish you had known going into this profession?

Being able to do your job proficiently isn't always enough. There's still harassment.

4. Are there many job opportunities in your profession? In what specific areas?

The four main areas in the elevator trade are construction, modernization, and service and maintenance. On the office end, there are administrative and sales jobs and state inspector jobs like mine. But it's dependent on the economy. There are many jobs in cities like New York, where so many buildings have elevators. People in the industry stay a long time because you make good money and get a good pension. Any overtime is double time. It's not unusual to make $120,000 a year. Who would want to leave that? According to Forbes magazine, elevator installation and repair is the highest paying blue collar job in the country.

5. How do you see your profession changing in the next five years? What role will technology play in those changes, and what skills will be required?

Elevators are becoming more sophisticated. There are all kinds of new things, like voice activation. Everything is touch-sensitive. The technology is pretty amazing. It can you tell you how many people are on the elevator, when they walked on the elevator, and when they walked off. If you know there's more demand for an elevator at a certain floor at a given time, you can dock the elevator there to sync with the schedule. It will be very helpful to have a computer background. You'll be using a laptop and USB drive on the job.

6. What do you enjoy most about your job? What do you enjoy least about your job?

One part of the job I've always liked is the climbing. When I was a kid, I always climbed trees and jumped across garage rooftops. The part of I've liked the most is the money! What I like least is when people work too fast and it becomes unsafe. And the razzing. As a woman, you have to be tough.

7. Can you suggest a valuable "try this" for students considering a career in your profession?

You should definitely take some automotive or industrial mechanical classes, because then you get your hydraulics. Take an electrical class. And take welding anywhere you can. That's very important. Call the local union and ask when their next hiring date is.

MORE INFORMATION

**Elevator and Escalator Safety
Foundation**
356 Morgan Avenue
Mobile, AL 36606
800.949.6442
www.eesf.org

**International Union of Elevator
Constructors**
7154 Columbia Gateway Drive
Columbia, MD 21046
410.953.6150
www.iuec.org

**National Association of Elevator
Contractors**
1298 Wellbrook Circle
Conyers, GA 30012
800.900.6232
www.naec.org

**National Association of Elevator
Safety Authorities**
NAESA International
6957 Littlerock Road SW, Suite A
Tumwater, WA 98512
360.292.4968
www.naesai.org

National Elevator Industry, Inc.
1677 County Route 64
P.O. Box 838
Salem, NY 12865-0838
518.854.3100
www.neii.org

John Pritchard/Editor

Heating & Cooling Technician

Snapshot

Career Cluster: Construction; Maintenance & Repair

Interests: Mechanics, working with your hands, communicating with others

Earnings (Yearly Average): $46,110

Employment & Outlook: Faster than Average Growth Expected

OVERVIEW

Sphere of Work

Heating and cooling technicians—also called heating, ventilation, air conditioning, and refrigeration (HVACR) technicians—install and maintain heating and cooling systems in homes and businesses. Some heating and cooling technicians are employed by large companies while others work as private contractors. The job of a heating and cooling technician is to repair and maintain the machines that control air temperature and air quality in homes and businesses and in buildings of various sizes. Heating and cooling technicians perform a variety of tasks, including the construction of ductwork and routine checks for

ventilation efficiency. They are also responsible for ensuring that a building or home is compliant with local air quality regulations.

Work Environment

The work environment of heating and cooling technicians varies from job to job. The work they perform is generally indoors, though some machines, such as large heat pumps or industrial air conditioning units, require them to work outside. Heating and cooling technicians must take proper precautions to minimize their risk of injuries related to both heating and cooling machines.

Profile

Working Conditions: Work both Indoors and Outdoors
Physical Strength: Medium Work
Education Needs: On-The-Job Training, High School Diploma with Technical, Education, Technical/Community College
Licensure/Certification: Required
Physical Abilities Not Required: N/A
Opportunities For Experience: Apprenticeship, Military Service
Holland Interest Score*: REC

* See Appendix A

Occupation Interest

Like engineers or engineering technicians, people who pursue a career as a heating and cooling technician enjoy science and mathematics. They also like taking things apart and putting them back together again. The job requires meticulous attention to detail and an extensive knowledge of heating and cooling mechanics.

A Day in the Life—Duties and Responsibilities

No two days are alike for a heating and cooling technician. Sometimes independent or residential contractors schedule projects in advance, while others receive a list of the day's jobs each morning. Heating and cooling technicians work eight to ten hours a day. Some heating and cooling technicians work overtime or weekends. Independent contractors have more control over how often and how long they work.

The responsibilities of heating and cooling technicians include reading and following blueprints and design specifications, installing electrical wiring, testing machine components, replacing old parts, and installing ductwork. In addition to doing repairs and installations, some heating and cooling technicians sell maintenance contracts to consumers. Because they often work independently, heating and cooling technicians must check their work on-site to ensure that technical and mechanical issues have been addressed.

Some heating and cooling technicians perform tasks as needed for heating and cooling systems, while others who work for a large company might be responsible for only one task such as the installation of a particular machine or system.

Duties and Responsibilities

- Diagnosing causes of breakdowns
- Installing and repairing units
- Lifting parts into position
- Disassembling and assembling parts
- Screwing, bolting, welding and brazing parts
- Cutting, threading and connecting pipes
- Connecting motors to control panels
- Connecting control panels to power sources
- Testing parts using instruments
- Adjusting valves
- Lubricating machinery

OCCUPATION SPECIALTIES

Refrigeration Technicians

Refrigeration Mechanics install, service and repair industrial and commercial refrigeration and cooling systems in supermarkets, freezer plants and other industrial establishments.

Furnace Installers and Repairers

Furnace Installers and Repairers install and repair oil, gas, electric, solid-fuel and multifuel heating systems.

WORK ENVIRONMENT

Physical Environment

Heating and cooling technicians sometimes work in tight or cramped spaces in homes, schools, offices, or factories. However, the daily activities of most technicians are varied enough that they spend equal amounts of time sitting and standing as they travel to jobs and communicate with colleagues and customers.

Relevant Skills and Abilities

Interpersonal/Social Skills
- Being able to work independently

Organization & Management Skills
- Following instructions
- Performing duties which change frequently

Research & Planning Skills
- Using logical reasoning

Technical Skills
- Performing technical work
- Working with machines, tools or other objects

Unclassified Skills
- Using set methods and standards in your work

Human Environment

On the job, heating and cooling technicians interact regularly with customers. Technicians and their customers discuss problems with air quality systems. If necessary, technicians will also explain the installation task. Some technicians do sales work, so a professional manner and a comfort in dealing with people is important. Heating and cooling technicians must be able to explain problems, repairs, and installations to the satisfaction of the customer.

Technological Environment

Heating and cooling technicians work with a number of technologies that range from simple hand tools (such as wrenches or screwdrivers) to acetylene torches and combustion analyzers that are built for testing machines. They also need to be familiar with computer hardware that is design to operate air quality systems as well as heating and cooling systems.

EDUCATION, TRAINING, AND ADVANCEMENT

High School/Secondary

An aspiring heating and cooling technician should enroll in physics, mathematics, science, and shop classes. A working knowledge of computers and electronics is also helpful. Most heating and cooling technicians are required by employers to earn a high school degree or pass a General Educational Development (GED) test.

Suggested High School Subjects
- Applied Math
- Applied Physics
- Blueprint Reading
- Chemistry
- Electricity & Electronics
- English
- Heating/Air Cond./Refrigeration
- Mechanical Drawing
- Metals Technology
- Physics
- Shop Math
- Trade/Industrial Education
- Welding

Famous First

The first successful refrigeration service for local customers began operating in 1889 in Denver, Colorado, under the name Colorado Automatic Refrigeration Company. A 50,000-square-foot cold storage warehouse and a 30-ton ice machine supplied area businesses with their refrigeration and ice-making needs. The system operated on liquid ammonia. Old fashioned system pictured.

College/Postsecondary

Most companies prefer to hire heating and cooling technicians with some postsecondary training. Aspiring heating and cooling technicians can apply for programs through a technical school. These programs can last anywhere for six to twenty-four months and will teach basic skills that are related to the field. Educational programs and vocational schools award graduates with certificates or associate's degrees in a specialized field related to heating and cooling.

After the completion of postsecondary training, heating and cooling technicians can apply for formal apprenticeships. Some technicians apply for a formal apprenticeship directly after high school. A number of organizations, including the Air Conditioning Contractors of America, the National Association of Home Builders, the Mechanical Contractors Association of America, the Plumbing-Heating-Cooling Contractors Association, and Associated Builders and Contractors offer apprenticeships under an experienced professional. Apprenticeship programs usually last three to five years.

Related College Majors
- Heating, Air Conditioning & Refrigeration Mechanics & Repair
- Heating, Air Conditioning & Refrigeration Technology

Adult Job Seekers

Adult job seekers who wish to begin a career as a heating and cooling technician should enroll in a postsecondary education program.

Individuals with transferrable skills, such as prior experience as a mechanic, should apply for an apprenticeship.

Professional Certification and Licensure

There are several tests and licenses available to heating and cooling technicians. Technician associations and trade groups offer licensing and certification for different stages of a technician's career. Many states require heating and cooling technicians to attain some form of licensure. Though they are not always required, certification and licensure makes a heating and cooling technician more employable. Technician certifications do not expire, though most are staggered to test both basic and more advanced knowledge and specializations. Heating and cooling technicians who work with refrigerants must be certified through the Environmental Protection Agency. Technicians must pass one of three written specialization exams servicing small appliances, high-pressure refrigerants, and low-pressure refrigerants. Other heating and cooling technicians are eligible to take exams after at least one year of installation experience and two years of experience in maintenance and repairs.

Additional Requirements

Heating and cooling technicians often have to lift heavy pieces of equipment or mechanical parts. They also often work in difficult physical positions and locations. For these reasons, heating and cooling technicians should maintain their physical fitness. They must also be adept at working with their hands and have good hand-eye coordination.

Fun Facts

The New York Stock Exchange building in New York was one of the first structures to use an air conditioning system, back in 1903.
Source: http://www.americanweathermakers.com/fun-facts.php

Population booms and economic growth in southern states like Texas and Florida would never have happened if not for air conditioning.
Source: http://www.americanweathermakers.com/fun-facts.php

EARNINGS AND ADVANCEMENT

Earnings depend on the employee's skill and experience, type of equipment being repaired and the geographic location and extent of unionization of the employer. Skilled electricians, pipefitters or sheet metal workers who have specialized in air conditioning, refrigeration and/or heating work usually earn higher wages.

In 2013, heating and cooling technicians had mean annual earnings of $46,110. The lowest ten percent earned less than $27,210, and the highest ten percent earned more than $69,740. Apprentices usually begin at about fifty percent of the wage rate paid to experienced workers. As they gain experience and improve skills, they receive periodic increases.

Heating and cooling technicians may receive paid vacations, holidays, and sick days; life and health insurance; and retirement benefits. These are usually paid by the employer. Uniforms and safety equipment may also be provided.

Metropolitan Areas with the Highest
Employment Level in this Occupation

Metropolitan area	Employment [1]	Employment per thousand jobs	Hourly mean wage
New York-White Plains-Wayne, NY-NJ	7,330	1.40	$27.35
Chicago-Joliet-Naperville, IL	5,460	1.48	$28.40
Houston-Sugar Land-Baytown, TX	5,380	1.95	$20.91
Dallas-Plano-Irving, TX	4,690	2.18	$22.49
Atlanta-Sandy Springs-Marietta, GA	4,660	2.02	$20.68
Washington-Arlington-Alexandria, DC-VA-MD-WV	4,520	1.91	$25.67
Phoenix-Mesa-Glendale, AZ	4,130	2.32	$23.12
Philadelphia, PA	4,050	2.20	$23.33
Los Angeles-Long Beach-Glendale, CA	4,040	1.02	$26.29
Boston-Cambridge-Quincy, MA	3,440	1.97	$28.49

[1]Does not include self-employ ed. Source: Bureau of Labor Statistics

EMPLOYMENT AND OUTLOOK

There were approximately 268,000 heating and cooling technicians employed nationally in 2012. Employment is expected to grow much faster than the average for all occupations through the year 2022, which means employment is projected to increase 20 percent or more. As the population and number of buildings grow, so does the demand for new residential, commercial, and industrial climate-control systems. In addition, a renewed concern about energy conservation should continue to prompt the development and installation of new energy-saving heating and air-conditioning systems.

Employment Trend, Projected 2012–22

Heating and Cooling Technicians: 21%

Total, All Occupations: 11%

Installation, Maintenance, and Repair Occupations: 10%

Note: "All Occupations" includes all occupations in the U.S. Economy. Source: U.S. Bureau of Labor Statistics, Employment Projections Program

Related Occupations
- Energy Auditor
- Energy Engineer
- Home Appliance Repairer
- Plumber & Pipe Fitter
- Renewable Energy Technician
- Sheet Metal Worker
- Solar Energy System Installer
- Stationary Engineer

Related Military Occupations
- Heating & Cooling Mechanic

Conversation With . . . *LOUIS SKAGGS, Sr.*

Owner, Zone Heating and Air Conditioning, 40 Years
New Orleans, LA
Heating and Cooling Business, 43 Years

1. What was your individual career path in terms of education/training, entry-level job, or other significant opportunity?

I was in the U.S. Marine Corps and also hold a BS in aerodynamics from Louisiana Tech. Originally, I wanted to go on and get a master's degree, and possibly a PhD. But I've always been an outside guy and mechanical. My father-in-law started this business with his brother in 1950. I bought it from him in 1975. He was retiring, his brother had passed away, they had built a good clientele, and I had worked for my father-in-law off and on going back to high school. I went on to build the business and improve it financially.

2. What are the most important skills and/or qualities for someone in your profession?

You've got to be mechanically- and electrically-inclined, a very logically-minded person who can ask yourself questions in order to work through a problem. You need to be able to read and understand schematics and go through them to deal with whatever is applicable for the problem at hand. For instance, you have to know where the current comes from, where it stops, and what's open and closed as far as diodes and resisters, safeties, pressure switches, and the like. You also have to be able to trace back; start at the problem and go back to see if everything else is functioning.

3. What do you wish you had known going into this profession?

As a business owner, you have three sources of stress you always have to be aware of: your role as the service guy, the liability standpoint, and the customers.

4. Are there many job opportunities in your profession? In what specific areas?

There's plenty of opportunity. Some companies allow for commissions, some pay bonuses. HVAC companies have slow seasons – here in New Orleans, it's winter – and you need to know that if you're the new guy and if your company doesn't plan ahead, you're going to be out of a job in the wintertime.

5. How do you see your profession changing in the next five years, what role will technology play in those changes, and what skills will be required?

Today, I would really consider going for an electrical engineering degree first since the technology is so high-level and complex. These systems are run by electronics; they go back to a solid state board like a motherboard. We've got WiFi thermostats now that you can set from your phone from anywhere in the world. We still have the mechanics – things like motors and coils – and that hardware is going to remain the same. The software is where the industry is going. Continuous training is a requirement, including seminars taught by engineering people from the different manufacturers so you know how something operates.

6. What do you enjoy most about your job? What do you enjoy least about your job?

I really enjoy that I'm making people comfortable in their atmosphere. When I repair a system, especially one that really has a tough problem, I feel great. The people are happy, and it's gratifying. For me, the worst part is in the winter when I have to go under houses in mud and slush to do troubleshooting. It's muddy, wet, and even though I take proper precautions, I feel I run a chance of getting electrocuted. That's the only thing I don't really like.

7. Can you suggest a valuable "try this" for students considering a career in your profession?

Get on the web or pick up a few books on heating and air conditioning – or just air conditioning, which really is the most complex side of this trade – and see if you can figure out how these systems function. See if you can solve a problem. Also volunteer to tag along with a service technician because this is a hands-on trade.

SELECTED SCHOOLS

A college degree is not necessary in most cases to work as a heating and cooling technician. For those interested in the field, however, a technical or community college is a good place to start. Many commercial trade schools are also available. Students are advised to consult with their school guidance counselor or research area post-secondary schools to find the right program.

MORE INFORMATION

Air Conditioning Contractors of America
2800 Shirlington Road, Suite 300
Arlington, VA 22206
703.575.4477
www.acca.org

Air-Conditioning, Heating and Refrigeration Institute
2111 Wilson Boulevard, Suite 500
Arlington, VA 22201
703.524.8800
www.ari.org

American Society of Heating, Refrigerating and Air-Conditioning Engineers
Education Department
1791 Tullie Circle, NE
Atlanta, GA 30329
800.527.4723
www.ashrae.org

Associated Builders and Contractors
4250 N. Fairfax Drive, 9th Floor
Arlington, VA 22203
703.812.2000
www.abc.org

HVAC Excellence
1701 Pennsylvania Avenue, NW
Washington, DC 20006
800.394.5268
www.hvacexcellence.org

Mechanical Contractors Association of America
1385 Piccard Drive
Rockville, MD 20850
301.869.5800
www.mcaa.org

National Association of Home Builders
1201 15th Street, NW
Washington, DC 20005
800.368.5242
www.nahb.com

National Center for Construction Education and Research
13614 Progress Boulevard
Alachua, FL 32615
888.622.3720
www.nccer.org

Plumbing-Heating-Cooling Contractors-National Association
180 South Washington Street
P.O. Box 6808
Falls Church, VA 22040
800.533.7694
www.phccweb.org

Refrigerating Engineers & Technicians Association
P.O. Box 1819
Salinas, CA 93902
831.455.8783
www.reta.com

Refrigeration Service Engineers Society
1666 Rand Road
Des Plaines, IL 60016-3552
847.297.6464
www.rses.org

Sheetmetal and Air Conditioning Contractors National Association
4201 Lafayette Center Drive
Chantilly, VA 20151-1209
703.803.2980
www.smacna.org

Molly Hagan/Editor

Insulation Worker

Snapshot

Career Cluster(s): Building & Construction, Architecture & Construction

Interests: Working with tools, working with your hands

Earnings (Yearly Average): $33,720

Employment & Outlook: Faster Than Average Growth Expected

Sphere of Work

Insulation workers measure, cut, install, and replace a building's insulation materials, including thermal insulated panels, fiberglass rolls, spray foam, and other types of insulating fibers. They may also insulate pipes and ductwork. Insulation helps maintain and control a building's temperature. Insulation workers may also participate in the renovation of old buildings. Besides installing insulation, an insulation worker must also remove old insulation during renovations and dispose of it safely.

Work Environment

Insulation workers generally work inside of buildings, sometimes in confined spaces. They can work at construction sites or at residential and commercial buildings. Insulation workers spend a lot of time on their feet, standing, kneeling, and bending. Depending on the job, they may need to crawl into small spaces or climb ladders.

There are several safety issues insulation workers must keep in mind. As they work, they must ensure they are properly protecting themselves from irritants and other hazardous substances.

Profile

Working Conditions: Work both Indoors and Outdoors
Physical Strength: Medium Work
Education Needs: On-The-Job Training, High School Diploma with Technical Education, Apprenticeship
Licensure/Certification: Usually Not Required
Opportunities For Experience: Apprenticeship, Part-Time Work
Holland Interest Score*: RCI

* See Appendix A

Occupation Interest

Insulation work attracts professionals who are interested in working with their hands as part of the drywall and construction industry. No two insulation jobs are alike, so someone interested in the profession should be able to adapt to different situations. Since insulation workers are required to work with a variety of tools and be on their feet much of the day, being in good physical shape is a great benefit.

A Day in the Life—Duties and Responsibilities

When an insulation worker is hired for a job, he or she must first assess the style of insulation to be installed and how much of it is needed. This can be figured out by reading blueprints or by collaborating with others in the industry to find a solution. Once the amount and style of insulation is determined, an insulation worker will evaluate the tools and safety equipment needed.

There is a variety of insulation tactics a worker can use, depending on the particular job. If the job calls for insulating a wall panel, an insulation worker will first install a wire screen onto the wall for the insulating foam to cling to. He or she will then use a spray gun to dispense the foam. Finally, drywall or plaster will be used to cover the insulation. If an attic or exterior wall is being insulated, the worker will commonly blow in fiberglass, rock wool, or cellulose insulation via a compressor hose. For this type of job, an insulation worker will need assistance to feed the insulation into the hose while it is being aimed. Other insulation jobs may require a worker to staple rolls of fiberglass or rock wool to the walls and ceilings before wall paneling can be put in place.

Sometimes insulation workers will have to remove old insulation before putting up new ones. If the old insulation contains asbestos, a cancer-causing material used frequently in the past, a specially trained worker must come in and remove it.

Duties and Responsibilities

- Selecting proper type of insulating material
- Binding wire netting around object being insulated
- Applying insulating materials over wire netting
- Measuring and cutting block or formed pipe insulation to the required size and shape
- Spot welding or screwing wire studs to surfaces and fastening insulating material to studs
- Brushing waterproofing cement over the surfaces and pressing material into place
- Coating joints with cement and wrapping them with tape to seal them
- Covering and sealing insulation

OCCUPATION SPECIALTIES

Pipe Coverers and Insulators

Pipe Coverers and Insulators cover boilers, pipes, tanks and refrigeration units with insulating materials to reduce loss or absorption of heat.

Blower Insulators

Blower Insulators use a hose attached to a blower to blow insulating material into spaces within walls, floors and ceilings of buildings.

WORK ENVIRONMENT

Physical Environment

Insulation workers perform their job in a variety of locations, including construction sites, residential and commercial buildings, and industrial zones. Jobs can sometimes be in confined spaces such as attics and basements.

Human Environment

As part of the construction, drywall, and insulation industry, insulation workers will often collaborate with other professionals in these trades. They frequently communicate with their clients on residential jobs as well.

Technological Environment

Insulation workers use a variety of tools to perform their job. These tools range from small hand tools, such as knives and commercial staplers, to industrial machinery, such as compressor hoses. Workers

Relevant Skills and Abilities

Interpersonal/Social Skills
- Having good judgment

Organization & Management Skills
- Paying attention to and handling details
- Following instructions

Research & Planning Skills
- Using logical reasoning

Technical Skills
- Working with your hands

Unclassified Skills
- Using set methods and standards in your work

Work Environment Skills
- Working both indoors and outdoors
- Working in high places
- Working under different weather conditions

handle different kinds of insulation materials, such as fiberglass, foam, and rock wool. Materials used to cover insulation include sheet metal, plaster, and drywall. Typical safety equipment includes gloves, goggles, and face masks.

EDUCATION, TRAINING, AND ADVANCEMENT

High School/Secondary

Most training to become an insulation worker is done on the job or through a formal apprenticeship, but it is common for employers to require a high school diploma or the equivalent. There are several high school courses that can benefit an insulation worker, including woodworking, mathematics, basic science, and mechanical drawing.

Suggested High School Subjects
- Blueprint Reading
- Building Trades & Carpentry
- English
- Shop Math
- Welding

Famous First

It was in 1928 that builders figured out how to incorporate air conditioning into a building as it was being built. The first fully air-conditioned building was the Milam Building in San Antonio, Texas which was 21 stories high and had nearly 250,000 square feet of floor space. This was an important breakthrough, as San Antonia has had temperatures reaching 111 degrees Fahrenheit.

Postsecondary

While employers do not usually require insulation workers to have a college degree, there are several courses that can be of use. An insulation worker should have a strong knowledge of mechanical drawing and the reading and altering of blueprints. The better a worker's understanding of the mathematical and mechanical aspects of a construction site, the more prepared he or she will be. These courses can usually be taken at community colleges and vocational schools.

Adult Job Seekers

Adults interested in becoming insulation workers should consider the physically demanding aspects of the job. Insulation workers spend nearly the entire workday on their feet, performing tasks such as bending, crawling, or climbing. They also frequently handle small and large tools, so a basic knowledge of mechanical skills is useful. Most insulation workers work standard forty-hour weeks, but sometimes overtime is needed to complete a job.

Professional Certification and Licensure

Insulation workers can learn their trade either on the job as a trainee or by going through a formal apprenticeship program. On-the-job training begins with the trainee helping out with simple tasks around a jobsite. These tasks can include running errands, transporting materials and tools, and holding insulation while an experienced insulation worker secures it. As the trainee progresses, the tasks become more advanced. Commonly, this form of training can last two years. At the end of training, a trainee will require less supervision and be paid more.

Workers who go through an apprenticeship will receive formal training from experienced insulation workers. Those seeking an apprenticeship program must be at least eighteen years old. Apprenticeships commonly last four or five years, depending on the program. During each year of the program, an apprentice must receive 144 hours of technical instruction in a classroom and 1,700 to 2,000 hours of paid on-the-job training. The technical instruction includes topics such as safety, components of insulation, and tools. Apprenticeship programs are often sponsored by local insulation contractors and the International Association of Heat and Frost Insulators and Allied Workers, of which many insulation workers are members.

Once an apprentice has completed his or her training and passed written tests, he or she can advance to a higher position, such as supervisor or contractor. If a worker wishes to remove and handle asbestos, he or she must pass a US Environmental Protection Agency (EPA) certification course. Some insulation-contractor organizations offer voluntary certification so insulation workers have proof of their skills and knowledge. Similarly, the National Insulation Association offers certification for mechanical insulators who wish to perform energy-efficiency appraisals for industrial customers.

Additional Requirements

This job attracts people who enjoy building things with their hands and not being stuck in an office all day. Since interaction with clients and others in the drywall and construction profession is necessary, an aspiring insulation worker should be outgoing and able to work well as part of a team. A clean driving record and valid driver's license is usually required.

EARNINGS AND ADVANCEMENT

Earnings depend on the type, geographic location, and extent of unionization of the employer. Those working in commercial and industrial settings earned substantially more than those working in residential construction, which does not require as much skill. Median annual earnings for insulation workers were $33,720 in 2014. The lowest ten percent earned less than $22,000, and the highest ten percent earned more than $61,450. Apprentices start at about fifty percent of the experienced insulation worker's wages.

Insulation workers may receive paid vacations, holidays, and sick days; life and health insurance; and retirement benefits. These are usually paid by the employer.

Metropolitan Areas with the Highest Employment Level in this Occupation

Metropolitan area	Employment	Employment per thousand jobs	Hourly mean wage
Houston-Sugar Land-Baytown, TX	1,690	0.59	$21.99
Baton Rouge, LA	1,640	4.29	$20.91
Chicago-Joliet-Naperville, IL	900	0.24	$37.38
Denver-Aurora-Broomfield, CO	650	0.49	$18.70
Richmond, VA	650	1.05	$16.76
San Antonio-New Braunfels, TX	610	0.67	$18.59
Virginia Beach-Norfolk-Newport News, VA-NC	570	0.79	$21.59
Seattle-Bellevue-Everett, WA	530	0.36	$22.25
Fort Worth-Arlington, TX	490	0.53	$17.27
Washington-Arlington-Alexandria, DC-VA-MD-WV	450	0.19	$23.40

Source: Bureau of Labor Statistics

EMPLOYMENT AND OUTLOOK

There were approximately 52,000 insulation workers employed nationally in 2012. Employment is expected to grow faster than the average for all occupations through the year 2022, which means employment is projected to increase 25 percent to 45 percent or more. Demand for insulation workers will be spurred by the continuing need for energy efficient buildings and power plant construction.

Employment Trend, Projected 2012–22

Insulation workers, mechanical: 47%

Insulation workers, floor, ceiling, and wall: 26%

Construction trades workers: 22%

Total, all occupations: 11%

Note: "All Occupations" includes all occupations in the U.S. Economy. Source: U.S. Bureau of Labor Statistics, Employment Projections Program

Related Occupations
- Carpenter
- Drywall Installer & Taper
- Plasterer

MORE INFORMATION

**Insulation Contractors
Association of America**
1321 Duke Street, Suite 303
Alexandria, VA 22314
703.739.0356
www.insulate.org

**International Association of Heat
& Frost Insulators & Asbestos
Wkrs.**
9602 M. L. King Jr. Highway
Lanham, MD 20706
301.731.9101
www.insulators.org

National Insulation Association
12100 Sunset Hills Road, Suite 330
Reston, VA 20190
703.464.6422
www.insulation.org

**North American Insulation
Manufacturers Association**
44 Canal Center Plaza, Suite 310
Alexandria, VA 22314
703.684.0084
www.naima.org

Patrick Cooper/Editor

Landscape Architect

OVERVIEW

Sphere of Work

Landscape architects are designers of exterior space. Much of the work they do is both decorative and functional. They plan the surrounding landscape for new buildings, deciding where to place walkways, lawns, trees, gardens, retaining walls, fountains, reflecting pools, and other natural and manmade objects. They also design bike trails, golf courses, playgrounds, highway and waterfront beautification projects, and other public spaces. In addition to planning aesthetically pleasing environments, they prepare environmental impact statements, solve environmental problems such as flooding or mudslides, and restore habitats back to their original condition.

Work Environment

Landscape architects work in government and in the private sector. Many landscape architects are self-employed or work in small architectural firms. They interact with clients, architects, urban planners, engineers, and other professionals involved in construction and development. They also often supervise the contractors and gardeners who carry out their landscaping plans. They frequently work long or odd hours to meet deadlines.

Profile

Working Conditions: Work both Indoors and Outdoors
Physical Strength: Light Work
Education Needs: Bachelor's Degree, Master's Degree
Licensure/Certification: Required
Physical Abilities Not Required: No Heavy Labor
Opportunities For Experience: Internship, Apprenticeship, Volunteer Work, Part-Time Work
Holland Interest Score*: AIR

* See Appendix A

Occupation Interest

Landscape architecture attracts people who value the harmony between humans and nature that can be achieved through thoughtful planning and manipulating the environment. They are imaginative, artistic problem-solvers who are solidly grounded in science and technology. They are both detail-oriented and able to envision large-scale projects. Successful landscape architects use their excellent communication skills to convey their design ideas to others.

A Day in the Life—Duties and Responsibilities

The duties and responsibilities of landscape architects are many and varied. Larger jobs usually involve carrying out a preliminary assessment, or feasibility study, performed in collaboration with the architect, engineers, and environmental scientists. At that time, the landscape architect might take photographs or a video of the area to be developed. He or she might also have to submit applications to government agencies for zoning permits and environmental approval.

After a site has been approved, the landscape architect studies the area's topographic features. The landscape architect then offers suggestions on how best to situate the project's buildings, walkways and roadways, and natural elements based on environmental factors such as sunlight and drainage. He or she then designs the landscape to complement the design of the building, harmonize with the surrounding environment, and accommodate the spatial needs of various stakeholders. Much of the design work is done with a computer-aided design (CAD) program, but it may also be sketched by hand. The landscape architect might also prepare a video simulation or build a 3-D model of the design. He or she then puts together a proposal that also includes a cost analysis, written reports, permits, and other materials.

On large projects, the approval process typically involves many meetings with the developer over the course of several months. During this time, the landscape architect might give several presentations to a board of shareholders or a government commission. He or she also submits construction designs to local building commissioners for approval.

Once approved, the landscape architect refines the drawings and details specific construction guidelines. After construction begins, he or she may return to the site to oversee the work.

Duties and Responsibilities

- **Preparing site plans, working drawings, specifications and cost estimates for land developments**
- **Presenting design sketches to clients and community interest groups**
- **Outlining in detail the methods of construction**
- **Drawing up a list of necessary materials**
- **Inspecting construction work in progress to make sure specifications are followed**
- **Conferring with clients, engineering personnel and architects on overall programs for project**
- **Compiling and analyzing data on site conditions such as geographic location, soil, vegetation and rock features, drainage and location of structures**

WORK ENVIRONMENT

Physical Environment

Landscape architects work in offices but also spend much time at job sites. Undeveloped sites may have safety issues such as uneven terrain, mud, or plant and animal pests, while those under construction may involve loud noise, fumes, chemicals, or other hazards.

Relevant Skills and Abilities

Communication Skills
- Expressing thoughts and ideas clearly
- Speaking and writing effectively

Creative/Artistic Skills
- Being skilled in art or design

Organization & Management Skills
- Making decisions
- Paying attention to and handling details

Research & Planning Skills
- Using logical reasoning

Technical Skills
- Performing technical work

Human Environment

Unless they are self-employed, landscape architects usually work in firms or departments with other architects, assistants, and staff, under supervision by the head architect or director. They may supervise drafters, surveyors, gardeners, and other employees or contractors. Their clients range from homeowners to residential and commercial developers to boards of directors.

Technological Environment

Landscape architects use computers equipped with CAD software, word processing, geographic information systems (GIS), and spreadsheets, among other programs. They might also use photo imaging, illustration, modeling, and other computer graphics or design software. In addition to conventional office equipment, they use large format copiers and a variety of drafting and art tools and supplies. They may also use surveying equipment.

EDUCATION, TRAINING, AND ADVANCEMENT

High School/Secondary

A well-rounded college preparatory program that emphasizes math, science, and courses that introduce CAD, such as mechanical drawing or drafting, will provide the best foundation for a career in landscape design. Especially relevant courses include geometry, trigonometry, environmental science, biology, geology, and botany. Speech communication and English courses help develop communication skills, while drawing, sculpture, photography, computer graphics, and other art courses encourage creativity. Part-time jobs in gardening, lawn care, or construction, or volunteering at a nature center or arboretum can provide valuable hands-on work experience.

Suggested High School Subjects
- Applied Biology/Chemistry
- Applied Math
- Arts
- Blueprint Reading
- Drafting
- English
- Landscaping
- Mathematics
- Mechanical Drawing
- Ornamental Horticulture
- Photography

Famous First

The first American landscape architect of note was Frederick Law Olmstead (1822-1903), designer of Central Park and Prospect Park in New York City as well as numerous other notable municipal parks, state parks, and college campuses. Olmsted was also active in the conservation movement, and during the Civil War he headed the US Sanitary Commission, which oversaw care of sick and wounded soldiers.

College/Postsecondary

A bachelor's degree in landscape architecture is the minimum requirement for licensing as a landscape architect; some employers require an advanced degree. The undergraduate degree in landscape architecture often takes five years and includes courses in surveying, CAD and modeling, ecology, horticulture, earth sciences, landscape planning, design, and construction, and management. Some programs require, or strongly suggest, an internship and offer hands-on opportunities as part of the curriculum.

Related College Majors
- Architectural Environmental Design
- Landscape Architecture

Adult Job Seekers

Adults with a background in horticulture, gardening, botany, geology, urban planning, or another related discipline would have an advantage when entering this career. Those with a bachelor's degree in a related field may be able to enroll directly in a three-year master's degree program, thus saving time and money. Qualified landscape architects should consider membership in professional associations, which often provide opportunities for networking, job-finding, and professional development.

Advancement opportunities depend on the place of employment and its size. Experienced landscape architects are given more difficult and higher-profile jobs. They may become project managers, partners in their firms, or establish their own firms. Some move into consulting or academic positions.

Professional Certification and Licensure

All states license landscape architects. In most cases, candidates are required to have a bachelor's degree from a Landscape Architectural Accreditation Board (LAAB) accredited program as well as one to four years of experience and a passing score on the Landscape Architect Registration Examination (LARE). Some states also administer their own test and have slightly different requirements for experience and education. Continuing education is a common requirement for license renewal. Interested individuals should check the requirements of their home state.

Additional Requirements:

Landscape architects must be familiar with local zoning regulations and environmental codes. Those who wish to establish their own landscape design firms should have business skills and motivation as well as experience in the field.

Fun Fact

A tree shading an outdoor air conditioner unit can increase its efficiency by as much as ten percent.
Source: signatureconcretedesign.com

EARNINGS AND ADVANCEMENT

Earnings of landscape architects depend on the type, size, and geographic location of the employer and the individual's education and experience. Mean annual earnings for landscape architects were $68,570 in 2013. The lowest ten percent earned less than $39,000, and the highest ten percent earned more than $104,000.

Landscape architects may receive paid vacations, holidays, and sick days; life and health insurance; and retirement benefits. These are usually paid by the employer.

Metropolitan Areas with the Highest Employment Level in This Occupation

Metropolitan area	Employment[1]	Employment per thousand jobs	Hourly mean wage
Seattle-Bellevue-Everett, WA	680	0.47	$30.19
Washington-Arlington-Alexandria, DC-VA-MD-WV	570	0.24	$39.84
Minneapolis-St. Paul-Bloomington, MN-WI	550	0.30	$26.51
Denver-Aurora-Broomfield, CO	530	0.42	$34.96
Santa Ana-Anaheim-Irvine, CA	440	0.30	$33.82
Boston-Cambridge-Quincy, MA	420	0.24	$43.54
Philadelphia, PA	420	0.23	$30.06
San Diego-Carlsbad-San Marcos, CA	410	0.32	$34.44
Oakland-Fremont-Hayward, CA	390	0.39	$42.97
Atlanta-Sandy Springs-Marietta, GA	350	0.15	$31.22

[1] Does not include self-employed. Source: Bureau of Labor Statistics

EMPLOYMENT AND OUTLOOK

There were approximately 24,000 landscape architects employed nationally in 2012. About one-fourth were self-employed. Employment of landscape architects is expected to grow about as fast as the average for all occupations through the year 2022, which means employment is projected to increase 10 percent to 16 percent. Employment will grow because of the expertise of landscape architects will be sought after in the planning and development of new construction. Growing interest in city and regional environmental planning, increased development of open space into recreation areas, wildlife refuges and parks and continued concern for the environment should also spur demand for landscape architects.

Employment Trend, Projected 2012–22

Architects, Surveyors, and Cartographers (All): 15%

Landscape Architects: 14%

Total, All Occupations: 11%

Note: "All Occupations" includes all occupations in the U.S. Economy. Source: U.S. Bureau of Labor Statistics, Employment Projections Program.

Related Occupations
- Architect
- Floral Designer
- Forester & Conservation Scientist
- Gardener & Groundskeeper
- Urban & Regional Planner

Conversation With . . .
JON CONNER

Vice President and Practice Leader
Landscape Architecture, JMT, Sparks MD
Landscape Architect, 28 years

1. What was your individual career path in terms of education/training, entry-level job, or other significant opportunity?

I started in the School of Architecture at the University of Maryland but after two years figured out that wasn't my cup of tea. I was more of a logical thinker and not quite so prepared for the artistic side of that profession. So, moving to design outside of buildings placed me in a design environment that was more scientifically-based. That's how I found my comfort level. I got my degree in horticulture with a landscape design option from the College of Agriculture. I was at my first job about five years and decided to get my Master's in Landscape Architecture at Morgan State University. I then moved here to JMT, which is historically a transportation engineering firm

Our projects range from conceptual planning to final design. We do many streetscape projects, which include not only planting design but also design for sidewalks, urban plazas and parks. We led the planning team to site stations in neighborhoods for the Baltimore City Red Line. We've done studies and reports and management plans for scenic byways, understanding what's particularly special about an historic road or corridor. I plan and design pedestrian and bicycle facilities.

In general, landscape architecture has historically suffered from an identity crisis because people tend to place emphasis on the word "landscape" and not the word "architecture." Landscape Architects can focus on ecological and stream restoration, historic preservation, parks and recreation, or even schools. I chose to pursue the transportation realm.

2. What are the most important skills and/or qualities for someone in your pro-fession?

You need to be well-equipped in terms of graphic capabilities. You communicate with drawings, and you still need to be able to sketch something out to depict what you're thinking. As you get into the working world, you have to be a good communicator and comfortable presenting in front of people.

3. What do you wish you had known going into this profession?

I wish I had known that landscape architecture was more diverse. It would have allowed me to hone in more quickly on a niche that I was interested in pursuing.

4. Are there many job opportunities in your profession? In what specific areas?

Job prospects and the future are really bright because of the growing emphasis on sustainability and green solutions. Engineers, architects, and private institutions hire us because of our experience understanding how the built environment must co-exist with the natural environment. Many times we are brought in to serve as the quarterback for a project because we understand how the full range of project issues and systems fit into the overall ecosystem of an area.

5. How do you see your profession changing in the next five years? What role will technology play in those changes, and what skills will be required?

We'll see even more emphasis on sustainable solutions. Also, computer graphics are a big part of our production work, so being able to graphically depict views of what you want to build is important. Higher end software products that can depict ideas — something that's completely photorealistic — are used in higher levels of design. Any of the computer mapping and graphic applications are essential.

6. What do you enjoy most about your job? What do you enjoy least about your job?

My job is rewarding because in the broadest sense it gives me an opportunity to make a difference to improve places where people live, work, play and learn. One of my more rewarding projects came when we asked to re-invent Main Street in Rehoboth Beach, DE, a popular East Coast beach town. The main street was showing years of design decisions geared towards moving cars, and was not particularly attractive or safe for pedestrians and bicyclists. Much of the infrastructure was deteriorating and in need of replacement. It cost the city $35 million and took six years, but now there's a traffic circle when you come into town —with a replica of the local Cape Henlopen Lighthouse —that slows traffic down for pedestrians and bicyclists. It says, "I have arrived." The overhead utilities went underground as part of that project.

My least favorite thing, probably because most of our work is with the public sector, is the bureaucracy. It can be mind-numbing at times, and you see how much money gets wasted just trying to move designs to construction.

7. Can you suggest a valuable "try this" for students considering a career in your profession?

Think of one or more of your favorite places to go, go there, and think what is it about that place that makes it one of your favorite places. Is it the sheer natural beauty, or something designed? There's a full range: you might go to the Grand Canyon and be in awe of natural beauty, or you might go to Disney World, an artificial environment created by man.

Also look for opportunities such as the one offered by my company, which participates in the local chapter of the American Society of Landscape Architects' annual job shadow program. That lets students experience what we do. We take them out to a couple of job sites and look at projects that are under construction as well as reviewing designs that are "on the boards."

A good resource is ASLA.org, which has a section called "Become a Landscape Architect."

SELECTED SCHOOLS

Many colleges and universities have bachelor's degree programs in art and architecture, design, and related subjects; some offer concentrations in landscape architecture. The student may also gain an initial grounding in the field at an agricultural, technical, or community college. For advanced positions, a master's is commonly obtained. Below are listed some of the more prominent schools in this field.

Cal Poly, Pomona
3801 W. Temple Avenue
Pomona, CA 91768
909.869.7659
www.csupomona.edu

Cornell University
410 Thurston Avenue
Ithaca, NY 14850
607.255.5241
www.cornell.edu

Kansas State University
119 Anderson Hall
Manhattan, KS 66506
785.532.6250
www.k-state.edu

Louisiana State University
1146 Pleasant Hall
Baton Rouge, LA 70803
225.578.1175
www.lsu.edu

Purdue University
445 Stadium Mall
West Lafayette, IN 47907
765.494.1776
www.purdue.edu

Ohio State University
281 West Lane Avenue
Columbus, OH 43210
614.292.3980
www.osu.edu

Texas A&M University
PO Box 30014
College Station, TX 77842
978.845.1060
www.tamu.edu

University of Georgia
Terrell Hall
210 South Jackson Street
Athens, GA 30602
706.542.8776
www.uga.edu

University of Pennsylvania
1 College Hall, Room 1
Philadelphia, PA 19104
215.898.7507
www.upenn.edu

Virginia Tech
925 Prices Forks Road
Blacksburg, VA 24061
540.231.6267
www.vt.edu

MORE INFORMATION

American Institute of Architects
1735 New York Avenue NW
Washington, DC 20006-5292
800.242.3837
www.aia.org

**American Nursery and
Landscape Association**
1000 Vermont Avenue NW, Suite 300
Washington, DC 20005
202.789.2900
www.anla.org

**American Society of Landscape
Architects**
636 Eye Street NW
Washington, DC 20001-3736
888.999.2752
www.asla.org

**Association of Collegiate Schools
of Architecture**
1735 New York Avenue, NW
Washington, DC 20006
202.785.2324
www.acsa-arch.org

**Council of Landscape
Architectural Registration
Boards**
3949 Pender Drive, Suite 120
Fairfax, VA 22030
571.432.0332
www.clarb.org

**Landscape Architecture
Foundation**
818 18th Street NW, Suite 810
Washington, DC 20006
202.331.7070
www.lafoundation.org

**Society of American Registered
Architects**
14 E. 38th Street
New York, NY 10016
888.385.7272
www.sara-national.org

Sally Driscoll/Editor

Painter and Paperhanger

Snapshot

Career Cluster(s): Building & Construction, Architecture & Construction, Arts, A/V Technology & Communications

Interests: Art, applied arts, decorative arts, construction, carpentry

Earnings (Yearly Average): $35,950

Employment & Outlook: Faster Than Average Growth Expected

OVERVIEW

Sphere of Work

Painting and paperhanging are considered finishing trades as they are among the last steps performed in new construction or remodeling jobs. By applying wallpaper, paint, stain, varnish, and other materials, painters and paperhangers finish and protect various surfaces, and, in many cases, add final touches to decorating schemes.

In addition to routine painting jobs, some painters provide a variety of decorative painting techniques, including faux finishes, texturing, rag-rolling, sponging, and marbling. Other painters are hired to paint numbers, letters, and symbols on roads, parking lots, and other outdoor locations.

Work Environment

Painters and paperhangers work in government agencies, for private contractors and construction companies, and in maintenance departments for colleges, hospitals, apartment complexes, and other institutions and businesses. Nearly half of painters and paperhangers are self-employed. Some painters specialize in automobiles, marine vehicles, or industrial facilities, such as water tanks and oil rigs. Their hours range from regular forty-hour weeks to seasonal work and part-time jobs. To accommodate client schedules, the painter or paperhanger may work some nights and weekends.

Profile

Working Conditions: Work both Indoors and Outdoors
Physical Strength: Medium Work
Education Needs: On-The-Job Training, High School Diploma or GED, High School Diploma with Technical Education, Apprenticeship
Licensure/Certification: Usually Not Required
Opportunities For Experience: Apprenticeship, Part-Time Work
Holland Interest Score*: RSE

* See Appendix A

Occupation Interest

Painting and paperhanging tend to attract people who value aesthetics. They must be physically fit, with good manual dexterity, a sense of balance, and a steady hand. Math skills, technical knowledge, and artistic ability are also important. Self-employed painters and paperhangers also need strong business and communication skills.

A Day in the Life—Duties and Responsibilities

The first steps undertaken in a painting or wallpapering job usually involve measuring and assessing the surface to be covered. The condition and type of surface, whether wood, metal, drywall, or plaster, determines the type of preparation needed. Old paint might have to be removed by scraping, wire-brushing, or sandblasting, while old wallpaper might need to be steamed off. Most surfaces at least need to be cleaned, and many need priming.

A paperhanger usually begins by marking a straight line using a level and plumb bob. He or she then measures and cuts strips of wallpaper. If pre-pasted, the paper is rolled in a trough filled with water before being applied to the surface. Otherwise, the paperhanger brushes on adhesive or runs each strip of wallpaper through a pasting machine.

He or she then attaches the pieces to the wall in an orderly fashion, aligning edges and patterns and smoothing out any wrinkles and bubbles. Each piece is wiped, trimmed with a knife, and allowed to dry. In addition to paper, wall coverings made from vinyl and fabric are used.

Painters select the most appropriate type of paint and method of application based on the surface, location, condition, and client needs. They might need to mix multiple cans of paint together to ensure consistent color coverage, or they might mix in additives that slow down the drying time. They usually begin by trimming with a brush and then roll the larger surfaces, taking care to cover brush strokes and roller marks. Depending on the surface, quality of paint, and color, a second or third coat might be applied. Painters also apply stains, varnishes, polyurethane, shellac, and other materials.

Self-employed painters and paperhangers also handle their own advertising, billing, purchasing, cost-estimates, and other business responsibilities.

Duties and Responsibilities

- Measuring walls and ceilings to determine the amount of paint or wallpaper required
- Removing old wallpaper
- Painting with brushes, rollers or spray guns
- Measuring and cutting strips from rolls of wallpaper or fabric and applying paste
- Smoothing joints with a seam roller
- Setting up scaffolds and ladders for work above ground level
- Estimating job costs

OCCUPATION SPECIALTIES

Shipyard Painters

Shipyard Painters prepare wood, fiberglass and metal surfaces for painting and paint equipment, interiors and exteriors of ships, boats and shipyard and marina buildings.

Bridge and Structure Painters

Bridge and Structure Painters remove old finishes and apply paints and coatings to existing bridges, oil rigs, and other exterior structures to prevent corrosion.

Artisan Painters

Artisan Painters specialize in creating distinct finishes by using one of many decorative techniques. One such technique is adding glaze for increased depth and texture. Other common techniques are sponging, distressing, rag rolling, color blocking, and faux finishing.

WORK ENVIRONMENT

Physical Environment

Painters work indoors year round and outdoors when weather permits. Most work performed by paperhangers is indoors. Painters and paperhangers are at risk for falls, knee, back, or neck problems, and exposure to toxic substances. Toxic fumes require the use of ventilation systems, while handling lead-based paint or asbestos mandates the use of full safety equipment and special treatment methods for removal.

Relevant Skills and Abilities

Organization & Management Skills
- Following instructions
- Making decisions
- Organizing information or materials
- Paying attention to and handling details

Technical Skills
- Performing scientific, mathematical and technical work
- Working with machines, tools or other objects

Human Environment

Unless they are self-employed, painters and paperhangers report to supervisors for job assignments and work under supervision until they become experienced. They may then supervise assistants or apprentices. Some work alone or with a partner, while others work with a team. They also interact with clients, paint or wallpaper store clerks, interior decorators, office personnel, and/or construction workers.

Technological Environment

To remove old wallpaper and paint, painters and paperhangers use various hand and power tools, including steamers, blowtorches, sanders, and scrapers. Tools used for applying paint include rollers, brushes, and sprayers, while paperhangers use various measuring devices, knives, seam rollers, pasting machines, and other tools. They should be able to set up and properly use ladders and scaffolds. They may use two-way radios and cell phones for communication.

EDUCATION, TRAINING, AND ADVANCEMENT

High School/Secondary

A high school diploma or its equivalent is the minimum required for most jobs. Whether enrolled in a vocational or academic program, aspiring painters and paperhangers should take courses in applied math and geometry, which are needed for measuring, calculating quantities of supplies, and handling cost-estimates, among other tasks. Chemistry can provide an understanding of the properties of paint and other materials, while art will be helpful for mixing colors and giving advice on color selection. English is necessary for reading labels, signs, and blueprints and for communicating with workers and the public. Experience in carpentry or construction and/or coursework in woodworking or metal shop provides useful skills in working with tools.

Suggested High School Subjects
- Applied Math
- Building & Grounds Maintenance
- Building Trades & Carpentry
- English

Famous First

Wallpaper was first manufactured by stamping the design with wood blocks onto sheets of paper that were joined together. A paintbrush was then used to apply the color. This process was first designed by Plunket Fleeson in 1739 in Philadelphia, PA. In the original ad, it was called "paperhanging." This slow method required a paperhanger and a painter. The process was later replaced by mass-produced, user-friendly printed rolls.

Postsecondary

Most painters and paperhangers learn on the job through formal or informal apprenticeships that last between two and five years. The Finishing Trades Institute (FTI), sponsored by the International Union of Painters and Allied Trades, and other trade associations offer apprenticeship programs. Courses may supplement or be taken in lieu of an apprenticeship and are offered through community colleges, continuing education programs, manufacturers, and trade associations. Those painters interested in learning decorative techniques might consider applied arts or finishing programs available through local schools of decorative arts, such as the School of Applied Arts in Denver.

Adult Job Seekers

Adults seeking employment in painting and paperhanging should enroll in apprenticeships or take courses to ensure they have learned the best techniques, regardless of prior personal experience. Painting and paperhanging might also appeal to those who already have part-time employment and are interested in earning extra money. Trained painters and paperhangers can seek out job listings and networking opportunities through professional associations.

Entry-level painters and paperhangers typically begin as helpers and then take on increasing responsibility until they move into independent and supervisory positions. Experienced workers might move into higher pay scales if unionized or employed by the government, or they can transfer to more lucrative specialties, such as industrial painting. Some establish their own companies.

Professional Certification and Licensure

There are no professional licenses or certifications required for general painting and paperhanging; however, painters who remove lead-based paint in homes, childcare facilities, and schools must be EPA Lead-Safe certified by taking an eight-hour training course. Several apprenticeship programs, schools, and trade associations provide optional certifications that may be required by some employers or give participants an advantage in their job searches. For example, the National Association of Corrosion Engineers offers the Protective Coating Specialist certification for those who work in industrial painting. Interested individuals should consult credible professional painting and paperhanging associations and research the relevancy and value of the certification program.

Additional Requirements

Painters and paperhangers must have good eyesight, maintain a clean driving record, and comply with Occupational Safety and Health Association (OSHA) health regulations. They must be at least eighteen years old. Some employers require special clearances or drug tests. Fluency in a second language and completion of a formal apprenticeship are advantages that may garner higher wages, salary increases, or promotions.

Fun Fact

Benjamin Moore has more than 3,500 colors in its line of paint, but the color of the year for 2016 may surprise you: Simply White.

Source: http://www.benjaminmoore.com/en-us/for-your-home/benjamin-moore-color-trends-2016?gclid=ClvsmaWU6sgCFYcTHwodyF4J0Q

EARNINGS AND ADVANCEMENT

Earnings depend on the type, size, geographic location and extent of unionization of the employer. Earnings of painters may be reduced on occasion because of bad weather and the short-term nature of many construction jobs.

Median annual earnings of painters were $35,950 in 2014. The lowest ten percent earned less than $23,730, and the highest ten percent earned more than $62,090. Median annual earnings of paperhangers were $32,930 in 2014. Wages for apprentices usually start at 30 to 50 percent of the rate for experienced workers.

Painters and paperhangers may receive paid vacations, holidays, and sick days; life and health insurance; and retirement benefits. These are usually paid by the employer. Painters and paperhangers usually provide their own tools and equipment.

Metropolitan Areas with the Highest
Employment Level in this Occupation

Metropolitan area	Employment	Employment per thousand jobs	Hourly mean wage
New York-White Plains-Wayne, NY-NJ	7,660	1.42	$24.53
Houston-Sugar Land-Baytown, TX	5,950	2.09	$16.07
Los Angeles-Long Beach-Glendale, CA	5,920	1.46	$21.83
Chicago-Joliet-Naperville, IL	5,120	1.36	$30.14
Seattle-Bellevue-Everett, WA	4,290	2.87	$21.14
Santa Ana-Anaheim-Irvine, CA	3,670	2.47	$19.24
Phoenix-Mesa-Glendale, AZ	3,590	1.97	$17.42
San Diego-Carlsbad-San Marcos, CA	3,590	2.72	$21.37
Washington-Arlington-Alexandria, DC-VA-MD-WV	3,470	1.46	$19.22
Riverside-San Bernardino-Ontario, CA	2,970	2.37	$21.10

Source: Bureau of Labor Statistics

EMPLOYMENT AND OUTLOOK

There were approximately 320,000 painters and paperhangers employed nationally in 2012. Most of these were painters. The majority of painters and paperhangers work for contractors doing new construction or remodeling work or for organizations that own or manage large buildings. About one-half of painters were self-employed.

Employment is expected to grow faster than the average for all occupations through the year 2022, which means employment is projected to increase 15 percent to 25 percent. This is due to new construction activity and the number of structures needing maintenance and repair. However, replacement of workers in this occupation will account for most job openings.

Employment Trend, Projected 2012–22

Construction trades workers: 22%

Painters, construction and maintenance: 20%

Total, all occupations: 11%

Note: "All Occupations" includes all occupations in the U.S. Economy. Source: U.S. Bureau of Labor Statistics, Employment Projections Program

Related Occupations
- Plasterer

Conversation With . . .
WENDY COLLINS

Owner, Creating Spaces with Wendy
North Grafton, Massachusetts
Painter/Wallpapering business, 31 years

1. What was your individual career path in terms of education/training, entry-level job, or other significant opportunity?

As a young teen, I began helping my father with his income properties. When a tenant moved, I would go in and clean, repaint, re-paper, and do repairs to the apartments. As far as training goes, I was self taught—trial and error, so to speak. When I was a child, I always enjoyed art: drawing, coloring, and painting. My mother was an artist and I believe I was fortunate enough to inherit her talents. In grade school, I went to an art school for drawing and painting.

By the time I reached high school, my aspirations were to go onto college and become an architect. I was passionate about drawing and creating buildings, along with other beautiful things. But as life would have it, I did not attend college. Instead, I started working with my dad. There, I was able to create in my own way, with colors, designs, patterns. I was able to express myself through painting and wallpapering.

I taught myself the tricks of the trade, along with the know-how to complete each task. As I grew older, I took my skills and made painting and wallpapering my full-time business.

2. What are the most important skills and/or qualities for someone in your profession?

I would have to say that the most important skill to have is customer service. Social skills for interacting with your clients are a must. You must be able to guide the homeowner through each task. Having the knowledge and physical skills to complete a job are one thing, but clients will need and rely on your expertise in choosing colors, finishes, and designs.

3. What do you wish you had known going into this profession?

The only thing that I can really say I wish I had known is that it's very difficult to find good help—workers who have the same skills and work ethic that I do. It seems that in this profession there are a lot of fly-by-nights. They seem to come and go at their leisure.

4. Are there many job opportunities in your profession? In what specific areas?

There are many job opportunities in this line of work. Starting your own business is one possibility, but there are many others, including maintenance work for large companies, hospitals, apartment complexes and colleges. There are always opportunities available for hard-working, skilled individuals who do painting.

5. How do you see your profession changing in the next five years? What role will technology play in those changes, and what skills will be required?

New equipment is always becoming available: better sprayers, updated tinting machines and mixers, etc. Computer programs help your customer with choosing colors and actually put them in a room scene to see how they will look. I can only imagine that in the future those types of things will become even more significant.

6. What do you enjoy most about your job? What do you enjoy least about your job?

What I enjoy most is developing relationships with my clients and building trust—having them confident that they can always count on me to help with any project. Over the years, my client list has grown significantly. Most of them repeat year after year and they know they can refer me to friends and relatives in confidence that the job will be done in a neat, clean, precise, and professional manner.

I least enjoy the paperwork. This profession is very physically demanding and requires a lot of working hours. Most days I work ten hours. When I get home in the evening, I'm usually exhausted, yet there are still materials to be ordered, schedules to be set up, estimates to be done, invoices to be sent, receipts that need to be organized and categorized by job, payroll that needs to be done, and taxes that need to be paid. One of these days, I just may hire someone to do all of that for me. That would be helpful!

7. Can you suggest a valuable "try this" for students considering a career in your profession?

For anyone considering this profession, I suggest trying a job at Home Depot or at a paint store where you can learn about the profession. You need to acquire knowledge of colors, finishes, and, most importantly, products. Many different products are available for each project. Knowing the correct products to use, the manner in which to use them, and the steps required to complete a job properly are extremely important. Also, being exposed to the public and learning customer service skills will help you develop the skills necessary to work with clients.

MORE INFORMATION

Associated General Contractors of America (AGC)
2300 Wilson Boulevard, Suite 400
Arlington, VA 22201
800.242.1767
www.agc.org

Building Trades Association
16th Street, NW
Washington, DC 20006
800.326.7800
www.buildingtrades.com

International Union of Painters & Allied Trades
7234 Parkway Drive
Hanover, MD 21076
410.564.5900
www.iupat.org

National Association of Corrosion Engineers (NACE International)
1440 South Creek Drive
Houston, TX
800.797.6223
www.nace.org

National Center for Construction Education and Research
13614 Progress Boulevard
Alachua, FL 32615
888.622.3720
www.nccer.org

National Finishing Contractors Association (FCA)
8120 Woodmont Avenue, Suite 520
Bethesda, MD 20814
301.215.7026
www.finishingcontractors.org

National Guild of Professional Paperhangers
136 South Keowee Street
Dayton, OH 45402
800.254.6477
www.ngpp.org

Painting & Decorating Contractors of America
1801 Park 270 Drive, Suite 220
St. Louis, MO 63146
800.332.7322
www.pdca.com

Professional Decorative Painters Association (PDPA)
P.O. Box 13427
Denver, CO 80201
www.pdpa.org

Sally Driscoll/Editor

Plasterer

Snapshot

Career Cluster: Building & Construction, Architecture & Construction

Interests: Construction, architecture, reading blueprints, mechanical drawing, mathematics

Earnings (Yearly Average): $37,550

Employment & Outlook: Average Growth Expected

OVERVIEW

Sphere of Work

Plasterers are tradesmen who apply coats of protective building material to walls and ceilings for both functional and aesthetic purposes. The most common materials used are plaster and stucco, but plasterers may also utilize gypsum and wire lathing for some plaster jobs. Their work provides the wall with a more finished look after drywall has been installed. Plasterers work in newly constructed commercial or residential buildings and also perform repair jobs in existing buildings.

Work Environment

Plasterers work in a wide range of buildings, both commercial and residential. Their work is done both indoors and outdoors and is physically demanding, requiring plasterers to constantly be on their feet. Workers are frequently stooping, kneeling, and climbing. For ceilings and jobs higher up, a plasterer must work on a ladder or scaffolding. Often the work environment can be dusty and dirty, so workers typically wear protective masks and goggles.

Profile

Working Conditions: Work Indoors, Work both Indoors and Outdoors
Physical Strength: Medium Work
Education Needs: On-The-Job Training, High School Diploma or G.E.D., High School Diploma with Technical Education, Apprenticeship
Licensure/Certification: Usually Not Required
Opportunities For Experience: Apprenticeship, Part-Time Work
Holland Interest Score*: RES

* See Appendix A

Occupation Interest

This job tends to attract individuals who enjoy working with their hands outside of an office environment. Those with an interest in the construction trade who are looking for a less physically demanding specialization should consider becoming a plasterer. Plasterers are good problem solvers who enjoy working in different environments, either solo or with a team of people.

Most plasterers work for construction contractors. After years of experience in the trade, a small percentage become self-employed.

A Day in the Life—Duties and Responsibilities

When a plasterer begins a job, he or she first assesses the amount of materials needed by visiting the jobsite or by reading blueprints. The floor area around the plaster job is covered with a blanket or a tarp, protecting the surface from dust and plaster. The plaster is mixed and prepared either at a workshop or on-site. The most common types of plaster are lime and gypsum.

If needed, a plasterer will secure a wire lathe to the wall before plaster is applied. This is commonly done for new construction projects. Layers of plaster are then applied over the lathe using a plastering hawk and a trowel or taping knife. A hawk is a flat board with a handle that is used to hold plaster while the worker scoops and applies it with the trowel or knife. Different sizes and shapes of trowels and taping knives are used depending on the job. The final coat of plaster normally has a lime base.

For some jobs with existing walls or ceilings, a worker will first apply a layer of gypsum-based plaster. This creates a surface for the lime-based plaster to stick to more easily. They can also use scratchers and sandpaper to roughen the undercoats to make the final coat adhere more easily. Before the final coat of plaster dries, a worker will either smooth the surface or create decorative designs, depending on the job. Sealants are then applied to protect the surface.

Duties and Responsibilities

- Mixing plaster and erecting scaffolds
- Installing guide wires and surfaces to indicate the thickness of plaster to be applied
- Spreading plaster over lath or masonry base and smoothing it with tools to create a uniform thickness
- Making decorative textures in the finish coat by marking it with a brush and trowel or by spattering it with small stones

OCCUPATION SPECIALTIES

Stucco Masons

Stucco Masons apply weatherproof, decorative coverings of portland cement or gypsum plaster to outside building surfaces.

Molding Plasterers

Molding Plasterers install ornamental plaster panels and trim and cast ornamental plaster cornices and moldings.

Spray Gun Plasterers

Spray Gun Plasterers use spray guns to apply plaster to ceilings, walls and partitions of buildings.

Rough and Finish Plasterers

Rough and Finish Plasterers specialize in applying rough and finishing coats of plaster to a designated area.

WORK ENVIRONMENT

Physical Environment

Plasterers work in a variety of commercial, business, and residential buildings, both indoors and outdoors. Sometimes plasterers must work high up on ladders or scaffolds. The use of different plasters can create dust and other irritants, so safety gear such as face masks and goggles is required.

Relevant Skills and Abilities

Organization & Management Skills
- Making decisions
- Paying attention to and handling details

Research & Planning Skills
- Creating ideas
- Developing evaluation strategies

Technical Skills
- Performing scientific, mathematical and technical work
- Working with machines, tools or other objects
- Working with your hands

Human Environment

Plasterers work closely with others in the construction industry, including other plasterers. Depending on the job, they may work as part of a team. Communication with others is essential to ensure jobs are completed correctly. Plasterers must also communicate with clients and contractors to ensure accuracy.

Technological Environment

Plasterers use a variety of hand tools, including hand sanders, hawks, trowels, taping knives, mixing pans, putty knives, wire lathes, ladders, and scaffolding. Tape and blankets are used to protect nearby surfaces that are not being plastered.

EDUCATION, TRAINING, AND ADVANCEMENT

High School/Secondary

In order to enter a formal training program, an applicant is usually required to have a high school diploma or the equivalent. There are some basic high school courses that can benefit an entry-level plasterer, including mathematics, shop class, and mechanical drawing. Art classes can help students develop creative and artistic skills and become accustomed to handling plaster-like materials such as clay and plaster of paris.

Suggested High School Subjects
- Applied Math
- Blueprint Reading
- Building Trades & Carpentry
- English
- Machining Technology
- Mathematics
- Mechanical Drawing

Famous First

Unlike plaster, which has been around for thousands of years as a wall covering, other common materials like bricks, terra cotta, and plywood have been manufactured in the United States only since 1825, 1841, and 1905, respectively. These building materials have different roles in the construction of large and small buildings, but all can be covered in the end by plaster in order to create a uniformed and decorative finish.

Postsecondary

Plasterers are usually not required to have a college degree, but there are some courses offered at community and technical colleges that can help individuals who have no experience in the construction industry. At a community college, an individual can take courses in mechanical drawing, advanced mathematics, and basic architecture. Technical colleges often offer courses in basic construction concepts, materials, and blueprint reading.

Some schools offer specific plastering courses, ranging from beginner to certification level. Basic courses cover everything from tools to the application of plaster to various surfaces. As students progress, they gain more in-depth knowledge and skills, such as how to create different textures on a surface. Hirers are more likely to employ someone who has completed a relevant training course.

Adult Job Seekers

Plasterers commonly work forty hours a week, but larger and more complex jobs may require some overtime, so individuals occasionally may need to be away from their families for longer than a normal work week. Transitioning to a job as a plasterer is easier if a worker has completed some courses on the trade. Some employers even look to these schools for new hires. Potential plasterers should try to network through their school, local trade organizations, and unions.

Professional Certification and Licensure

Many plasterers learn the trade through on-the-job training. Some start out as helpers on construction sites, where they run errands and aid more experienced workers. When they start to learn plastering, they usually begin by learning how to mix and apply different types of plaster.

Some trade associations and unions offer apprenticeship programs for plasterers. These programs last three to four years, during which time apprentices are required to complete 144 hours of formal instruction and 2,000 hours of hands-on training. The formal instruction covers blueprint reading, safety standards and practices, and building-code regulations. Hands-on training starts with the basics, such as mixing and applying plaster, and gradually builds up to more complex tasks. After an apprentice successfully completes the program, plasterers become journey workers and may perform jobs without supervision.

Several trade organizations offer certification in specialized fields of masonry, including plastering. Most of these certification programs last for up to twelve weeks and end with a competency exam.

Plasterers can apply to join a union after completing their apprenticeship. Applying to a union requires proof of hours worked and a fee. Once a plasterer is in a union, he or she is ensured medical benefits, a pension, and fair work standards.

Additional Requirements

A plasterer needs to have a keen eye for detail to ensure plaster is applied correctly. Workers who apply decorative touches to plaster also need to have artistic and creative skills. Plasterers should be physically fit and able to work several hours on their feet.

Fun Fact

The palaces and pyramids of ancient Egypt had plaster surfaces. The word "plaster" meant "to daub on" to the ancient Greeks, and they were doing it at least 500 years before the birth of Christ.
Source: http://www.oren-usa.com/page2.html

EARNINGS AND ADVANCEMENT

Earnings depend on the geographic location and extent of unionization of the employer and the employee's skills. Poor weather conditions and periodic declines in construction may limit their work time. Plasterers are employed an average of ten months a year.

Median annual earnings of plasterers were $37,550 in 2014. The lowest ten percent earned less than $24,940, and the highest ten percent earned more than $71,710. Apprentice wages start at about half the rate paid to experienced workers.

Plasterers may receive paid vacations, holidays, and sick days; life and health insurance; and retirement benefits. In unionized construction, these are usually paid by the employer. Plasterers may have to purchase their own hand tools.

Metropolitan Areas with the Highest
Employment Level in This Occupation

Metropolitan area	Employment	Employment per thousand jobs	Hourly mean wage
Houston-Sugar Land-Baytown, TX	850	0.30	$13.16
Santa Ana-Anaheim-Irvine, CA	850	0.57	$13.45
Los Angeles-Long Beach-Glendale, CA	520	0.13	$14.60
Portland-Vancouver-Hillsboro, OR-WA	350	0.33	$14.40
Oakland-Fremont-Hayward, CA	320	0.31	$13.01
Dallas-Plano-Irving, TX	250	0.11	$11.92
Seattle-Bellevue-Everett, WA	240	0.16	$15.66
Nassau-Suffolk, NY	190	0.15	$13.17
Baton Rouge, LA	190	0.50	$13.31
Philadelphia, PA	160	0.09	$10.93

Source: Bureau of Labor Statistics

EMPLOYMENT AND OUTLOOK

There were approximately 25,000 plasterers employed nationally in 2012. Most plasterers worked on new construction sites, while others repaired and renovated old buildings. About one-fourth were self-employed. Employment of plasterers is expected to grow about as fast as the average for all occupations through the year 2022, which means employment is projected to increase 10 percent to 15 percent. A large amount of plastering work is done in Florida, California and the Southwest, where exterior plasters and decorative finishes are especially popular.

Employment Trend, Projected 2012–22

Construction trades workers: 22%

Plasterers: 15%

Total, all occupations: 11%

Note: "All Occupations" includes all occupations in the U.S. Economy. Source: U.S. Bureau of Labor Statistics, Employment Projections Program.

Related Occupations
- Brickmason/Stonemason
- Carpenter
- Cement Mason
- Drywall Installer & Taper
- Insulation Worker
- Painter & Paperhanger

Conversation With . . .
ROSIE BERNARD

Plaster Education Director/Apprenticeship Instructor
Cement Masons and Plasterers
Local 528, Seattle, Washington
Plastering industry, 25 years

1. What was your individual career path in terms of education/training, entry-level job, or other significant opportunity?

I actually dropped out of high school and I went into Job Corps when I was 17 or 18 to do their "business-clerical" program, but instead got introduced to the construction trades. I thought working outside and being physical would be a better fit for me. I liked that it's physically challenging, as compared to sitting at a desk all day typing. So I went through their pre-apprenticeship program for plastering. I've been working in the trade ever since.

I've been in the union since I was 19, and it's been a good 26 years. I served my apprenticeship in Washington State. Being in the union, you can make a living with decent wages and receive health insurance and a pension.

Now I'm an instructor for students who go through our apprenticeship program. I teach plastering skills to apprentices and help them advance their skills to become a better worker.

Plastering is a specialty trade. Plaster is a versatile material that has lots of uses. There are types of plaster that have specific uses and require special skill for those applications. We do interior and exterior walls. Plasterers can apply decorative finishes. Veneer plaster is an interior product; it can be a smooth or textured wall with color, no paint needed. We also apply gypsum plaster for interior wall and ceiling, stucco for exterior surfaces, and EIFS (Exterior Insulation Finish System). There is also fireproofing, which is a sprayed applied insulation on steel structures exposed to heat and fire.

2. What are the most important skills and/or qualities for someone in your profession?

Being a hard worker, and the ability to pay attention to details.

You can't learn plastering overnight. You have to learn to use your tools. Most material is applied with a hawk and trowel, and it's also machine-applied. There are many tools for different applications.

3. **What do you wish you had known going into this profession?**

    The unpredictable impact that the economy can have on the building trades in general.

4. **Are there many job opportunities in your profession? In what specific areas?**

    There's always new construction or remodeling. There is always going to be the opportunity to become a foreman, supervisor, even an estimator for a company.

5. **How do you see your profession changing in the next five years, what role will technology play in those changes, and what skills will be required?**

    With the new energy codes that are more energy efficient, EIFS (Exterior Insulation Finish System) will be the most viable system to meet the standards. EIFS is an exterior cladding system that uses an EPS (expanded polystyrene board) which is adhesively attached to substrate that has a liquid WRB (weather resistant barrier).

6. **What do you enjoy most about your job? What do you enjoy least about your job?**

    I like the challenges of working on projects in the industry. I like to see a building come together, from start to finish, and know it's going to be there forever.

7. **Can you suggest a valuable "try this" for students considering a career in your profession?**

    You can always can always visit an apprenticeship class and get a tour of an apprenticeship program. Or, there's always the Job Corps centers.

MORE INFORMATION

Association of the Wall and Ceiling Industries, International
513 West Broad Street, Suite 210
Falls Church, VA 22046
703.538.1600
www.awci.org

International Masonry Institute
42 East Street
Annapolis, MD 21401
410.280.1305
www.imiweb.org

International Union of Bricklayers and Allied Craftworkers
620 F Street NW
Washington, DC 20004
202.783.3788
www.bacweb.org

National Association of Home Builders
1201 15th Street, NW
Washington, DC 20005
800.368.5242
www.nahb.com

Operative Plasterers' & Cement Masons' Intl. Association
11720 Beltsville Drive, Suite 700
Beltsville, MD 20705
301.623.1000
www.opcmia.org

Patrick Cooper/Editor

Plumber & Pipe Fitter

Snapshot

Career Cluster(s): Building & Construction, Architecture & Construction, Manufacturing

Interests: Plumbing, construction work, hydraulics, piping systems, sanitation systems

Earnings (Yearly Average): $50,660

Employment & Outlook: Faster Than Average Growth Expected

OVERVIEW

Sphere of Work

Plumbers and pipe fitters are specialized construction workers. They contribute to the construction of buildings by installing plumbing fixtures; installing and maintaining pipes for water, sanitation, and fuels (plumbers); and installing and maintaining piping systems for chemicals, fuels, and high- and low-pressure liquids (pipe fitters). If not for plumbers and pipe fitters, the health of society would suffer. Well-maintained pipes

keep drinking water clean and prevent disease-carrying sewage from leaking into the open.

Work Environment

Plumbers and pipe fitters work anywhere pipes exist or need to be installed: indoors, outdoors, in cramped environments, in basements, on ground floors, and on ladders or scaffolding, to name a few. The work is potentially dangerous, but rigorous safety precautions minimize injuries.

Profile

Working Conditions: Work Indoors, Work both Indoors and Outdoors
Physical Strength: Heavy Work
Education Needs: High School Diploma or G.E.D., High School Diploma with Technical Education, Apprenticeship
Licensure/Certification: Required
Opportunities For Experience: Apprenticeship, Military Service, Part-Time Work
Holland Interest Score*: RCE, REI, RES

* See Appendix A

Occupation Interest

Plumbers and pipe fitters have physically demanding responsibilities, so anyone considering a career as a plumber or a pipe fitter should enjoy manual labor and be in good shape. There is an intellectual element to plumbing and pipe fitting as well, so a potential plumber or pipe fitter should find critical thinking and problem solving appealing.

A Day in the Life—Duties and Responsibilities

It is not uncommon for plumbers to experience variation between daily responsibilities. They may split their time between residential and commercial projects, spending a morning installing a water heater at a house and an afternoon repairing or installing plumbing fixtures at a business. On larger projects, they may spend much more time at a single jobsite and may even supervise a plumbing crew.

For pipe fitters, there can be a great deal of variation between daily responsibilities, depending on where they are in a particular pipe-fitting project. At the start of a project, pipe fitters may be expected to choose the materials they need, inspect the work site, and schedule the order in which pipes must be installed. Then they cut, assemble, and install the piping system. They may be expected to test the system at the end of a project and clean up the jobsite by loading materials onto trucks and transporting them back to their shop.

Duties and Responsibilities

- Studying building plans and work drawings
- Inspecting worksites to determine possible obstructions
- Selecting type and size of pipe and other materials
- Planning sequence of installation
- Cutting openings in walls and floors for pipes and pipe fittings
- Cutting thread and bend pipes
- Assembling and installing valves, pipe fittings, and pipes
- Soldering, brazing, welding or caulking pipes
- Reading pressure gauges to determine if system is leaking

OCCUPATION SPECIALTIES

Maintenance Plumbers, Industrial

Industrial Maintenance Plumbers specialize in the repair and maintenance of heating, water and drainage systems in industrial or commercial establishments.

Maintenance Plumbers, Residential

Residential Maintenance Plumbers specialize in the repair and maintenance of heating, water and drainage systems in residential settings.

WORK ENVIRONMENT

Physical Environment

Both plumbers and pipe fitters work in commercial and industrial settings, but plumbers are more likely than pipe fitters to handle projects in the residential sector.

Relevant Skills and Abilities

Interpersonal/Social Skills
- Being able to work independently
- Working as a member of a team

Organization & Management Skills
- Making decisions
- Paying attention to and handling details

Research & Planning Skills
- Developing evaluation strategies

Technical Skills
- Performing scientific, mathematical and technical work
- Working with machines, tools or other objects
- Working with your hands

Human Environment

The type of plumbing or pipe-fitting project dictates the size of the work force needed for it. Large-scale projects generally require crews of plumbers and pipe fitters. Small, simple projects, on the other hand, such as an appliance installation, may be handled by a single plumber. Plumbers and pipe fitters who are in apprenticeship training programs have much less autonomy than journeymen—those who have completed their apprenticeship—and master plumbers.

Technological Environment

Plumbers and pipe fitters have a number of new electronic technologies at their disposal. Micro inspection cameras mounted on long, flexible cables allow plumbers to examine the insides of pipes and other tight spaces. Water-leak detectors use ultrasonic sensors to detect pressure or vacuum leaks in piping systems. Touch-screen tablet computers enable communication between construction-crew members in the field, and piping calculators facilitate the calculation of pipe dimensions.

EDUCATION, TRAINING, AND ADVANCEMENT

High School/Secondary

A high school diploma or general educational development (GED) certificate is necessary to be an apprentice, journeyman, or master plumber or pipe fitter.

Suggested High School Subjects
- Applied Math
- Applied Physics
- Blueprint Reading
- Building & Grounds Maintenance
- Building Trades & Carpentry
- English
- Mechanical Drawing
- Science
- Shop Math
- Welding
- Woodshop

Famous First

Illinois was the first state to create a law regarding plumbing in 1881. The law stated that in cities of 500,000 or more, the commissioner had to give written permission to plumbers before they could start work. The law called for regulation of plumbing in housing, but also required that plumbers have a plan of action before they started a job. They could be fined $100 or more for not having a plan, and were subject to fines of $10 per day until they came into compliance.

Postsecondary

The first step to becoming a licensed plumber or pipe fitter is entering one of the many accredited apprenticeship training programs offered by plumbers' associations and union chapters. To do so, the applicant must have a high school diploma or GED, be eighteen years of age or older, and be an American citizen. Plumbing and pipe-fitting apprenticeships consist of at least four years of on-the-job training and 144 hours of classroom study a year. The United Association of Journeymen and Apprentices of the Plumbing and Pipe Fitting Industry of the United States and Canada, for example, offers a five-year-long apprenticeship program with 216 hours of classroom training per year. Apprentice plumbers and pipe fitters study physics, hydraulics, mechanical drawing, piping systems, sanitation systems, and plumbing materials in the classroom, and they work alongside licensed plumbers and pipe fitters in the field.

Related College Majors
• Plumbing & Pipefitting

Adult Job Seekers

Entering an apprenticeship training program with the United Association guarantees a salary for the duration of the apprenticeship. For plumbers and pipe fitters who have completed their apprenticeship training and are looking for employment, the Internet is an excellent resource. Online job boards, some of which offer free registration, post plumbing and pipe-fitting job openings and are easily accessible. Licensed master plumbers and pipe fitters have the option of starting their own businesses.

Professional Certification and Licensure

Each state has its own licensing rules, but most call for plumbers to be licensed in some way to legally perform their trade. A journeyman license is issued to plumbers who complete their apprenticeship training and pass a journeyman plumber exam. A plumber with a journeyman license is restricted to working under the supervision of a master plumber.

For a plumber to be able to work independently as a contractor, most states require that he or she have a master plumber license. Obtaining a master plumber license is not easy; it requires many years of experience and additional training as a journeyman and passing a master plumber exam. Applicants for journeyman and master plumber licenses may have to meet other qualifications as well.

Additional Requirements

Many plumbers and pipe fitters choose to join a building-trades union such as the United Association. While not an industry requirement, union membership is favorable to plumbers and pipe fitters in terms of salary and benefits. Union members earn more than nonmembers and often receive health insurance and pension packages.

Fun Fact

When Albert Einstein said he'd become a plumber if he had to do it all over again, the Plumbers and Steamfitters Union made him an honorary member.

Source: http://www.lexingtonplumbing.com/fun_facts.php

EARNINGS AND ADVANCEMENT

Earnings depend on the type, size and geographic location of the employer, and the employee's experience and skills. Plumbers and pipefitters had median annual earnings of $50,660 in 2014. The lowest ten percent earned less than $29,470, and the highest ten percent earned more than $88,160. Apprentices usually begin earning 30 to 50 percent of the wages paid to experienced plumbers and pipefitters.

Plumbers and pipe fitters may receive paid vacations, holidays, and sick days; life and health insurance; and retirement benefits. These are usually paid by the employer. Plumbers and pipefitters usually purchase their own hand tools, hard hats and safety shoes.

Metropolitan Areas with the Highest
Employment Level in this Occupation

Metropolitan area	Employment	Employment per thousand jobs	Hourly mean wage
New York-White Plains-Wayne, NY-NJ	13,710	2.54	$35.23
Houston-Sugar Land-Baytown, TX	11,640	4.09	$23.05
Chicago-Joliet-Naperville, IL	9,980	2.66	$36.06
Los Angeles-Long Beach-Glendale, CA	7,590	1.87	$31.07
Washington-Arlington-Alexandria, DC-VA-MD-WV	6,140	2.58	$26.73
Baltimore-Towson, MD	6,070	4.69	$25.52
Minneapolis-St. Paul-Bloomington, MN-WI	5,740	3.14	$34.22
Dallas-Plano-Irving, TX	5,540	2.47	$19.12
Nassau-Suffolk, NY	5,410	4.28	$39.49
Boston-Cambridge-Quincy, MA	5,300	2.95	$39.16

Source: Bureau of Labor Statistics

EMPLOYMENT AND OUTLOOK

There were approximately 385,000 plumbers and pipe fitters employed nationally in 2012. Over one-half worked for plumbing contractors doing new construction, repair, modernization or maintenance work. Others worked for industrial, commercial and government employers. About 15 percent of plumbers and pipefitters were self-employed.

Employment is expected to grow faster than the average for all occupations through the year 2022, which means employment is projected to increase 20 percent or more. Demand for plumbers will stem from new construction and building renovation, including the retrofitting involved in conserving water due to the increasing awareness of how water conservation impacts the environment.

Employment Trend, Projected 2012–22

Construction trades workers: 22%

Plumbers, pipefitters, and steamfitters: 21%

Total, all occupations: 11%

Note: "All Occupations" includes all occupations in the U.S. Economy. Source: U.S. Bureau of Labor Statistics, Employment Projections Program

Related Occupations
- General Maintenance Mechanic
- Heating & Cooling Technician
- Solar Energy System Installer

Related Military Occupations
- Plumber & Pipe Fitter
- Water & Sewage Treatment Plant Operator

Conversation With . . .
TIM HALEY

Training Director
Plumbing & Gasfitters UA Local 5 Training Facility
Lanham, Maryland
Plumber, 32 years

1. What was your individual career path in terms of education/training, entry-level job, or other significant opportunity?

Originally I wanted to be a veterinarian, but between the cost and time it would take to get through vet school, I decided to go for the trades and the money I could earn. After high school I worked five years for a non-union boiler maker, but I ran into a friend from high school who told me about the union helper's program with the local. It's like a pre-apprenticeship, assisting journeyman plumbers.

From there I applied to the plumber's apprenticeship program as well as the 602 steamfitter's program, was accepted into both, and chose the plumbing field because I made a commitment to the training director. He said, "If we accept you, we want to know we have a commitment from you."

I was in a four-year apprenticeship (that is now five years), then went from an apprentice to journeyman to foreman to supervisor. Then opportunities opened up with companies to move into estimating, on to project manager, to senior project manager, and eventually owning my own business. Then the opportunity at the UA Local 5 Training Facility opened up. I gave the company to my wife when I first started, but we closed it down last year.

I've done everything from being that guy working in your house to being the guy working at government buildings. I've been in the street running a twelve-inch water main, retrofitting hospitals, and doing things like working on oxygen cryogenic systems.

What I'm doing now is setting up courses and curricula and scheduling and bringing new technologies to training so we can stay proactive about the training needs for the future instead of having to react. I do a lot of career building with community colleges, high schools, and trade centers.

2. What are the most important skills and/or qualities for someone in your profession?

Math skills are very important—everything we do is math, such as weights and measures or offsets. You also need mechanical aptitude, a positive attitude, regular attendance—punctuality is huge—communications skills (verbal, not necessarily texting), and a thick skin.

3. What do you wish you had known going into this profession?

I would have liked to have known the academic requirements. I had no idea there was a school attached to being a plumber. I thought I would just learn my trade out in the field but the reality was five years of apprenticeship school along with the field experience.

4. Are there many job opportunities in your profession? In what specific areas?

Yes, from helper-entry level to apprenticeship jobs to journeyman, foreman, and superintendent. You have to look for opportunities to move up in an office. Positive attitudes will reach high altitudes.

We start our first-year apprentices at $32,000 a year with benefits, with a 5% increase every six months. If you own your own business, it's a great way to go, but it comes with long hours and a lot of stress. There's profit to be made, but it's very competitive so profit margins are shrinking due to competition.

5. How do you see your profession changing in the next five years? What role will technology play in those changes, and what skills will be required?

I see a lot of technology coming into the field now. The industry is going digital, from the old CAD coordination to BIM, 3D models, 4D, 5D, and 6D. The draftsman in the office can modify drawings and the field gets those changes in minutes instead of days. We can now design a building and know exactly how it's going to operate.

We use robotic layout tools that work off GPS. And a lot of guys on service trucks have a tablets or iPad, so they go straight to the manufacturer's website and pull up material and equipment specification data sheets, availability of parts, and contact web-based support teams for equipment and technical support.

We can even access building control systems and trouble shoot equipment without even being on the job. These areas are prime for the generation coming up; they are all gamers and they get the interactive resources that are now in our industry.

6. What do you enjoy most about your job? What do you enjoy least about your job?

The best part is that I get to help the next generation of plumbers. The worst is having to deal with the ignorance and apathy of people who really don't understand their potential and the career opportunity they have.

7. Can you suggest a valuable "try this" for students considering a career in your profession?

A helper is the ideal way to get in at entry level; there's no commitment or attachment to further schooling and you can see if you're really suited.

MORE INFORMATION

Building and Construction Trades Department
815 16th Street, Suite 600
Washington, DC 20006
202.347.1461
www.bctd.org

Mechanical Contractors Association of America
1385 Piccard Drive
Rockville, MD 20850
301.869.5800
www.mcaa.org

National Center for Construction Education and Research
13614 Progress Boulevard
Alachua, FL 32615
888.622.3720
www.nccer.org

Plumbing-Heating-Cooling Contractors Association
180 S. Washington Street
Falls Church, VA 22046
800.533.7694
www.phccweb.org

United Association of Journeymen and Apprentices of the Plumbing and Pipe Fitting Industry of the United States and Canada
3 Park Place
Annapolis, MD 21401
410.269.2000
www.ua.org

Jamie Aronson Tyus/Editor

Roofer

Snapshot

Career Cluster(s): Building & Construction, Architecture & Construction

Interests: Construction, architecture, computer drafting, design, working outdoors

Earnings (Yearly Average): $35,760

Employment & Outlook: Average Growth Expected

OVERVIEW

Sphere of Work

Roofers install and repair roofs on buildings, homes, and other structures. Roofing is a dangerous occupation involving the movement, application, and repositioning of building materials far off the ground. As such, professional roofers are additionally skilled at operating safety equipment and constructing scaffolding that allows them to install and repair roofs properly without jeopardizing their own or others' safety. Roofing materials and support substructures vary from building to building and

project to project depending on intended building use, location, and surrounding climate.

Work Environment

Roofers work primarily outdoors, and as such, contractors and construction companies traditionally plan jobs so that roofs are complete before the onset of harsh weather conditions such as extreme temperatures and heavy precipitation. Roofs are almost always constructed significantly above ground, requiring workers to be comfortable with heights. Roofers generally work traditional business hours and have weekends off. However, overtime work on weekends and holidays may be required to complete projects.

Profile

Working Conditions: Work Outdoors
Physical Strength: Medium Work
Education Needs: On-The-Job Training, High School Diploma or G.E.D., High School Diploma with Technical Education, Apprenticeship
Licensure/Certification: Required
Opportunities For Experience: Apprenticeship, Part-Time Work
Holland Interest Score*: REC

* See Appendix A

Occupation Interest

Roofers generally enter the occupation from previous positions in carpentry and construction. Many roofers learn the skills of the trade through apprenticeship programs or by working as entry-level laborers for roofing firms. Since the majority of training for roofing is acquired on the job and does not require an extensive educational background, roofing is a common transitional field for laborers, students, and building professionals who aspire to careers in other realms of the construction industry.

A Day in the Life—Duties and Responsibilities

The daily duties of roofers vary based on the type of construction site and the materials used. Traditionally, a roofing project begins with an on-the-ground survey of the structure at hand. This is common for both new construction and renovation projects. Once the building and architectural plans have been inspected, the roofer begins constructing methods of access to the building's roof area. This work can entail the construction of scaffolding, placement of ladders, use of temporary elevators, and creation of other temporary means of access that best suit a particular project.

A roof replacement begins with the dismantling of the existing roof structure. Roofers must carefully remove the old roofing material layer by layer and dispose of the waste without posing a threat to workers and other individuals on the ground. When working on shorter structures, workers may simply toss debris down into adjacent dumpsters. In other cases, they may use elevators, carts, and other methods to remove old roofs, depending on the particular job at hand.

Roofing professionals construct roofs out of all kinds of materials, including wood, asphalt, fabricated metal, slate, rubber, and high-density plastic. The particular nature of roof construction varies from building to building. Materials are typically layered together with tar to create watertight roofs on flat-topped buildings such as apartment complexes and retail facilities, while for most homes, roofers position strips of waterproof materials and then nail shingles or tiles over them. Regardless of the type of roof being built, the roofer must measure the area, determine how much material to use and its cost, replace damaged structural elements and clean the work area as needed, cut and position the roofing materials to ensure the roof is watertight and conforms to the shape of the building, and seal and insulate the roof to prevent leaks and corrosion.

Duties and Responsibilities

- Cutting roofing paper to size
- Fastening roofing paper to roof
- Lining up roof material with edge of roof
- Fastening composition shingles or sheets to roof
- Punching holes in slate, tile or wooden shingles
- Applying roofing materials in stages and layers
- Mopping or pouring hot asphalt or tar onto roof base
- Applying gravel or pebbles over asphalt or tar
- Hammering and chiseling away rough spots on walls and floors
- Painting or spraying waterproofing material on prepared walls and floors

WORK ENVIRONMENT

Physical Environment

Roofers work on residential, commercial, and industrial construction and building sites. Much of the work of a roofer is conducted on ladders and from scaffolding. It is common practice for roofers to work in harsh environments and inclement conditions, but most avoid working in the rain or snow when surfaces are likely to be slick.

Human Environment

As roofers often work alongside other construction laborers, excellent teamwork and communication skills are crucial, particularly given the numerous hazards present when working at high altitudes.

Relevant Skills and Abilities

Organization & Management Skills
- Following instructions
- Making decisions
- Organizing information or materials
- Paying attention to and handling details
- Performing duties which change frequently

Research & Planning Skills
- Developing evaluation strategies
- Using logical reasoning

Technical Skills
- Working with machines, tools or other objects
- Working with your hands

Work Environment Skills
- Working in high places
- Working outdoors

Technological Environment

Roofers use nearly all hand tools associated with light carpentry and contracting work, including saws, hammers, nail removers, hatchets, utility knives, and pry bars. They also use a variety of power tools, including electric saws, sawzalls, blow torches, soldering irons, drills, nail guns, and staple guns, as well as heavy machinery such as cranes and lifts. They may also rely on modeling software, word processors, databases, spreadsheets, and analytical applications.

EDUCATION, TRAINING, AND ADVANCEMENT

High School/Secondary

High school students can best prepare for careers in the trades with coursework in algebra, geometry, chemistry, design, physics, and computer drafting. Industrial arts and traditional art classes can also prepare students for future design and building work.

Suggested High School Subjects
- Applied Math
- Blueprint Reading
- Building Trades & Carpentry
- English
- Mathematics
- Mechanical Drawing
- Woodshop

Famous First

The first large-scale retractable roof was the Civic Arena and Exhibit Hall in Pittsburgh, PA, and was finished on September 17, 1961. The roof, which was made of two stationary sections and six rotating sections, was made of 2,950 tons of structural steel and rested on a reinforced concrete ring girder.

Postsecondary

Postsecondary education is not required for a career in roofing, as many of the basic skills are gained through apprenticeships and on-the-job training. Individuals interested in becoming construction or project managers may benefit from taking postsecondary courses in business management, finance, and architecture.

Related College Majors
• Carpentry

Adult Job Seekers

Transitioning into roofing is relatively easy, as there are few educational requirements and on-the-job training is common. Those interested in entering the field are advised to seek out local apprenticeship programs. Apprentices must be over eighteen, have completed high school or an equivalent program, and have the necessary stamina to perform the work. During their training, apprentice roofers study the tools and techniques of the trade, learn government building requirements and safety practices, assist with site setup, and gain hands-on practice applying roofing materials. Fully trained roofers may work for construction firms or choose to go into business for themselves.

Professional Certification and Licensure

Licensure requirements vary by state. A roofer may need to have a minimum number of years' training or hands-on experience, pay an application fee, and successfully complete a written exam to obtain licensure. In some cases, a criminal background check may be performed, and continuing education may be necessary for license renewal. Professional organizations such as the National Roofing Contractors Association (NRCA) offer voluntary roofing certifications. Work permits are normally required for each construction project.

Additional Requirements

Roofers must be physically fit, sure on their feet, and able to work well under stress. Maintaining a safe environment for team members working in high places and for those on the ground is one of the top priorities of all roofing teams.

Fun Fact

EARNINGS AND ADVANCEMENT

Earnings depend on the type and geographic location of the employer and the employee's experience and skill. Earnings of roofers are sometimes reduced by bad weather limiting the time they can work. Median annual earnings of roofers were $35,760 in 2014. The lowest ten percent earned less than $23,410, and the highest ten percent earned more than $61,240. Apprentices generally start at about 30 to 50 percent of the rate paid to experienced roofers and receive raises as they learn the skills of the trade.

Roofers may receive paid vacations, holidays, and sick days; life and health insurance; and retirement benefits. These are usually paid by the employer.

Metropolitan Areas with the Highest
Employment Level in this Occupation

Metropolitan area	Employment	Employment per thousand jobs	Hourly mean wage
Chicago-Joliet-Naperville, IL	2,800	0.75	$23.04
Tampa-St. Petersburg-Clearwater, FL	2,230	1.88	$15.74
Phoenix-Mesa-Glendale, AZ	2,140	1.17	$15.66
New York-White Plains-Wayne, NY-NJ	1,850	0.34	$31.67
Santa Ana-Anaheim-Irvine, CA	1,840	1.24	$24.05
Los Angeles-Long Beach-Glendale, CA	1,670	0.41	$22.48
Dallas-Plano-Irving, TX	1,500	0.67	$14.71
Oakland-Fremont-Hayward, CA	1,450	1.41	$23.23
San Diego-Carlsbad-San Marcos, CA	1,430	1.08	$21.00
Orlando-Kissimmee-Sanford, FL	1,420	1.31	$15.17

Source: Bureau of Labor Statistics

EMPLOYMENT AND OUTLOOK

There were approximately 133,000 roofers employed nationally in 2012. About one-third of roofers were self-employed. Many self-employed roofers specialize in working on homes. Employment is expected to grow about as fast as the average for all occupations through the year 2022, which means employment is projected to increase 9 percent to 13 percent. Roofs deteriorate faster and are more susceptible to weather damage than most other parts of buildings and periodically need to be repaired or replaced.

Turnover is high in the roofing industry as the work is hot, dirty and strenuous. Jobs should be easiest to find during spring and summer, when most roofing is done.

Employment Trend, Projected 2012–22

Construction trades workers: 22%

Roofers: 11%

Total, all occupations: 11%

Note: "All Occupations" includes all occupations in the U.S. Economy. Source: U.S. Bureau of Labor Statistics, Employment Projections Program

Related Occupations
- Carpenter
- Construction Laborer

Conversation With . . .
BRADFORD D. BELDON

CEO, Beldon Roofing Company
& the Beldon Group of Companies
San Antonio, Texas
Roofing industry, 39 years

1. What was your individual career path in terms of education/training, entry-level job, or other significant opportunity?

My grandfather founded this business in 1946 and I grew up wanting to be in the family business. My first job was cutting the grass when I was 12 years old, then I eventually followed that by working on the roofs. I spent days learning about safety before I was allowed on a roof when I was 16. I was trained to install every system we were installing at that time. After I went to college at the University of Texas in Austin, I decided to work for someone outside of the family business and went to work for Prospect Enterprises, in Sterling, Virginia, in their sales and estimating departments. After two years, I went home and started doing residential sales, then moved into production, followed by commercial sales. Later, I started overseeing all the operations. I'm now chief executive officer (CEO) of the organization, which has 600 employees.

We always focused mainly on getting the roof installed properly; today you'll see some people in the industry focus on how quickly you can get it done. Safety and proper installation is more important to us than speed.

We recently developed Roof Monitor technology, which includes a sensor that triggers an alarm monitored by a call center when there's too much snow or water on the roof. We also developed a safety mat placed at the edge of the roof, called Edge Defense, which protects workers on the roof. An alert goes off the minute you step on it. We're always looking for ways to make the roof safer.

2. What are the most important skills and/or qualities for someone in your profession?

Integrity. It's the only thing no one can give or take from you.

3. What do you wish you had known going into this profession?

There have been no surprises, as I grew up in the roofing industry and wouldn't want to do anything else. I love solving people's problems and making their headaches go away.

4. Are there many job opportunities in your profession? In what specific areas?

Yes, there are numerous opportunities within the roofing industry. They range from the top to the bottom. Unfortunately, not everyone sees the roofing industry as glamorous; thus, it's really hard to recruit. However, once you've been exposed, you don't want to leave it. You get a good feeling every time you solve somebody's problems, and your efforts are tangible. Every day is a different day. We have a lot of long-term employees.

5. How do you see your profession changing in the next five years? What role will technology play in those changes, and what skills will be required?

We've been using technology for many years and were among the first roofers in our area to use computers. The roofing industry itself doesn't use a lot of technology, but you can use technology to figure out better ways to keep up with the competition. The Roof Monitor is an example of using technology and real-time data to prevent a problem from happening in the first place.

6. What do you enjoy most about your job? What do you enjoy least about your job?

Working with our team. They are top notch, and I truly love coming to work every day. What I don't love about the industry is that not everybody plays by the rules. It's frustrating when you are doing so; it's hard to explain to your customer why your price is higher. People don't view the roof as the fifth wall of your building, but it's the most important wall and not every roofer spends the time to fix or install it properly.

7. Can you suggest a valuable "try this" for students considering a career in your profession?

If I was looking to get into the industry, I'd research the cities I wanted to work in and go to the National Roofing Contractors Association website (www.NRCA.net) to look for a professional roofing contractor. I'd write a letter asking if they would consider hiring me as an intern. Once in the door, if you prove yourself, you'll likely have a job for life. In our small family business, we just awarded our 59th twenty-year service award to an employee!

MORE INFORMATION

Associated General Contractors of America
Director, Construction Education Services
2300 Wilson Boulevard, Suite 400
Arlington, VA 22201
703.548.3118
www.agc.org

Building and Construction Trades Department
815 16th Street, Suite 600
Washington, DC 20006
202.347.1461
www.bctd.org

National Association of Home Builders
1201 15th Street, NW
Washington, DC 20005
800.368.5242
www.nahb.com

National Center for Construction Education and Research
13614 Progress Boulevard
Alachua, FL 32615
888.622.3720
www.nccer.org

National Roofing Contractors Association
10255 W. Higgins Road, Suite 600
Rosemont, IL 60018-5607
847.299.9070
www.nrca.net

United Union of Roofers, Waterproofers and Allied Workers
1660 L Street NW, Suite 800
Washington, DC 20036-5646
202.463.7663
www.unionroofers.com

John Pritchard/Editor

Solar Energy System Installer

Snapshot

Career Cluster(s): Building & Construction, Architecture & Construction, Manufacturing

Interests: Electrical installation and repair, alternative and green energy, wiring, electrical systems, general contracting

Earnings (Yearly Average): $40,020

Employment & Outlook: Faster Than Average Growth Expected

OVERVIEW

Sphere of Work

Solar energy system installers are members of the larger electrical installation and maintenance industry, as well as the growing green and alternative energy industry. Professional solar energy installation workers must also have expertise in home alteration and familiarity with roofing, wiring, and general home-remodeling procedures. Many solar energy system specialists also work as electricians or general home contractors and handle solar energy as a facet of their contracting business.

Solar energy system installers visit homes and businesses to evaluate the physical and technical requirements for installing solar panels and to rewire existing electrical systems to accept input from solar energy collectors. In addition, solar energy workers must perform routine maintenance and repair at sites where solar energy systems have already been installed.

Work Environment

Solar energy system installers typically work for private companies or as independent subcontractors. They may work in teams, with several installers working on a single site at one time. Installers also often work closely with general contractors and other home-repair specialists. In many cases, solar energy system installers need to develop and maintain working relationships with state and local licensing officials in order to obtain the proper permits for various projects.

Because solar energy systems are installed on-site, installers must visit a variety of different work environments. In addition, most homes and businesses install solar panels on the roof, so workers must be comfortable working on top of buildings and homes of various sizes.

Profile

Working Conditions: Work both Indoors and Outdoors
Physical Strength: Heavy Work
Education Needs: Junior/ Technical/Community College
Licensure/Certification: Recommended
Opportunities For Experience: Apprenticeship
Holland Interest Score*: RCI

* See Appendix A

Occupation Interest

Those best suited to a career in solar energy system installation have a strong interest in electronics installation and repair. Experience working as a general contractor or home-remodeling specialist is beneficial. In addition, solar energy technology may appeal to those with an interest in alternative and green energy, who often enter the profession partly out of a desire to help combat the detrimental effects of traditional energy use.

A Day in the Life—Duties and Responsibilities

There are several stages to every solar energy system installation project, beginning with a site evaluation. During this stage, one or more installers and solar energy specialists examine the physical site to evaluate the difficulties involved and materials needed to perform the installation. In addition, the solar energy team examines the current energy usage of the home or business to determine if a solar energy system will be effective and establishes the optimal layout and design for the proposed system.

After performing a site evaluation, installers must coordinate with other contractors to arrange for any additional site alterations before the installation begins. The installation team typically obtains permits for the project and coordinates with utility companies in the area to manage the transfer of power. The team also assembles and prepares solar-panel arrays and other equipment needed for the specific project before beginning the installation.

Once preparations have been made, the installation team must work on-site for periods ranging from several days to several months, depending on the scope of the project and the degree to which the site needs to be altered to permit installation. Solar energy systems are typically installed on rooftops, and workers must take steps to ensure their safety during the installation. To complete the work safely, installers typically use a temporary rope-and-harness system, especially when working on steep surfaces.

Installers mount supporting structures, secure panels, and wire the electrical components. Each solar panel that is installed must be tested to confirm that the panel and connected electrical system are functioning properly and efficiently. Solar energy system installers may also install specialized equipment within the home to collect, store, and transfer solar energy to power home appliances.

A solar energy system installer also spends a certain amount of time maintaining and repairing solar energy equipment from previous installation projects. Solar panels are fragile and can be damaged by projectiles and inclement weather. In some cases, workers may have to conduct maintenance and repair on the support structures or electronics systems connected to the solar energy collectors.

Duties and Responsibilities

- Locating and marking the desired positions for solar collectors according to specifications
- Cutting holes in the roof, walls and ceiling to permit installation of solar equipment
- Installing supports and brackets to anchor solar collectors
- Connecting electrical wires between controls and the pumps that recirculate water to the solar collectors for reheating
- Testing electrical circuits and repairing or replacing defective equipment
- Testing plumbing for leaks using pressure gauges
- Repairing or replacing worn or damaged parts
- Directing activities of helpers

OCCUPATION SPECIALTIES

Solar Energy System Installer Helpers

Solar Energy System Installer Helpers assist installation and repair of residential, commercial and industrial solar energy systems.

WORK ENVIRONMENT

Physical Environment

Solar energy system installers work both outdoors and indoors in a variety of environments and often work on rooftops and the tops of buildings. Because solar energy systems require sunlight, installers typically work in areas that are frequently exposed to intense sun.

Relevant Skills and Abilities

Organization & Management Skills
- Making decisions
- Paying attention to and handling details
- Performing duties which change frequently

Research & Planning Skills
- Developing evaluation strategies

Technical Skills
- Performing scientific, mathematical and technical work
- Working with machines, tools or other objects

Plant Environment

Solar energy system installers do most of their work on-site, but they may also utilize a workshop at their company to prepare and assemble systems prior to installation. Workshops contain specialized equipment needed for testing the electronic components of solar energy panels and other equipment.

Human Environment

Some solar energy system installers work alone on projects, but extensive installations often require teams of installers who must work together to handle different aspects of the job. In addition, installers must work closely with home contractors, designers, and other construction specialists to integrate solar technology into the existing building plan.

Technological Environment

Installers often use hand and power tools such as hammers and drills to complete installation projects. They also rely on project-management and basic office software to plan and organize installation projects.

EDUCATION, TRAINING, AND ADVANCEMENT

High School/Secondary

High school students can prepare for a career in solar energy installation by taking classes in electronics and mathematics. Familiarity with basic physics and mechanics can also be helpful in planning installation projects. In addition, computer classes can be helpful for understanding the software used to test and develop solar energy systems.

Suggested High School Subjects
- Applied Math
- Blueprint Reading
- Building Trades & Carpentry
- Electricity & Electronics
- English
- Heating/Air Cond./Refrigeration
- Machining Technology
- Mechanical Drawing
- Science
- Shop Math
- Shop Mechanics

Famous First

The first solar-powered battery was invented in 1954 and was intended to convert the sun's energy into useful electricity. Gerald Leondus Pearson was the inventor and he worked at Bell Telephone Laboratories. The battery was theorized to be able to last forever, especially because there were no moving parts that could break, nor was anything destroyed internally during its usage.

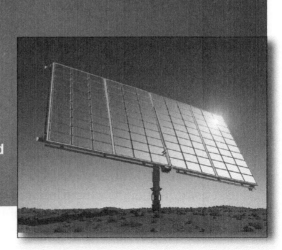

Postsecondary

Many colleges and trade schools offer basic electronics classes that can be helpful for obtaining work in solar energy systems. Trade and technical schools are more likely to offer specific programs in solar energy technology and other specialized skills involved in the field. Most solar energy system installers also work as general contractors or electricians, and training in these fields can be obtained through a variety of technical institutions. Some technical schools may offer classes that train contractors specifically in the use of software and equipment used in solar energy technology.

Many individuals who work as solar energy contractors begin by working alongside experienced installers in apprenticeship programs that last from several months to a year. A number of companies offering solar energy installation services provide training and apprenticeship programs for those interested in the field.

Related College Majors
- Heating, Air Conditioning & Refrigeration Mechanics & Repair
- Solar Technology

Adult Job Seekers

Many solar energy system installers work as general contractors before becoming involved in the solar energy field. For those with backgrounds in electrical installation or repair, becoming qualified to work with solar energy may involve taking an extension course at a technical institute or through a company specializing in solar energy equipment. Many companies that manufacture and sell solar energy technology offer training programs that are open to interested individuals from a variety of backgrounds.

Professional Certification and Licensure

General contractor groups such as the North American Board of Certified Energy Practitioners (NABCEP) may provide optional certification programs for electricians and solar energy technicians and often offer training courses for those interested in the field. NABCEP requires candidates to be eighteen years old, have a combination of educational and work experience, complete a written exam, and adhere to a code of professional ethics.

Depending on local regulations, solar energy installers may be required to hold a general contractor's license or electrician's license from the state or city in which they typically operate. Those interested in solar energy system installation should check with local companies to determine the licensing requirements for their region.

Additional Requirements

Solar energy system installation can be demanding work that requires significant endurance and physical ability. Solar panels and other equipment may be heavy, and contractors often work on top of buildings and in other locations where safety is a prime consideration. In addition, solar energy system installers should be knowledgeable about a variety of home repair and modification procedures, as each project may present new challenges that must be addressed before the installation can proceed. Strong time-management, problem-solving, and communication skills are also key.

EARNINGS AND ADVANCEMENT

Earnings of solar energy system installers depend on the geographic location and union affiliation of the employer and the employee's skill, experience and training. Median annual earnings of solar energy system installers were $40,020 in 2014. The lowest ten percent earned less than $28,420, and the highest ten percent earned more than $58,340.

Solar energy system installers may receive paid vacations, holidays, and sick days; life and health insurance; and retirement benefits. These are usually paid by the employer.

Metropolitan Areas with the Highest
Employment Level in this Occupation

Metropolitan area	Employment	Employment per thousand jobs	Hourly mean wage
Oakland-Fremont-Hayward, CA	320	0.32	$21.18
Edison-New Brunswick, NJ	180	0.18	$22.38
San Luis Obispo-Paso Robles, CA	100	0.91	$18.11
Honolulu, HI	90	0.20	$23.14
Tucson, AZ	60	0.16	$16.23

Source: Bureau of Labor Statistics

EMPLOYMENT AND OUTLOOK

Solar energy system installers held about 5,000 jobs nationally in 2012, and the field continues to grow. Employers of solar energy system installers include heating and cooling contractors, manufacturers of solar equipment, engineering and architectural firms, wholesale and retail establishments, and electrical and gas utilities. About 20 percent of all firms involved in solar energy were located in four states: California, Nevada, Arizona and Hawaii.

Employment is expected to grow much faster than the average for all occupations through the year 2022, which means employment is projected to increase 25 percent or more. This growth is due to consumers continuing to seek out alternative forms of energy. The best opportunities will be in the southern and western states which have sunshine during most of the year.

Employment Trend, Projected 2012–22

Solar energy system installers: 24%

Construction trades workers: 22%

Total, all occupations: 11%

Note: "All Occupations" includes all occupations in the U.S. Economy. Source: U.S. Bureau of Labor Statistics, Employment Projections Program

Related Occupations
- Carpenter
- Energy Auditor
- Energy Engineer
- Glazier
- Heating & Cooling Technician
- Plumber & Pipe Fitter
- Renewable Energy Technician
- Sheet Metal Worker

Conversation With . . .
SUSAN HOLLINGSHEAD

Chief Administrative & People Officer
Sungevity, Oakland, California
Solar business, 5 years

1. What was your individual career path in terms of education/training, entry-level job, or other significant opportunity?

I put myself through Mount Holyoke College and graduated with a liberal arts degree in psychology. Initially I worked at a group home for juvenile delinquents in California, but it was a precarious situation for a number of reasons, including lack of state funding. So I sort of stumbled into a job in the recruiting department at Bechtel, which was then the largest engineering company in the world. I was promoted to a position that involved running employee relations for a large organization within the company. I did a couple of short-term, international assignments and we created one of the first job-posting programs within a major company in the U.S. But, at that time I wanted to start a family and my career trajectory at Bechtel would have required more international assignments in the role I held at the time.

So, I moved to a large bank and within a year became its youngest vice president, for their operations centers. The bank was in the midst of a union organizing effort, and it was one of the more fascinating situations I've found myself in. I also found myself pregnant. The bank needed someone full-time, given the union situation. Since that was before the days of a legal structure for maternity leave, I took six months off. I ended up going to work for a regional insurance carrier, initially in human resources, then in operations, where I gained good experience in sales, field marketing, claims management, and customer service, and then I became a regional manager. About 500 people in eight different offices reported to me.

Still, I wanted to do something that mattered to me, so I went to work for the first environmental insurance company. I quickly discovered opportunities to buy contaminated companies and created insurance policies to create a degree of financial certainty for those who agreed to clean up the properties. I started my first real estate company in 1993 and sold it in 1999 to the largest environmental construction company in the country. We redeveloped brownfields, a significant environmental leap forward and an opportunity to invest large amounts of money in community redevelopment. I went on to start a second, similar real estate company. It was a phenomenal journey until two things happened: the recession hit, and my youngest child was diagnosed with brain cancer.

This was a difficult time. I sat back and reflected. Two things became clear, career-wise: I absolutely loved the energy of emerging markets, of going someplace in a business context that nobody had ever been before. And it was incredibly important to me to make a difference—to make life better.

I spent about two years consulting with socially-conscious businesses. During that process, I found Sungevity, where I was able to take all my different experiences and meld them into one job. We had 52 people when I started and have 1200 today. If you were to look at my career, I would say the most fun aspect is that the experience never ends. If you're up for doing so, you can experience transition, learning, and growth throughout your career.

2. What are the most important skills and/or qualities for someone in your profession?

Having the ability to learn technical information, and being really inquisitive are both essential qualities. In any relatively new market sector, everybody is on a path of continuous learning.

Don't underestimate the importance of communications skills. Every day I deal with somebody whose career may well be foreshortened because they can't write a decent email or speak in front of a group. Bad grammar can make someone appear to be less than what they are.

3. What do you wish you had known going into this profession?

The importance of math and science. The world of tomorrow is a world dominated by technology, math, and science. A basic background in finance is critical for almost any management position.

4. Are there many job opportunities in your profession? In what specific areas?

Solar offers burgeoning opportunities in almost every field you can imagine. People think only of the installation process, but marketing, sales, legal, finance, and software development are all a huge part of what we do. Solar will continue to redefine itself with evolving technology. It's a growing industry that can change the future by helping to control climate change.

5. How do you see your profession changing in the next five years? What role will technology play in those changes, and what skills will be required?

Solar today is very much where cell phones were fifteen years ago. It's ready to explode in terms of market penetration.

6. What do you enjoy most about your job? What do you enjoy least about your job?

I enjoy the amazing opportunity of a growth industry; to have participated in creating 1,100 jobs is the greatest joy you can imagine. I like the long hours least. A job at my level, and certainly in an emerging business, requires long days.

7. Can you suggest a valuable "try this" for students considering a career in your profession?

Volunteer. Great organizations in every major community are available to support and train people for solar jobs. In California, for instance, you can participate in a community installation.

MORE INFORMATION

Energy Efficiency & Renewable Energy Network
Mail Stop EE-1
Department of Energy
1000 Independence Avenue, SW
Washington, DC 20585
202.586.5000
www.eere.energy.gov

North American Board of Certified Energy Practitioners
56 Clifton Country Road, Suite 202
Clifton Park, NY 12065
800.654.0021
www.nabcep.org

Renew the Earth
Global Environment & Technology Foundation
2900 S. Quincy Street, Suite 375
Arlington, VA 22206
703.379.2713
www.getf.org

Solar Energy Industries Association
575 7th Street, NW, Suite 400
Washington, DC 20004
202.682.0556
www.seia.org

Solar Energy International
520 S. Third Street, Room 16
Carbondale, CO 81623
970.963.8855
www.solarenergy.org

Micah Issitt/Editor

Structural Metal Worker

Snapshot

Career Cluster(s): Building & Construction, Architecture & Construction, Manufacturing

Interests: Construction, engineering, architecture, physics, mathematics

Earnings (Yearly Average): $36,570

Employment & Outlook: Average Growth Expected

OVERVIEW

Sphere of Work

Structural metal workers construct and install iron and steel structures that are utilized in construction, ship building, and other areas of heavy industry and architecture. The design and construction of structural metal forms is a highly specialized construction process that requires strict adherence to the unique design specifications, which vary from project to project. Structural metal installations are a crucial part of commercial buildings, as well as roads, dams, bridges, and other major infrastructure projects. Metal forms are extremely dangerous because of their size

and weight, and their installation requires extensive planning and communication to ensure the safety of the workers.

Work Environment

Structural metal workers traditionally work outdoors on large-scale construction sites. Structural metal forms are typically one of the first installments in the construction of large buildings and other structures. Metal workers utilize a wide range of heavy machinery, including trucks and large cranes to position the structures into place. Much of the work takes place at great heights and in all types of weather conditions. The work environment of structural metal workers also includes frequent exposure to potentially hazardous equipment such as shears, drill presses, and welding guns.

Profile

Working Conditions: Work Outdoors
Physical Strength: Heavy Work
Education Needs: On-The-Job Training, High School Diploma or G.E.D., High School Diploma with Technical Education, Apprenticeship
Licensure/Certification: Usually Not Required
Opportunities For Experience: Apprenticeship, Military Service
Holland Interest Score*: REI

* See Appendix A

Occupation Interest

Structural metal work attracts professionals who enjoy intense physical activity, such as climbing, lifting, and balancing. Given the team-oriented nature of many of the tasks inherent to structural metal work, professionals in the field tend to be collaborative in nature. Metal workers are also analytical thinkers who thrive in environments where quality standards and safety measures is top priority.

A Day in the Life—Duties and Responsibilities

The construction, transport, and installation of structural metal support beams and joists is a complex and highly intricate process.

The architectural designs that call for structural metal reinforcement vary in scope and complexity. Structural metal works whose expertise lies in the conception of parts for structures will study blueprints and layout specifications in an attempt to create pieces that conform to design specifications, building codes, and budgetary constraints. This design phase requires professionals to be well versed in mathematics, engineering, and physics.

Once the design specifications are finalized, metal pieces are constructed in steel mills and inspected by engineers, who may make markings on individual pieces to indicate necessary adjustments prior to installation. Adjustments include cuts, adhesion of plates and pivots, and other structural changes.

The transport of structural metal pieces from foundries to the construction site can also pose a tremendous challenge for workers. The large size of structural metal elements often requires special ground transport via a flat-bed truck. Speed restrictions are often placed on oversized loads, which can require several days of transport depending on their distance from a particular construction site.

The installation of structural metal pieces is another intricate process, often requiring extensive collaboration and communication between workers on the ground and at great heights. Pieces are often temporarily fitted before welding to ensure compliance with design specifications. Many times, pieces must be removed and adjusted by workers on the ground prior to their permanent installation.

Duties and Responsibilities

- Setting up hoisting equipment
- Fastening steel parts to the cables of hoisting equipment
- Guiding steel parts with ropes
- Pulling, pushing or prying steel parts into approximate position while supported by hoisting devices
- Forcing steel parts into final position
- Positioning rivet holes in steel parts and driving drift pins through holes
- Checking the vertical and horizontal position of steel parts
- Bolting positioned steel parts to keep them in place until permanently riveted, bolted or welded
- Cutting and welding steel parts to make alterations

OCCUPATION SPECIALTIES

Structural Steel Workers

Structural Steel Workers raise, place and unite large beams, columns and other structural steel parts to form framework or complete structures.

Reinforcing Metal Workers

Reinforcing Metal Workers position and secure steel bars in concrete forms to reinforce concrete.

WORK ENVIRONMENT

Physical Environment

Structural metal workers primarily work at construction sites. Structural metal workers who specialize in engineering and architecture, however, often work in office settings. They may also work at foundries, steel mills, or other industrial sites where metal pieces are formed prior to their transport to a construction site.

Relevant Skills and Abilities

Organization & Management Skills
- Managing time
- Meeting goals and deadlines
- Paying attention to and handling details

Technical Skills
- Performing scientific, mathematical and technical work
- Working with machines, tools or other objects

Human Environment

Work with heavy-duty construction materials requires extensive collaboration skills in design, transport, and installation. Extensive communication helps to eliminate design flaws and ensures the structural integrity of projects upon completion, as well as the safety of the workers.

Technological Environment

Structural metal work requires the extensive use of tools and technology. While blow torches, punches, surface gauges, and shears are common tools in the field, a variety of software and digital technologies are also utilized, ranging from computer-aided design tools, spreadsheet software, and resource-planning programs.

EDUCATION, TRAINING, AND ADVANCEMENT

High School/Secondary

High school students can prepare for a career in structural metal work with courses in algebra, calculus, geometry, trigonometry, chemistry, physics, and introductory computer science. Drafting or industrial arts classes can also provide a foundation for a future career in construction design. English composition and scholastic sports help to equip students with the communication and leadership skills that are needed in collaborative professional arenas such as construction.

Pre-employment exposure to the construction industry, through internships or volunteerism, can also provide important insights into the basics of the industry.

Suggested High School Subjects
- Applied Physics
- Blueprint Reading
- English
- Mathematics
- Mechanical Drawing
- Metals Technology
- Shop Math
- Shop Mechanics
- Welding

Famous First

The first skyscraper was a ten-story-high building with a steel frame erected in Chicago, Ill. It was developed by the Home Insurance Company and designed by Major William Le Baron Jenney in 1884. The frame supported the entire weight of the building, allowing it to be built high. Previously, the walls themselves supported the weight of a building, thus limiting height.

Postsecondary

Postsecondary course work is not traditionally a prerequisite for employment as a structural metal worker, given that large amount of training, particularly for entry-level positions, is provided on the job. However, candidates interested in a career in the design, fabrication, and engineering aspects of structural metal work and heavy-duty construction will benefit tremendously from bachelor's and associate's degree programs in subjects ranging from civil engineering, construction management, technology, and civic planning.

Related College Majors
- Welding

Adult Job Seekers

Structural metal work is a feasible option for adult job seekers interested in transitioning careers, particularly those who have previous experience in trades or construction. Many structural metal firms undertake jobs at on a national level, which may require workers to travel for certain projects. While structural metal workers traditionally work normal business hours, certain projects may require extensive overtime and weekend work.

Professional Certification and Licensure

No specific licensure or certification is required for a career as a structural metal worker, though applicants with commercial licenses and welding certification typically have an employment advantage.

Additional Requirements

Professionals who work with structural metal fabrications and other heavy-duty construction elements are team-oriented individuals who possess a respect for the rules and regulations that protect workers and civilians during large construction projects.

Fun Fact

New York City boasts the world's largest collection of cast-iron architecture. Cheaper than brick or stone and easy to cast into decorative designs, it has been used for decorative or structural purposes in the early 19th century.

Source: http://www.castironnyc.org/history.htm

EARNINGS AND ADVANCEMENT

Earnings for structural metal workers fluctuate because work time can be affected by both bad weather and the loss of time between jobs. Median annual earnings of structural metal workers were $36,570 in 2014. The lowest ten percent earned less than $24,690, and the highest ten percent earned more than $55,040. Apprentices usually start at about sixty percent of the wages paid to experienced workers.

Structural metal workers may receive paid vacations, holidays, and sick days; life and health insurance; and retirement benefits. These are usually paid by the employer.

Metropolitan Areas with the Highest
Employment Level in this Occupation

Metropolitan area	Employment	Employment per thousand jobs	Hourly mean wage
Houston-Sugar Land-Baytown, TX	3,450	1.21	$17.89
Los Angeles-Long Beach-Glendale, CA	2,160	0.53	$20.07
Wichita, KS	1,380	4.76	$22.17
Minneapolis-St. Paul-Bloomington, MN-WI	1,200	0.66	$18.87
Philadelphia, PA	1,180	0.64	$19.88
Chicago-Joliet-Naperville, IL	1,160	0.31	$18.81
Atlanta-Sandy Springs-Marietta, GA	1,000	0.42	$16.88
Kansas City, MO-KS	1,000	0.99	$23.48
Seattle-Bellevue-Everett, WA	890	0.60	$20.05
Portland-Vancouver-Hillsboro, OR-WA	870	0.83	$19.37

Source: Bureau of Labor Statistics

EMPLOYMENT AND OUTLOOK

There were approximately 79,000 structural metal workers employed nationally in 2012. Employment is expected to as fast as the average for all occupations through the year 2022, which means employment is projected to increase 9 percent to 13 percent. This is primarily due to the continued growth of industrial and commercial construction. In addition, job growth will occur as a result of the need to repair and maintain this country's increasing number of older buildings, factories, highways and bridges.

Employment Trend, Projected 2012–22

Construction trades workers: 22%

Structural metal workers: 11%

Total, all occupations: 11%

Note: "All Occupations" includes all occupations in the U.S. Economy. Source: U.S. Bureau of Labor Statistics, Employment Projections Program

Related Occupations
- Metal/Plastic Working Machine Operator
- Sheet Metal Worker
- Welder

Related Military Occupations
- Construction Equipment Operator

Conversation With . . .
MIKE RELYIN

General Organizer, International Association of Bridge,
Structural, Ornamental and Reinforcing Ironworkers
Washington, DC
Reinforcing Ironworker, 27 years

1. What was your individual career path in terms of education/training, entry-level job, or other significant opportunity?

After I graduated from high school, I worked as an auto mechanic for about two years and also worked on maintaining industrial equipment. These jobs taught me to work with my hands, as well as manage the maintenance side of things. I had family in the ironwork trade, so when I heard about the opportunity to become an apprentice through our local in Detroit, I knew it was a good one. I did a two-year apprenticeship, became a journeyman, and worked as a journeyman, foreman, and general foreman in the field. Then I got an opportunity to apply for an instructor's position at the apprenticeship program in Detroit and did that for two and a half years before I became the apprenticeship coordinator. I did that for about ten years, and then I was offered a position at union headquarters in Washington, D.C. in the apprenticeship and training department working to provide training materials, resources, and assistance to training centers across the US and Canada.

I spent my career in the field working in the reinforcing part of the industry, placing reinforced steel and post-tensioning cables for concrete construction. We build bridges, foundations, sewage treatment plants, factories, power plants...anything that's got concrete in it.

A typical workday involved unloading, handling, and placing reinforcing steel. This included the use of cranes to get the material close to where we were working. Much of the material is placed by hand, while cranes are sometimes used to hoist larger pieces or partially assembled sections into place. Reinforcing steel is fastened together using wire that is tied using pliers, and occasionally welded.

My job now has two major functions: assisting and providing resources to local unions to help them provide training, and providing training programs for the union apprenticeship programs. I do a lot of support, creating training materials and curricula for our different certification programs.

2. What are the most important skills and/or qualities for someone in your profession?

People who gravitate toward our industry need to like to work with their hands and be good at it. You'll be working outside, so there is weather to deal with and it's physically very demanding. You need a good basic math background because you'll work with drawings and blueprints.

You need to pace yourself for the long haul and work smarter and take care of yourself because this work does wear and tear on the body.

3. What do you wish you had known going into this profession?

Ironwork's very rewarding, and for the most part I knew what I was getting into. I get to work with some great people and you build a great camaraderie because you rely on them and trust them. You create something. And you do neat stuff like working on a 30-story building, or being 100 feet in the ground, or working with cranes with 200-foot booms.

4. Are there many job opportunities in your profession? In what specific areas?

Job opportunities vary with the economy. Things have been getting better over the last year or two. All facets of ironwork need workers.

5. How do you see your profession changing in the next five years? What role will technology play in those changes, and what skills will be required?

One of the biggest things is safety and specialty certification for work such as welding. This continues to change; owners and certain contractors are adding their own training and certification requirements. Also, general foremen need more computer skills. Blueprints aren't always rolled out; sometimes guys are given iPads and use CAD or BIM software.

6. What do you enjoy most about your job? What do you enjoy least about your job?

What I like most in the field is that the fact you're always going to different projects. You meet new people and you solve problems every day. In my job now, I enjoy the fact that what we're doing has a positive influence at the local level and in how workers benefit.

What I like least in the field are the cold days, and being laid off can be trying at times. In my job now, I least like that on top of having many large projects going at once, things are always popping up that need immediate attention; it is easy to get frustrated and burned out from the workload.

7. Can you suggest a valuable "try this" for students considering a career in your profession?

Take a vocational class in welding or any of the building trades. That will give you a flavor of what the work is like, although most classes are geared toward residential construction, which is quite a bit different than the commercial and industrial side of the industry. Other vocational classes may also help a person decide if a hands-on physical career is for them, even though they may not be quite as demanding as working in the construction industry.

MORE INFORMATION

Associated General Contractors of America
Director, Construction Education Services
2300 Wilson Boulevard, Suite 400
Arlington, VA 22201
703.548.3118
www.agc.org

International Association of Bridge, Structural, Ornamental, and Reinforcing Iron Workers
1750 New York Avenue NW
Suite 400
Washington, DC 20006
202.383.4800
www.ironworkers.org

National Association of Home Builders
1201 15th Street, NW
Washington, DC 20005
800.368.5242
www.nahb.com

National Association of Reinforcing Steel Contractors
P.O. Box 280
Fairfax, VA 22030
703.591.1870
www.narsc.com

National Center for Construction Education and Research
13614 Progress Boulevard
Alachua, FL 32615
888.622.3720
www.nccer.org

NEA
The Association of Union Constructors
1501 Lee Highway, Suite 202
Arlington, VA 22209-1109
703.524.3336
www.nea-online.org

United Steelworkers of America
Five Gateway Center
Pittsburgh, PA 15222
412.562.2400
www.usw.org

John Pritchard/Editor

Surveyor & Cartographer

Snapshot

Career Cluster(s): Building & Construction, Architecture & Construction, Science, Technology, Engineering & Mathematics
Interests: Geography, maps and map-making, engineering, spatial data, demographics, mathematics
Earnings (Yearly Average): $57,050
Employment & Outlook: Average Growth Expected

OVERVIEW

Sphere of Work

Surveyors measure, record, and interpret features on and above the surface of the earth using specialized equipment. Cartographers are mapmakers: they use survey data, photographs, and satellite images to create digital or graphical maps and charts of geographical and demographic information. Government agencies, utility companies, architectural and engineering firms, publishers, and other employers hire surveyors and cartographers to provide information necessary to their business operations or sales. The work that surveyors and cartographers produce leads to defining the earth's surface

and position and to locating boundaries of countries, states, and properties.

Work Environment

Surveyors and cartographers typically work forty hours or more each week, both at the field sites and in the office. Cartographers tend to do more solitary, sedentary office work than fieldwork. Field measurements are often taken by groups working together to adjust and operate surveying equipment. Travel to remote field sites may be required. Fieldwork can be physically demanding, requiring long periods of standing, walking long distances, and climbing with heavy loads of survey instruments.

Profile

Working Conditions: Work both Indoors and Outdoors
Physical Strength: Medium Work
Education Needs: Bachelor's Degree
Licensure/Certification: Required
Opportunities For Experience: Apprenticeship, Military Service, Part-Time Work
Holland Interest Score*: IER, IRE

* See Appendix A

Occupation Interest

Individuals interested in becoming surveyors and cartographers are usually detail-oriented, fascinated by geography, and interested in maps and map-making. Prospective surveyors and cartographers tend to be adept at understanding spatial information, demonstrate an ease with numbers and mathematical functions, and enjoy the outdoors. Surveyors and cartographers have a great deal of responsibility as they provide critical geographical data for defense, first responders, and government agencies at all levels. They should be physically fit enough to meet the demands of fieldwork.

A Day in the Life—Duties and Responsibilities

Surveyors research land, air, and water features, primarily in the field but also in office settings. In the field, surveyors use a wide variety of tools to measure and record spatial information, such as latitude, longitude, elevation, position, and contour, among other physical characteristics. At the office, they analyze the collected data to write descriptions and reports and to create maps, charts, and other graphical representations. Since survey data is often used in legal documents and proceedings, surveyors or their work may occasionally be called upon in court. Surveyors may also research existing survey records, deeds, and boundaries to check their validity or gather information prior to conducting a new survey of an area. Experienced surveyors often focus on a single type of surveying, such as marine surveying or geodetic surveying, and supervise the work of technicians, apprentices, or assistants.

Cartographers make new maps and update old ones. They use aerial photography, satellite imagery, ground survey data, and GIS technology to compile data, which is often stored in databases. Computer-aided design (CAD) programs, mathematical formulas, and analytical processes help them produce graphical and digital charts, maps, and graphs. They also analyze and interpret non-spatial data about land-use, climate patterns, population density, and political, social, and economic demographics, and are responsible for determining a map's aesthetic presentation. Cartographers proofread their work before publication and revise existing maps as needed. In some cases, cartographers may also work with and troubleshoot photographic materials and processes in the course of drafting and replicating maps. Experienced cartographers may train and oversee less experienced cartographers.

Duties and Responsibilities

- Studying physical evidence, notes, maps, deeds or other records
- Checking the accuracy of the information gathered using complex mathematical computations
- Adjusting instruments to maintain accuracy
- Keeping notes and preparing sketches, maps, reports and legal descriptions of the survey
- Coordinating results with the work of engineering and architectural personnel, clients and others
- Calculating and adjusting survey data and planning survey systems

OCCUPATION SPECIALTIES

Geodetic Surveyors

Geodetic Surveyors plan, direct and conduct surveys of large areas of land such as states and counties.

Mine Surveyors

Mine Surveyors make surface and underground surveys for mine locations, tunnels, subways and underground storage facilities.

Marine Surveyors

Marine Surveyors make surveys of harbors, rivers and other bodies of water to determine shore lines, topography of bottom or other features to determine navigable channels.

Land Surveyors

Land Surveyors establish official land and water boundaries, write descriptions of land for deeds, leases and other legal documents, and measure construction and mineral sites.

Field-Map Editors

Field-Map Editors prepare maps using data provided by geodetic surveys, aerial photographs and satellite data.

WORK ENVIRONMENT

Physical Environment

Surveyors spend a great deal of time outdoors, in all types of weather conditions and across all kinds of terrain. Cartographers work mostly indoors in an office sitting in front of a computer, but fieldwork may also be required.

Human Environment

Surveyors must have strong communication skills as they often work in a team called a "survey party." Cartographers work with survey parties as well as independently. They may interact with survey technicians, assistants or apprentices, survey party chiefs, cartographic drafters, and supervisors.

Relevant Skills and Abilities

Interpersonal/Social Skills
- Working as a member of a team

Organization & Management Skills
- Coordinating tasks
- Following instructions
- Managing people/groups
- Organizing information or materials
- Paying attention to and handling details

Research & Planning Skills
- Using logical reasoning

Technical Skills
- Performing scientific, mathematical and technical work
- Working with machines, tools or other objects
- Working with your hands

Work Environment Skills
- Working outdoors

Technological Environment

Surveyors and cartographers use a vast range of equipment. They use global positioning system (GPS) instruments to locate various distance segments as well as total stations to measure and record angles and distances. Geographic information systems (GIS) allow surveyors and cartographers to collate, analyze, and store data in a digital platform. Light-imaging detection and ranging (LIDAR) helps them gather accurate spatial data, usually from aircraft. Cartographers also use CAD and imaging software, databases, film processors, copy cameras, and photographs.

EDUCATION, TRAINING, AND ADVANCEMENT

High School/Secondary

High school students interested in pursuing a career in surveying and cartography should prepare themselves by studying mathematics, technical drawing, computer science, and the sciences. Extracurricular activities that familiarize students with these subjects are also useful. While in high school, there may be opportunities to become an apprentice or assistant to a surveyor or cartographer to get work experience; however, postsecondary school training is usually required for surveyors and cartographers.

Suggested High School Subjects
- Algebra
- Applied Math
- Calculus
- College Preparatory
- English
- Geography
- Geometry
- Mechanical Drawing
- Physical Science
- Statistics
- Trigonometry

Famous First

The Present State of New England, being a narrative of the troubles with the Indians of New England, from the first planting thereof in the year 1607 to 1677 was the first book published in America to contain a map. The map was a woodcut print, showing the topographical details of the "Wine Hills," the White Hills of New Hampshire. The book describes the issues resulting from the Protestant invasion of Native tribal lands over the course of colonial history.

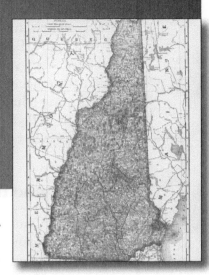

Postsecondary

To become a surveyor or cartographer, most states require a bachelor's degree from an Accreditation Board for Engineering and Technology (ABET) accredited school. Many colleges and universities have both surveying and cartography degree offerings. Most aspiring surveyors and cartographers study surveying, cartography, or a related field such as geography, engineering, or forestry. Postsecondary coursework should include statistics, CAD, earth sciences, satellite-assisted navigation, geography, and topographical surveying.

Related College Majors
- Geography
- Surveying

Adult Job Seekers

Adults seeking surveying and cartography jobs have generally earned a bachelor's degree. However, adults can join a survey crew or the armed forces and, with on-the-job training, work their way up. Many surveyors begin their careers as surveyor technicians or assistants. It may be useful to contact professional associations for networking, apprenticeships, continuing education opportunities, and licensing requirements.

Professional Certification and Licensure

All surveyors and some cartographers must obtain licensure from the National Council of Examiners for Engineering and Surveying (NCEES), which involves passing two written examinations taken four years apart. Between the two exams, candidates work under experienced surveyors. In addition, most states require surveyors to pass a state licensing board exam. Education prerequisites and continuing education requirements for renewal vary from state to state. The National Society of Professional Surveyors certifies surveyor technicians, which may be useful or necessary for promotions.

Additional Requirements

Visualization, accuracy, physical fitness and stamina, keen analytical abilities, and strong collaborative skills are essential qualities in surveyors and cartographers. Familiarity with computer technology and a college degree can provide a competitive edge in the field.

Fun Fact

The art of surveying, which goes back to Egyptian times, includes such historical luminaries as George Washington and Capt. James Cook among its practitioners.
Source: http://www.interestingreality.com/interesting-facts-surveying/

EARNINGS AND ADVANCEMENT

Earnings depend on the size and geographic location of the employer and the employee's education and experience. Median annual earnings of surveyors and cartographers were $57,050 in 2014. The lowest ten percent earned less than $32,740, and the highest ten percent earned more than $93,370.

Surveyors and cartographers may receive paid vacations, holidays, and sick days; life and health insurance; and retirement benefits. These are usually paid by the employer. Surveyors and cartographers may also receive reimbursement for business-related travel expenses, but may be required to purchase their own uniforms and other work-related equipment.

Metropolitan Areas with the Highest Employment Level in this Occupation

Metropolitan area	Employment	Employment per thousand jobs	Hourly mean wage
Houston-Sugar Land-Baytown, TX	2,290	0.80	$28.06
New York-White Plains-Wayne, NY-NJ	720	0.13	$34.84
Washington-Arlington-Alexandria, DC-VA-MD-WV	670	0.28	$30.72
Atlanta-Sandy Springs-Marietta, GA	570	0.24	$25.47
Pittsburgh, PA	560	0.50	$26.89
Los Angeles-Long Beach-Glendale, CA	550	0.14	$41.02
Chicago-Joliet-Naperville, IL	550	0.15	$30.20
Denver-Aurora-Broomfield, CO	540	0.41	$26.35
Phoenix-Mesa-Glendale, AZ	520	0.29	$26.52
Santa Ana-Anaheim-Irvine, CA	510	0.35	$38.20

Source: Bureau of Labor Statistics

EMPLOYMENT AND OUTLOOK

There were approximately 65,000 surveyors and cartographers employed nationally in 2012. Engineering and architectural firms employed about three-fourths of workers, while federal, state and local governments employed most of the rest. Employment is expected to grow as fast as the average for all occupations through the year 2022, which means employment is projected to increase 9 percent to 12 percent. Increasing demand for fast, accurate and complete geographic information will be the main source of growth for these occupations. Job openings will also result from the need to replace workers who transfer to other occupations or leave the labor force.

Employment Trend, Projected 2012–22

Architects, surveyors, and cartographers: 15%

Total, all occupations: 11%

Surveyors: 10%

Note: "All Occupations" includes all occupations in the U.S. Economy. Source: U.S. Bureau of Labor Statistics, Employment Projections Program

Related Occupations
- Architect
- Civil Engineer
- Engineering Technician
- Geologist & Geophysicist
- Mathematician
- Mining & Geological Engineer

Related Military Occupations
- Surveying & Mapping Manager
- Surveying, Mapping & Drafting Technician

Conversation With . . .
CURT SUMNER, LS

Executive Director
National Society of Professional Surveyors
Frederick, Maryland
Professional Surveyor, 35 years

1. What was your individual career path in terms of education/training, entry-level job, or other significant opportunity?

I began working as a survey technician for the Virginia Department of Transportation the day after I graduated from high school. I worked on projects such as the layout of I-77 where it passes through the mountains of Virginia into North Carolina, near where I grew up. I realized if I was going to do this for a living and be more than one of the guys on the crew, I'd have to get more education. I did that at community college and a university, although I didn't finish my bachelor's degree. I needed to work, and Virginia doesn't require a four-year degree for licensure—though some states do. I went to work for Anderson & Associates in Blacksburg, Virginia, and became a partner after I got my license.

In 1987, I decided to take a position near Washington, DC. At the same time, the Virginia Association of Surveyors chose me to represent them on the National Society of Professional Surveyors (NSPS) Board of Governors. I went on to chair its Board of Directors and to serve as President. In 1998, NSPS asked me to manage the national office for three months while they did an executive search. That three months has turned into a lot of years. I think what got me the job I have today is communication skills. I have been fortunate to meet surveyors all over the country and the world.

Although licensure as a professional surveyor is done on a state-by-state basis, and not all require a four-year degree, as far as I'm concerned, in today's environment an undergraduate degree is essential to prepare yourself for the technical and business aspects of the field.

2. What are the most important skills and/or qualities for someone in your profession?

You need good math and science skills, and for many jobs you must like being outside. But to be really successful, you must have a high level of interpersonal skills in order to communicate well and operate a business. I sometimes humorously say that professional surveyors must possess the skills of a detective, puzzle worker, and mind reader, due the job's equally important components of research, problem-solving, and interaction with others. Surveyors interact with the public on a daily basis.

It's not a profession based on technology alone. It's based on evidence analysis, the history of a property, and how people have bought and used the land over time.

3. What do you wish you had known going into this profession?

This profession offers the opportunity to make a really good living. Most people think of surveyors as somebody who comes out and sets your property boundaries, but it can be much more than that. A surveyor is the only person involved in a project from beginning to end. At the beginning, they define boundaries. They go back and put down markers for construction of everything the project requires, down to the utilities. When it's finished, the surveyor returns and confirms it's been done the right way. This creates an opportunity to build relationships with an entire set of people: property owners, realtors, attorneys, contractors, and government officials.

4. Are there many job opportunities in your profession? In what specific areas?

One could perform boundary surveys in a small town or expand his/her business to incorporate every new technology that comes along related to measurement, spatial positioning, and data management. The average age of professional surveyors is approximately 58. The demand for surveyors is increasing, so job opportunities should remain high.

5. How do you see your profession changing in the next five years? What role will technology play in those changes, and what skills will be required?

Advancements will require both professional surveyors and surveying technicians to continually adapt to new technologies. Any new technology that has anything to do with data is going to impact surveying. The more rapidly, efficiently, and accurately you can gather and process data, the more effective you will be.

This is a job you'll be drawn to if you like technologies such as GPS, digital collection tools, drones, etc. You get many opportunities to play with really cool "toys."

6. Can you suggest a valuable "try this" for students considering a career in your profession?

Try pulling up a GIS map or parcel map from your local jurisdiction. Think about who provides the accurate positioning of the property lines, the alignment and grading instructions for roads, airport runways, walking trails, etc., and construction of shopping centers, houses, or office parks. You could try to find the historical documents for the property on which your house is located. It may have been owned at one time by someone famous or notorious!

MORE INFORMATION

American Society for Photogrammetry and Remote Sensing
5410 Grosvenor Lane, Suite 210
Bethesda, MD 20814-2160
301.493.0290
www.asprs.org

National Council of Examiners for Engineering and Surveying
280 Seneca Creek Road
Seneca, SC 29678
800.250.3196
www.ncees.org

National Society of Professional Surveyors
6 Montgomery Village Avenue
Suite 403
Gaithersburg, MD 20879
240.632.9716
www.nspsmo.org

Susan Williams/Editor

Telecommunications Line Installer/ Repairer

Snapshot

Career Cluster(s): Building & Construction
Interests: Technology, working outdoors, solving problems
Earnings (Yearly Average): $54,450
Employment & Outlook: Slower Than Average Growth Expected

OVERVIEW

Sphere of Work

Telecommunications line installers and repairers install and maintain the lines and cables, including fiber-optic cables, used to transmit communication signals for telephones, cable television, the Internet and other communications networks. They install utility poles and string cables and also use construction equipment to lay underground cables. They also maintain existing cables by using remote monitoring equipment and responding in person to customers when there are services outages.

Telecommunications line installers and repairers must be able to handle heights while working inside of bucket trucks, climb poles and towers and also work in tunnels and trenches. Special safety equipment is used to minimize the risk of injury.

Work Environment

Telecommunications line installers and repairers work in and around any setting that uses cable television, Internet, or other telecommunications devices. Many telecommunications line installers work in residential neighborhoods, while others specialize in implementing cable television, Internet, or security-system networks in businesses, organizations, or government agencies. Much of the work of telecommunications line installers and repairers takes place outdoors, at external utility boxes or telephone poles.

Profile

Working Conditions: Work Outdoors
Physical Strength: Medium Work
Education Needs: On-The-Job Training, Junior/Technical/Community College
Licensure/Certification: Usually Not Required
Opportunities For Experience: Internship, Volunteer Work
Holland Interest Score*: RSE

* See Appendix A

Occupation Interest

Jobs pertaining to field and utility work in the telecommunications industry traditionally appeal to technologically savvy problem solvers who enjoy working on complex issues individually or in small groups. They should enjoy working outdoors and be comfortable performing duties in different situations, such as high up in the air or underground in trenches.

A Day in the Life—Duties and Responsibilities

Telecommunications line installers and repairers traditionally work out of centralized headquarters that house cable, Internet, or other communications systems. Those employed by Internet and cable service providers work in the field and begin their day reviewing the day's project list with supervisory staff. It is customarily the job of installation and repair workers to load their repair vans or trucks with the necessary equipment and tools needed for each of the day's installations or repairs.

Telecommunications line installers and repairers must work quickly and efficiently, prioritizing jobs by both complexity and need. They can often complete several simple repairs in a day; however, system overhauls and large repairs can take from several days to several weeks to complete, depending on their size and scope. Time management and the ability to stay on task are major facets of the job.

Professionals who work in and around telecommunications systems must also be well versed in the potential dangers of working around high-voltage electronics and public utility poles. Patience and adherence to basic safety procedures are important parts of a telecommunications line installer and repairer's job, in order to protect both their own safety and the safety of those around them.

Another major responsibility of telecommunications line installers and repairers is to follow through once a job is complete to ensure that all systems are responding appropriately and that any previous issues have been resolved.

Duties and Responsibilities

- Installing and repairing telecommunications lines and cables
- Laying underground cables in tunnels and trenches
- Operating construction equipment
- Setting up new services and troubleshooting malfunctioning equipment

OCCUPATION SPECIALTIES

Radio Mechanics

Radio Mechanics install and maintain radio transmitting and receiving equipment, excluding cellular communications systems.

WORK ENVIRONMENT

Physical Environment

Telecommunications line installers and repairers typically work at external communications hubs, which may be located on utility poles or rooftops. They are often employed by cable television and Internet service providers and telephone companies.

Relevant Skills and Abilities

Communication Skills
- Speaking effectively
- Writing concisely

Interpersonal/Social Skills
- Cooperating with others
- Representing others
- Working as a member of a team

Organization & Management Skills
- Managing time
- Organizing information or materials

Research & Planning Skills
- Analyzing information
- Gathering information
- Solving problems
- Using logical reasoning

Technical Skills
- Performing scientific, mathematical and technical work

Human Environment

Telecommunications line installers and repairers primarily work alone or with small groups of coworkers. Given the complexity of the systems that they work on, however, major projects and repairs sometimes require extensive collaboration. Residential and commercial telecommunications repairs require extensive interaction with customers and business owners.

Technological Environment

Telecommunications professionals work in a highly specialized technological environment. They must be familiar with network applications, telephone systems, Internet protocol setup, and exchange switchboards.

EDUCATION, TRAINING, AND ADVANCEMENT

High School/Secondary

High school students can best prepare for a career as a
telecommunications line installer and repairer by taking courses in
algebra, calculus, geometry, trigonometry, physics, and introductory
computer science. Drafting, architecture, and traditional art classes
can also serve as an important foundation for future system design
work. Exposure to computer technology through internships,
volunteerism, and extracurricular activities such as science and
technology fairs is useful as well.

Suggested High School Subjects
- Accounting
- Applied Communication
- Business Law
- Business Math
- College Preparatory
- Computer Science
- Electricity & Electronics
- English

Famous First

Telegraph cable made out of insulated copper wire and was first laid from Battery
to Governors Island, both in New York Harbor, in 1842.
Samuel Finley Breese Morse's first line was cut the
day after (October 19) being laid because the anchor
of a passing vessel caught and destroyed it. The next
year, Samuel Colt insulated the wire more thoroughly
using cotton yarn, beeswax, asphaltum, and lead pipe to
reduce the prospect of similar mishaps.

Postsecondary

Employers in the telecommunications industry are increasingly giving preference to applicants with at least some formal training in computer science, media, or technology. Many colleges across the United States offer certificate and two-year associate's programs in telecommunications systems, digital electronics repair, and networking. Many telecommunications professionals use whatever formal training they have and adapt it to the systems, technology, and tools used by their employers through preemployment training sessions and on-the-job field training.

The constant evolution of technology is a challenge for all workers in telecommunications. Many telecommunications professionals hone their skills at annual training seminars, either voluntarily or through educational programs sponsored by their employers.

Related College Majors
* Radio & Television Broadcasting Technology

Adult Job Seekers

Telecommunications line installation and repair is a fairly simple profession to transition to for adult job seekers interested in a career change. Much of the basics of the field can be learned through certificate training programs. Telecommunications professionals traditionally work regular business hours with major holiday and weekends off, though some employees may work emergency and on-call shifts, depending on their employer.

Professional Certification and Licensure

No specific certification or licensure is required.

Additional Requirements

Telecommunications line installers and repairers must be patient with sophisticated problems that often require a significant amount of analysis to solve.

EARNINGS AND ADVANCEMENT

Advancement is based on ability and years of service. Median annual earnings of telecommunications line installers and repairers were $54,450 in 2014. The lowest ten percent earned less than $28,530, and the highest ten percent earned more than $81,860.

Telecommunications line installers and repairers may receive paid vacations, holidays, and sick days; life and health insurance; and retirement benefits. These are usually paid by the employer.

Metropolitan Areas with the Highest Employment Level in this Occupation

Metropolitan area	Employment	Employment per thousand jobs	Hourly mean wage
New York-White Plains-Wayne, NY-NJ	9,660	1.79	$34.73
Washington-Arlington-Alexandria, DC-VA-MD-WV	5,020	2.11	$28.55
Philadelphia, PA	3,130	1.68	$29.57
Los Angeles-Long Beach-Glendale, CA	3,080	0.76	$29.16
Houston-Sugar Land-Baytown, TX	2,220	0.78	$23.70
Chicago-Joliet-Naperville, IL	2,150	0.57	$30.84
Edison-New Brunswick, NJ	1,960	1.96	$27.94
Baltimore-Towson, MD	1,880	1.46	$27.32
Dallas-Plano-Irving, TX	1,740	0.78	$22.14
Nassau-Suffolk, NY	1,710	1.36	$34.50

Source: Bureau of Labor Statistics

EMPLOYMENT AND OUTLOOK

There were approximately 250,000 telecommunications line installers and repairers employed nationally in 2012. Employment is expected to grow slower than the average for all occupations through the year 2022, which means employment is projected to increase 4 percent to 8 percent. Any job growth will be driven by the need for new telephone, cable and Internet services, especially the demand for more long-distance fiber-optic lines.

Employment Trend, Projected 2012–22

Total, all occupations: 11%

Electrical power-line installers and repairers: 9%

Line installers and repairers: 7%

Telecommunications line installers and repairers: 6%

Note: "All Occupations" includes all occupations in the U.S. Economy. Source: U.S. Bureau of Labor Statistics, Employment Projections Program

Related Occupations
- Telecommunications Equipment Repairer

MORE INFORMATION

**Society of Cable
Telecommunications Engineers**
140 Philips Road
Exton, PA 19341-1318
800.542.5040
www.scte.org

**TCA-Information Technology &
Telecommunications Association**
P.O. Box 910668
Lexington, KY 40591
859.276.4989
www.tca.org

USTelecom
607 14th Street NW, Suite 400
Washington, DC 20005
202.326.7300
www.ustelecom.org

John Pritchard/Editor

Tile Setter

Snapshot

Career Cluster: Building & Construction, Architecture & Construction
Interests: Design, Architecture, Patterns, Puzzles, Construction
Earnings (Yearly Average): $38,980
Employment & Outlook: Faster Than Average Growth Expected

OVERVIEW

Sphere of Work

Tile setters, also called tile installers, apply tile in residential, commercial, and industrial settings. The most common types of tile

are made of ceramic or porcelain, but glass, slate, stone, marble, and metal tile have become popular as well. Tile setters work on new construction sites as well as renovations. They tile a variety of surfaces, including bathroom floors and walls, kitchen backsplashes, hotel lobbies, and restaurant floors and walls.

Work Environment

Tile setters usually work alone or with a partner or assistant. For some projects, tile setters may be employed on a job site with other contractors. Tile may be installed indoors or outdoors, as tiled pool decks, patios, and walkways are becoming more common. Most tile setters work daytime hours from Monday to Friday, with occasional overtime.

Profile

Working Conditions: Work both Indoors and Outdoors
Physical Strength: Medium Work
Education Needs: On-The-Job Training, High School Diploma with Technical Education, Apprenticeship
Licensure/Certification: Recommended
Opportunities For Experience: Apprenticeship, Part-Time Work
Holland Interest Score*: CRE, RSE

* See Appendix A

Occupation Interest

The work performed by a tile setter attracts project-oriented people with good mechanical and mathematical skills and an aptitude for spatial thinking. Tiling also requires patience, good eyesight, pattern recognition, the ability to follow charts, and good eye-hand coordination. Although tile setters might work alone on many projects, they must have good communication skills. They must also be in good physical condition, with upper body strength to carry heavy boxes and equipment, and able to endure the physical exertion of the job. Successful tile setters who work as independent contractors must also have strong business skills in order to manage their businesses, maintain a schedule, and market their services.

A Day in the Life—Duties and Responsibilities

Tile setters typically work on one job at a time, seeing each project through to completion before beginning another. Most jobs require a minimum of a few days or a week to account for necessary drying times between steps. Large jobs may take weeks to complete and require the help of several tile setters and assistants.

A tile setter is often responsible for transporting all the necessary materials and equipment to the job site. Before tiling, he or she takes care of important preliminary work, such as double-checking the tile's technical specifications to make sure it complies with the intended use and measuring the surface to ensure that enough tile and other supplies have been ordered. The tile setter begins by preparing the surface, ensuring that the surface is clean of debris and level. Next, he or she cuts and attaches the appropriate backing material for proper adhesion and, if necessary, to act as a vapor barrier. Once the surface is ready, the setter uses a level and/or a plumb bob to mark lines to use as guides and prearrange the tile on a flat surface, anticipating where he or she will need to make cuts in the tile to achieve the design. Wooden battens are sometimes attached to prevent the tile from slipping.

The tile setter then spreads mastic or thin-set on the surface in a workable section and taps pieces of tile into place with a rubber mallet. Pieces are custom cut with an electric tile saw or trimmed with tile nippers as needed. Some tiling surfaces may pose unusual challenges and require many custom-cut pieces. Once the mastic has dried, the tile is grouted with a float, left to cure, and sealed or polished, if necessary.

As a tile setter gains proficiency and familiarity with the different types of tile, he or she may be asked for special technical or creative advice. Independent contractors have additional business responsibilities to take care of when not tiling.

Duties and Responsibilities

- Examining blueprints
- Measuring and marking surfaces to be covered
- Spreading concrete on subfloors
- Spreading mortar, mastic or other adhesives to form a bed for the tiles
- Cutting and shaping tiles to fit into spaces and corners
- Filling the joints with grout
- Cleaning the tile surfaces
- Positioning tile and tapping it into the adhesive

WORK ENVIRONMENT

Physical Environment

Tile setters install tile in residential, commercial, and industrial settings, where variations in temperature, humidity, safety factors, and other environmental conditions may require different surface preparations. Ear, skin, and eye protection, as well as proper ventilation, are necessary. Construction sites are somewhat messy and require work clothes and proper footwear. Setting tile can be especially hard on the back and knees.

Relevant Skills and Abilities

Organization & Management Skills
- Performing routine work

Research & Planning Skills
- Creating ideas
- Developing evaluation strategies

Technical Skills
- Working with machines, tools or other objects
- Working with your hands

Human Environment

A tile setter often reports to a supervisor and may work with other tile setters on larger jobs. Interaction with customers can vary from none at all to friendly conversations, requests for professional opinions, or discussion about project delays and completion. An experienced tile setter may supervise other employees. When working on new construction, a tile setter may interact with other contractors, technicians, architects, and clients.

Technological Environment

Tile setters use many different hand tools, including hammers, floats, saws, levels, trowels, and machine tools, such as power grinders, drills, and saws. Some tile setters may also use a computer and software for computer-aided design and/or project management. Scaffolding and ladders are used when necessary.

EDUCATION, TRAINING, AND ADVANCEMENT

High School/Secondary

A high school diploma is required for most jobs. Either a college preparatory program, with some industrial arts courses, or a vocational program that emphasizes math, English, and computer technology, can provide a good background. Design and art courses help develop creative skills.

Suggested High School Subjects
- Applied Math
- Blueprint Reading
- Building Trades & Carpentry
- English
- Mechanical Drawing
- Shop Mechanics

Famous First

Vitrolite was originally created in 1907 by the Meyercord-Carter Company in Parkersburg, WV, and is an opaque structural flat glass. It was cut into tiles and used as the original walling material for the early 1900s New York City Interborough Rapid Transit System. While at first it came only in white, in 1922 colored tiles were created by added sand, soda ash, and other ingredients into the mix.

Postsecondary

Traditionally, tile setters have learned their skills on the job, through apprenticeships. This remains the most common way to learn tile setting skills. For those tile setters interested in becoming an independent contractor, business courses in an adult education setting may be helpful in setting up the business.

Related College Majors
* Masonry & Tile Setting

Adult Job Seekers

An adult interested in starting a new career as a tile setter should have little difficulty, assuming one is in good health and meets other personal qualifications. A background in construction or art is especially useful.

Advancement opportunities include working on more difficult or prestigious jobs, moving into a supervisory position, or taking on office, sales, or design responsibilities. An experienced tile setter may also become an independent contractor or consultant.

Professional Certification and Licensure

There is no special license needed to install tile; however, certification as a Certified Tile Installer (CTI) is becoming more relevant in the industry since its introduction in 2008. Some employers will pay for new tile setters to attend this program. Certification programs typically have specific education and work experience requirements. As with any optional certification program, it is helpful to consult credible professional associations within the field, and follow professional debate as to the relevancy and value of the certification program.

Additional Requirements

Successful tile setters are able to advise their clients on the best flooring options based on function, durability, price, and design. An eye for color and design is a benefit. Because the process of tile setting requires time for materials to set, it is important that tile setters manage their time well in order to achieve high quality results in a timely manner.

Most tile setters need a driver's license. Tile setters should be familiar with the American National Standards for the Installation of Tile (ANSI) as provided in various industry publications.

Fun Fact

The oldest McDonald's in the world, in Downey, California, still boasts the original red and white tile exterior from 1953.

Source: http://www.downeyca.org/visitors/attractions/mcdonalds.asp

EARNINGS AND ADVANCEMENT

Earnings depend on the type and geographic location of the employer and the employee's experience. In 2014, median annual earnings of tile and marble setters were $38,980. The lowest ten percent earned less than $23,570, and the highest ten percent earned more than $74,550. Apprentices usually start at 30 to 50 percent of the rate of experienced tile and marble setters.

Tile setters may receive paid vacations, holidays, and sick days; life and health insurance; and retirement benefits. These are usually paid by the employer.

Metropolitan Areas with the Highest
Employment Level in this Occupation

Metropolitan area	Employment	Employment per thousand jobs	Hourly mean wage
New York-White Plains-Wayne, NY-NJ	1,290	0.24	$35.21
Los Angeles-Long Beach-Glendale, CA	1,160	0.28	$19.24
Riverside-San Bernardino-Ontario, CA	1,090	0.87	$20.94
Seattle-Bellevue-Everett, WA	1,020	0.69	$25.97
San Diego-Carlsbad-San Marcos, CA	810	0.61	$21.75
Chicago-Joliet-Naperville, IL	790	0.21	$27.53
Sacramento--Arden-Arcade--Roseville, CA	770	0.90	$22.47
Las Vegas-Paradise, NV	710	0.81	$19.53
Phoenix-Mesa-Glendale, AZ	660	0.36	$16.42
Washington-Arlington-Alexandria, DC-VA-MD-WV	630	0.26	$21.42

Source: Bureau of Labor Statistics

EMPLOYMENT AND OUTLOOK

There were approximately 40,000 tile setters employed nationally in 2012. Employment of tile setters is expected to grow faster than the average for all occupations through the year 2022, which means employment is projected to increase 12 percent to 18 percent. Job growth will occur as a result of increased construction of shopping malls, hospitals, schools, restaurants and other buildings where tile is used. In addition, tile is expected to continue to increase in popularity as a building material used widely in the growing number of more expensive homes.

Employment Trend, Projected 2012–22

Construction trades workers: 22%

Tile and marble setters: 15%

Total, all occupations: 11%

Note: "All Occupations" includes all occupations in the U.S. Economy. Source: U.S. Bureau of Labor Statistics, Employment Projections Program

Related Occupations
- Brickmason/Stonemason
- Carpet Installer
- Cement Mason

Conversation With . . .
JOHN COX

Owner, Cox Tile, Inc.
San Antonio, Texas
Residential tile contractor, 35 years

1. What was your individual career path in terms of education/training, entry-level job, or other significant opportunity?

I learned the trade by working for a builder as a laborer, then meeting a tile flooring professional and working for him as a helper. After ten years of learning the trade, I went into business for myself. I now employ twenty installers in the San Antonio area and have been the owner of my business for twenty-five years.

2. What are the most important skills and/or qualities for someone in your profession?

As a tile installer, one of most important skills is the ability to follow directions. A basic aptitude for math and numbers is a plus. Geometry and working with different shapes and designs is also a benefit. But most importantly, you should be willing to work hard to succeed at what can be a high-paying and rewarding job.

3. What do you wish you had known going into this profession?

I learned most of the job from many different people. Some taught me the right way; others didn't. I wish there had been well-developed training programs and resources available to me, but there weren't. Some excellent training programs today include the union apprenticeship programs offered by the International Union of Bricklayers and Allied Craftworkers (IUBAC) and online apprenticeship courses offered by the National Tile Contractors Association (www.tile-assn.com) as well as programs at vocational schools and community colleges. And many contracting companies will train workers in the field.

I also wish I had known sooner to join the National Tile Contractors Association sooner. It is one of the best business decisions I've made. The benefits include being part of a forum of industry peers that I can interact with daily, staying on top of industry standards, certification of my crews, and marketing my business by promoting my association membership.

4. Are there many job opportunities in your profession? In what specific areas?

Overall, the job opportunities in the tile industry are excellent. It's a growing industry. Installers who have the skills and training and get certified have a lot of work available to them in both residential and commercial tile work. Certification is offered by the Ceramic Tile Education Foundation, which offers a program approved by the tile industry. Its website is www.tilecareer.com. Besides installation, other jobs available in the world of tile include estimating, project management, sales, design, and warehousing.

5. How do you see your profession changing in the next five years? What role will technology play in those changes, and what skills will be required?

We are moving from a skill-based industry to a knowledge-based industry. We can teach the skills to install tile products. Technology is changing materials rapidly and you need to become aware of standards and product data information in order to properly sell and install them. For instance, large-format thin tile will change the whole industry. It's a thin tile that's lightweight, durable, flexible, and easy to cut and handle.

6. What do you enjoy most about your job? What do you enjoy least about your job?

I love working with my hands and creating. Tile installation is really like an art. You're creating something with different shapes. You are also taking someone's vision, whether it's a designer's or a homeowner's, and making it a reality with an installation that will last the lifetime of the home—or until someone wants to change it.

7. Can you suggest a valuable "try this" for students considering a career in your profession?

Go to a new construction site where a lot of houses are being built to see tile installers at work. Or visit a tile store in your area and see the showroom sales people and ask them about the industry. Getting a summer job or part-time job in a tile showroom or as a helper to a tile installer will give you great exposure to the industry and help you decide if it's right for you.

MORE INFORMATION

Building Trades Association
16th Street, NW
Washington, DC 20006
800.326.7800
www.buildingtrades.com

Ceramic Tile Education Foundation
5326 Highway 76
Pendleton, SC 29670
864.222.2131
www.tilecareer.com

International Masonry Institute
The James Brice House
42 East Street
Annapolis, MD 21401
410.280.1305
www.imiweb.org

National Association of Home Builders
1201 15th Street, NW
Washington, DC 20005
800.368.5242
www.nahb.com

National Center for Construction Education and Research
13614 Progress Boulevard
Alachua, FL 32615
888.622.3720
www.nccer.org

National Tile Contractors Association
626 Lakeland East Drive
Jackson, MS 39232
601.939.2071
www.tile-assn.com

Resilient Floor Covering Institute
115 Broad Street, Suite 201
LaGrange, GA 30240
www.rfci.com

Tile Contractors Association of America
10434 Indiana Avenue
Kansas City, MO 64137
800.655.8453
www.tcaainc.org

United Brotherhood of Carpenters & Joiners of America
101 Constitution Avenue, NW
Washington, DC 20001
202.546.6206
www.carpenters.org

United Union of Roofers, Waterproofers & Allied Workers
1660 L Street, NW, Suite 800
Washington, DC 20036-5646
202.463.7663
www.unionroofers.com

Sally Driscoll/Editor

What Are Your Career Interests?

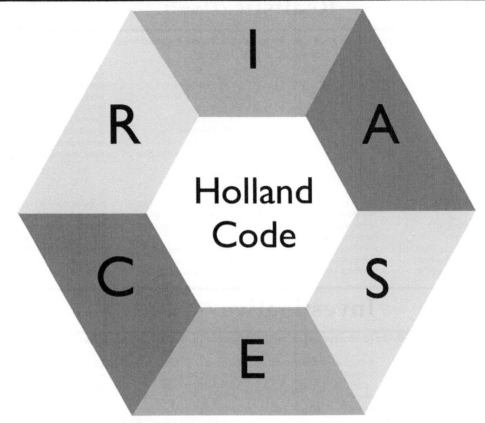

Holland Code

This is based on Dr. John Holland's theory that people and work environments can be loosely classified into six different groups. Each of the letters above corresponds to one of the six groups described in the following pages.

Different people's personalities may find different environments more to their liking. While you may have some interests in and similarities to several of the six groups, you may be attracted primarily to two or three of the areas. These two or three letters are your "Holland Code." For example, with a code of "RES" you would most resemble the Realistic type, somewhat less resemble the Enterprising type, and resemble the Social type even less. The types that are not in your code are the types you resemble least of all.

Most people, and most jobs, are best represented by some combination of two or three of the Holland interest areas. In addition, most people are most satisfied if there is some degree of fit between their personality and their work environment.

The rest of the pages in this booklet further explain each type and provide some examples of career possibilities, areas of study at MU, and co-curricular activities for each code. To take a more in-depth look at your Holland Code, take a self-assessment such as the SDS, Discover, or a card sort at the MU Career Center with a Career Specialist.

Realistic *(Doers)*

People who have athletic ability, prefer to work with objects, machines, tools, plants or animals, or to be outdoors.

Are you?		**Can you?**	**Like to?**
practical	independent	fix electrical things	tinker with machines/vehicles
straightforward/frank	ambitious	solve electrical problems	work outdoors
mechanically inclined	systematic	pitch a tent	be physically active
stable		play a sport	use your hands
concrete		read a blueprint	build things
reserved		plant a garden	tend/train animals
self-controlled		operate tools and machine	work on electronic equipment

**Career Possibilities
(Holland Code):**

Air Traffic Controller (SER)	Dental Technician (REI)	Laboratory Technician (RIE)	Property Manager (ESR)
Archaeologist (IRE)	Farm Manager (ESR)	Landscape Architect (AIR)	Recreation Manager (SER)
Athletic Trainer (SRE)	Fish and Game Warden (RES)	Mechanical Engineer (RIS)	Service Manager (ERS)
Cartographer (IRE)	Floral Designer (RAE)	Optician (REI)	Software Technician (RCI)
Commercial Airline Pilot (RIE)	Forester (RIS)	Petroleum Geologist (RIE)	Ultrasound Technologist (RSI)
Commercial Drafter (IRE)	Geodetic Surveyor (IRE)	Police Officer (SER)	Vocational Rehabilitation
Corrections Officer (SER)	Industrial Arts Teacher (IER)	Practical Nurse (SER)	Consultant (ESR)

Investigative *(Thinkers)*

People who like to observe, learn, investigate, analyze, evaluate, or solve problems.

Are you?		**Can you?**	Like to?
inquisitive	intellectually self-confident	think abstractly	explore a variety of ideas
analytical	Independent	solve math problems	work independently
scientific	logical	understand scientific theories	perform lab experiments
observant/precise	complex	do complex calculations	deal with abstractions
scholarly	Curious	use a microscope or computer	do research
cautious		interpret formulas	be challenged

**Career Possibilities
(Holland Code):**

Actuary (ISE)	Chemical Engineer (IRE)	Geologist (IRE)	Physician, General Practice (ISE)
Agronomist (IRS)	Chemist (IRE)	Horticulturist (IRS)	Psychologist (IES)
Anesthesiologist (IRS)	Computer Systems Analyst (IER)	Mathematician (IER)	Research Analyst (IRC)
Anthropologist (IRE)	Dentist (ISR)	Medical Technologist (ISA)	Statistician (IRE)
Archaeologist (IRE)	Ecologist (IRE)	Meteorologist (IRS)	Surgeon (IRA)
Biochemist (IRS)	Economist (IAS)	Nurse Practitioner (ISA)	Technical Writer (IRS)
Biologist (ISR)	Electrical Engineer (IRE)	Pharmacist (IES)	Veterinarian (IRS)

<u>A</u>rtistic *(Creators)*

People who have artistic, innovating, or intuitional abilities and like to work in unstructured situations using their imagination and creativity.

Are you?
creative
imaginative
innovative
unconventional
emotional
independent
Expressive

original
introspective
impulsive
sensitive
courageous
complicated
idealistic
nonconforming

Can you?
sketch, draw, paint
play a musical instrument
write stories, poetry, music
sing, act, dance
design fashions or interiors

Like to?
attend concerts, theatre, art
  exhibits
read fiction, plays, and poetry
work on crafts
take photography
express yourself creatively
deal with ambiguous ideas

**Career Possibilities
(Holland Code):**

Actor (AES)
Advertising Art Director (AES)
Advertising Manager (ASE)
Architect (AIR)
Art Teacher (ASE)
Artist (ASI)

Copy Writer (ASI)
Dance Instructor (AER)
Drama Coach (ASE)
English Teacher (ASE)
Entertainer/Performer (AES)
Fashion Illustrator (ASR)

Interior Designer (AES)
Intelligence Research Specialist
  (AEI)
Journalist/Reporter (ASE)
Landscape Architect (AIR)
Librarian (SAI)

Medical Illustrator (AIE)
Museum Curator (AES)
Music Teacher (ASI)
Photographer (AES)
Writer (ASI)
Graphic Designer (AES)

<u>S</u>ocial *(Helpers)*

People who like to work with people to enlighten, inform, help, train, or cure them, or are skilled with words.

Are you?
friendly
helpful
idealistic
insightful
outgoing
understanding

cooperative
generous
responsible
forgiving
patient
kind

Can you?
teach/train others
express yourself clearly
lead a group discussion
mediate disputes
plan and supervise an activity
cooperate well with others

Like to?
work in groups
help people with problems
do volunteer work
work with young people
serve others

**Career Possibilities
(Holland Code):**

City Manager (SEC)
Clinical Dietitian (SIE)
College/University Faculty (SEI)
Community Org. Director
  (SEA)
Consumer Affairs Director
  (SER)Counselor/Therapist
  (SAE)

Historian (SEI)
Hospital Administrator (SER)
Psychologist (SEI)
Insurance Claims Examiner
  (SIE)
Librarian (SAI)
Medical Assistant (SCR)
Minister/Priest/Rabbi (SAI)
Paralegal (SCE)

Park Naturalist (SEI)
Physical Therapist (SIE)
Police Officer (SER)
Probation and Parole Officer
  (SEC)
Real Estate Appraiser (SCE)
Recreation Director (SER)
Registered Nurse (SIA)

Teacher (SAE)
Social Worker (SEA)
Speech Pathologist (SAI)
Vocational-Rehab. Counselor
  (SEC)
Volunteer Services Director
  (SEC)

Enterprising *(Persuaders)*

People who like to work with people, influencing, persuading, leading or managing for organizational goals or economic gain.

Are you?
self-confident
assertive
persuasive
energetic
adventurous
popular

ambitious
agreeable
talkative
extroverted
spontaneous
optimistic

Can you?
initiate projects
convince people to do things
    your way
sell things
give talks or speeches
organize activities
lead a group
persuade others

Like to?
make decisions
be elected to office
start your own business
campaign politically
meet important people
have power or status

Career Possibilities
(Holland Code):

Advertising Executive (ESA)
Advertising Sales Rep (ESR)
Banker/Financial Planner (ESR)
Branch Manager (ESA)
Business Manager (ESC)
Buyer (ESA)
Chamber of Commerce Exec
    (ESA)

Credit Analyst (EAS)
Customer Service Manager
    (ESA)
Education & Training Manager
    (EIS)
Emergency Medical Technician
    (ESI)
Entrepreneur (ESA)

Foreign Service Officer (ESA)
Funeral Director (ESR)
Insurance Manager (ESC)
Interpreter (ESA)
Lawyer/Attorney (ESA)
Lobbyist (ESA)
Office Manager (ESR)
Personnel Recruiter (ESR)

Politician (ESA)
Public Relations Rep (EAS)
Retail Store Manager (ESR)
Sales Manager (ESA)
Sales Representative (ERS)
Social Service Director (ESA)
Stockbroker (ESI)
Tax Accountant (ECS)

Conventional *(Organizers)*

People who like to work with data, have clerical or numerical ability, carry out tasks in detail, or follow through on others' instructions.

Are you?
well-organized
accurate
numerically inclined
methodical
conscientious
efficient
conforming

practical
thrifty
systematic
structured
polite
ambitious
obedient
persistent

Can you?
work well within a system
do a lot of paper work in a short
    time
keep accurate records
use a computer terminal
write effective business letters

Like to?
follow clearly defined
    procedures
use data processing equipment
work with numbers
type or take shorthand
be responsible for details
collect or organize things

Career Possibilities
(Holland Code):

Abstractor (CSI)
Accountant (CSE)
Administrative Assistant (ESC)
Budget Analyst (CER)
Business Manager (ESC)
Business Programmer (CRI)
Business Teacher (CSE)
Catalog Librarian (CSE)

Claims Adjuster (SEC)
Computer Operator (CSR)
Congressional-District Aide (CES)
Cost Accountant (CES)
Court Reporter (CSE)
Credit Manager (ESC)
Customs Inspector (CEI)
Editorial Assistant (CSI)

Elementary School Teacher
    (SEC)
Financial Analyst (CSI)
Insurance Manager (ESC)
Insurance Underwriter (CSE)
Internal Auditor (ICR)
Kindergarten Teacher (ESC)

Medical Records Technician
    (CSE)
Museum Registrar (CSE)
Paralegal (SCE)
Safety Inspector (RCS)
Tax Accountant (ECS)
Tax Consultant (CES)
Travel Agent (ECS)

BIBLIOGRAPHY

Design, Engineering, and Construction Management

Allen, Edward and Joseph Iano. *Fundamentals of Building Construction: Materials and Methods*, 6th ed. Hoboken, NJ: Wiley, 2013.

Ching, Francis D. *Building Construction Illustrated*, 5th ed. Hoboken, NJ: Wiley, 2014.

Ching, Francis D.K. and James F. Eckler. *Introduction to Architecture*. Hoboken, NJ: Wiley, 2012.

Frederick, Matthew. *100 Things I Learned in Architecture School*. Cambridge, MA: MIT Press, 2007.

Gopi, Satheesh. *Basic Civil Engineering*. Boston: Pearson, 2009.

Gould, Frederick and Nancy Joyce. *Construction Project Management*, 4th ed. Upper Saddle River, NJ: Prentice Hall, 2013.

Jackson, Barbara J. *Construction Management Jumpstart*, 2d ed. Indianapolis: Sybex/Wiley, 2010.

Jeffries, Alan, David A. Madsen, and David P. Madsen. *Architectural Drafting and Design*, 6th ed . Clifton Park, NY: Delmar, 2010.

Mahoney, William D. *Construction Inspection Manual*. Vista, CA: Building News, 2008.

Mehta, Medan, Walter Scarborough, and Diane Armpriest. *Building Construction: Principles, Materials, and Systems*, 2d ed. Upper Saddle River, NJ: Prentice Hall, 2012.

Oles, Thomas. *Go With Me: 50 Steps to Landscape Thinking*. Amsterdam: Academy of Architecture, 2014.

Rogers, Leon. *Basic Construction Management: The Superintendant's Job*, 5th ed. Washington, DC: Builder Books, 2008.

Taylor, Gil. *Construction Codes and Inspection Handbook*. New York: McGraw Hill Education, 2006.

Thompson, Ian. *Landscape Architecture: A Very Short Introduction*. New York: Oxford University Press, 2014.

Building Trades

Bynum, Richard T. *Insulation Handbook*. New York: McGraw Hill, 2009.

Ferguson, Myron R. *Drywall: Hanging and Taping*. Newtown, CT: Taunton Press, 2004.

Glencoe/McGraw Hill. *Carpentry and Building Construction*. New York: McGraw Hill Education, 2008.

Goetz, Alisa. *Up, Down, and Across: Elevators, Escalators, and Moving Sidewalks*. London: Merrell, 2003.

Hauck, John. *Electrical Design of Commercial and Industrial Buildings*. Sudbury, MA: Jones & Bartlett, 2009.

Kavanagh, Barry F. *Surveying with Construction Applications*, 6th ed. Upper Saddle River, NJ: Prentice Hall, 2006.

Kicklighter, Clois E. *Modern Masonry*, 7th ed. Tinley Park, IL: Goodheart-Willcox, 2009.

Lemmer, Tom. *The Complete Guide to Finishing Walls and Ceilings*. Minneapolis, MN: Cool Springs Press, 2006.

Mayfield, Ray. *Photovoltaic Design and Installation for Dummies*. Hoboken, NJ: Wiley, 2010.

Mullin, Ray C. and Phil Simmons. *Electrical Wiring: Residential*, 14th ed. Clifton Park, NY: Delmar, 2014.

NCCR. *Heavy Equipment Operations*, 3d ed. Upper Saddle River, NJ: Prentice Hall, 2012.

Newman, Alexander. *Metal Building Systems: Design and Specifications*, 3rd ed. New York: McGraw Hill Education, 2014.

Novo, Robert. *How to Tile Floors*. Spring Valley, NY: Crossroads Publishing, 2011.

PHHC Educational Foundation. *Plumbing 101*, 6th ed. Clifton Park, NY: Delmar, 2012.

Roberts, Dave and Dan Atcheson. *Pipe and Excavation Contracting*. Carlsbad, CA: Craftsman Books, 2011.

RS Means. *The Gypsum Construction Handbook*, 7th ed. Hoboken, NJ: Wiley, 2014.

Spence, William P. *Roofing: Materials and Installation*. New York: Sterling, 2004.

USG. *The Gypsum Construction Handbook*, 7th ed. Hoboken, NJ: Wiley, 2014.

INDEX